Issues in Economic Theory and Public Policy

Professor Tapas Majumdar

Issues
in Economic Theory
and Public Policy

Essays in Honour of
Professor Tapas Majumdar

Editors

Amitava Bose
Mihir Rakshit
Anup Sinha

DELHI
OXFORD UNIVERSITY PRESS
CALCUTTA   CHENNAI   MUMBAI
1997

Oxford University Press, Walton Street, Oxford OX2 6DP

Oxford   New York
Athens   Auckland   Bangkok   Calcutta
Cape Town   Chennai   Dar es Salaam   Delhi
Florence   Hong Kong   Istanbul   Karachi
Kuala Lumpur   Madrid   Melbourne   Mexico City
Mumbai   Nairobi   Paris   Singapore
Taipei   Tokyo   Toronto
and associates in
Berlin   Ibadan

© Oxford University Press 1997

ISBN 0 19 563949 9

Typeset by Resodyn, New Delhi 110070
Printed in India at Pauls Press, New Delhi 110020
and published by Manzar Khan, Oxford University Press
YMCA Library Building, Jai Singh Road, New Delhi 110001

Preface

Professor Tapas Majumdar: An Appreciation

This book is a tribute to Professor Tapas Majumdar from some former students of Presidency College, Calcutta. Though the main activity at Presidency College is undergraduate teaching, a distinguishing feature of its Economics Department has been the high quality of research carried out by its faculty and a tradition which inextricably linked the quality of undergraduate teaching to the research interests of the teachers. As a result, undergraduates got a taste of the research being carried out at the frontiers of the subject. The Department has produced a long and impressive list of internationally renowned economists, giving it the reputation of being a nursery for breeding future teachers and scholars. Tapas Majumdar was one of the main architects of this tradition. He has been a source of inspiration to us in terms of his academic, administrative and personal qualities.

Tapas Majumdar comes from a family with a strong academic culture. His father, Nanigopal Majumdar, who passed away when Tapas Majumdar was only nine, was one of India's most well-known archaeologists. His maternal grandfather, Nalinimohan Shastri, himself a renowned scholar, influenced the young Tapas Majumdar greatly. Educated at Mitra Institution and Presidency College, he had a uniformly brilliant academic record. After a short stint at the Indian Statistical Institute, Calcutta, he joined Presidency College at the age of 21, as Assistant Professor. From 1955 to 1957 he worked on his doctoral thesis under the supervision of Lionel Robbins at the London School of Economics. This work was later published as his first book, *The Measurement of Utility*, which received wide acclaim. He returned to Presidency College as Professor and went on to become the Head of the Department of Economics. He moved to Jawaharlal Nehru University, New Delhi, in 1972, as Professor of Economics and Head of

the Zakir Hussain Centre for Educational Studies in the School
of Social Sciences. He is currently Emeritus Professor at the Zakir
Hussain Centre.

As a teacher at Presidency College, Tapas Majumdar (TM to
his students) provided a perfect foil to Bhabatosh Datta who had
already become a legend by the 1950s. Professor Datta's lucidity
in explaining intricate theoretical problems was unsurpassed and
left the students awestruck. Tapas Majumdar, on the other hand,
would raise issues which were at once elementary and open-
ended, making the students feel that they too could join the fray
in identifying problems and searching for solutions. This sense
of participation was fostered by his unfailing encouragement of
students.

It is difficult to overemphasize Tapas Majumdar's contribution
in building the tradition of research in economic theory in India.
His paper on 'Choice and Revealed Preference' written in his early
twenties for *Econometrica* (1956), and his dissertation on 'The
Measurement of Utility and Welfare Economics' played an important role in initiating research into the foundations of the theory
of choice by a number of his students beginning with Amartya
Sen. His own research interests were primarily in the areas of
demand theory, welfare economics, and economics of education.
He has written extensively in these areas and made significant
contributions in well-known international journals.

Tapas Majumdar's involvement with economics covers a wide
domain. The different sections in this book reflect his interests in
both theory and policy. The two essays in the section 'Welfare
Economics' discuss some of the most important issues at the
frontiers of research in this area, examining the possibilities and
implications of going beyond the narrow utility calculus of welfarism towards richer ethical constructs of well-being.

The section 'Working of the Market Economy', which is more
general yet fundamental, covers a range of current issues from
complexities that can arise even in simple models of general equilibrium, to the choice theoretic micro foundations of macroeconomics. Concerns about the working of markets and consequent

policy implications, in developing countries and the emerging market economies in the former planned socialist countries, are also addressed.

Tapas Majumdar's intellectual concerns have centred around understanding the workings of the economy, and what is more, in using this understanding to suggest more effective public policies. The last two sections contain essays on the economics of education, the provision of public goods and the efficacy of public policy. These essays address a number of issues ranging from the 'brain drain' and investment choices in education to voluntary contributions for enjoying public goods. The remaining essays focus on questions of enforcement, and some aspects of taxation and planning.

Apart from setting a very high standard in his own teaching and research, Tapas Majumdar proved his capabilities as an academic administrator as well. He had dreams for the future. What is more, he took the initiative in giving shape to his ideas, going about it in the quiet and decisive manner one has come to associate with him. He was instrumental in expanding the opportunities and facilities for conducting research, and attracting young scholars to the Economics Department at Presidency College. He played a leading role in setting up the Centre for Economic Studies at Presidency College with the help of the University Grants Commission. It was the first time in India that the UGC assisted in setting up a research centre in an undergraduate department. This not only expanded the resource base of the Department, but also brought formal recognition to it as a centre of academic excellence. His commitment to higher education is also reflected in the time he spared to be the Dean at Jawaharlal Nehru University from 1980 to 1982. He served as a member in various important bodies such as the UGC, National Council of Educational Research and Training, the Indian Council of Social Science Research, and the Justice Punnayya Committee on UGC Funding of Institutions of Higher Education.

Tapas Majumdar's personality is marked by elegance, charm and warmth. These qualities are evident in the way he dresses, talks, and receives friends and students. Students are welcome in his house at any time, to discuss anything they choose to. In the event of students becoming victims of an erratic examination system, he would be the first to encourage them, often by visiting their homes. Such encouragement has been a major factor contributing to the success of many of these students in their later life. The rapport he established with students was apparent during the Naxalite movement in the late 1960s, when students of all political affiliations seemed to have deep faith in his sense of justice and overriding concern for their welfare.

Tapas Majumdar made it easy for us. Within a few days of joining the undergraduate programme in economics at Presidency College, students just out of high school and with no prior exposure to economics, were introduced to Relation Algebra and Axiomatic Demand Theory as if that was the most natural thing to do. Professor Majumdar never treated undergraduates as customers with a final demand for a high placed B.A. degree. In the best tradition of Presidency College teachers, he taught us how to find our way to the events taking place at the frontiers of the discipline and what is more, how to learn to set that as our goal.

Contents

Tables

Figures

Contributors

Amit Bhaduri	Jawaharlal Nehru University, New Delhi
Amitava Bose	Indian Institute of Management, Calcutta
Dipankar Dasgupta	Indian Statistical Institute, New Delhi
Bhaskar Dutta	Indian Statistical Institute, New Delhi
Mukul Majumdar	Cornell University, USA
Tapan Mitra	Cornell University, USA
Dilip Mookerjee	Boston University, USA
Anjan Mukherji	Jawaharlal Nehru University, New Delhi
Mihir Rakshit	Indian Statistical Institute, Calcutta
Alok Ray	Indian Institute of Management, Calcutta
Ranjan Ray	University of Tasmania, Australia
Amal Sanyal	Lincoln University, New Zealand
Amartya Sen	Harvard University, USA
Ramprasad Sengupta	Jawaharlal Nehru University, New Delhi

I

Welfare Economics

Many contributors to the recent literature on welfare economics have argued extensively on the limitations of *welfarism* which uses individual utility information alone, in evaluating states of affairs. The exclusive reliance on individual utility limits the usefulness of welfare economics for purposes of policy making. The concept of utility, as satisfaction or desire-fulfilment, provides a narrow view of human well-being. In particular, the agency aspect of 'personhood' is neglected entirely, or, at best, reduced to instrumental value to the extent that it affects the level of utility. Many economists have emphasized the need to go beyond welfarism. The chapters by Amartya Sen and Bhaskar Dutta examine different aspects of using non-utility information.

Policy Making and Social Choice Pessimism

Economic policy-making seldom combines positive arguments with the welfare considerations of underlying social-choice questions. Majumdar, in his own research, had argued for the necessity of such considerations being taken into account in the process of policy-making. Sen, agreeing with Majumdar's position, argues that it is indeed possible to use a variety of information in combining important welfare considerations in the policy-making process.

A major reason for the separation of policy-making with its pragmatism, from welfare economics with its impossibility theorems, is the informational basis of the latter. Sen provides a new proof of Arrow's impossibility Theorem and demonstrates how the result is sensitive to the non-use of interpersonal comparisons of utility. Exclusive reliance on utility information and the Pareto criteria make the information base too narrow.

Broadening of this base, according to Sen, is both possible and desirable. Non-utility information on distributional inequality, or positive rights and freedoms, for instance, can enrich a modified Arrow framework. The mathematics of social welfare functionals can be used in this context to make welfare economics more practical and effective for policy purposes.

Interest, Well-Being and Advantage

One approach to a broader notion of well-being, focuses on *capabilities* as functioning. Functioning, according to this approach, is of intrinsic value, distinct from the commodities that can be instrumental in achieving the functioning, as well as the happiness or satisfaction achieved from the functioning. A Capability Set is the functioning *possibilities* available to an individual. This reflects the advantage an individual possesses. In this context the freedom of choice, in pursuing one's interest, attains greater importance than under the utility approach in the sense that a wider range of opportunities imply a greater freedom independent of the choice-induced outcome.

Dutta discusses some problems of ranking Capability Sets and Opportunity Sets. If the valuation ranking over all possible functionings is complete and admits a numerical representation, then there is no problem, except that the valuation is not to be interpreted as utility, since the judgement of interest is based on more objective criteria. If the valuation ranking is incomplete, and Dutta asserts its plausibility, then the only non-controversial ranking follows from a dominance-ranking axiom. This makes it difficult to compare 'most' pairs of capability sets, posing a practical difficulty with the capabilities approach. The ranking of opportunity sets, on the other hand, bears a close similarity to the Arrow problem of constructing a social ordering from individual orderings.

1

Policy Making and
Social Choice Pessimism

D71

D78

Amartya Sen

1 INTRODUCTION

It was, I think, in July 1951 that I first met Tapas Majumdar, when I had just arrived at Presidency College in Calcutta, as an undergraduate. Tapasda was impeccably dressed in a beige suit and a spotted tie, and looked amazingly comfortable despite the heat and humidity. He lectured to us, with unwavering skill and elegance, on macroeconomics. His interest in welfare economics was, however, already very clear, even though he did not lecture on it.[1] Welfare considerations seeped into his macroeconomics as well. Unemployment was not a piece of inert statistics, nor just a 'social mechanism' that kept wages from rising 'too fast' (the 'natural rate of unemployment' had not yet formally emerged but its precursors were plentifully there). Rather, it was the real phenomenon of people not having work — nor any income from work. Connections with individual welfare and social choice were strongly present in Tapasda's thought even then (it was striking how often they came up in our discussions), although it was some years later that he began writing on that subject.[2]

[1] We were taught welfare economics — with superb mastery — by Professor Bhabatosh Datta, who had earlier taught Tapas Majumdar as well. That the breathtaking clarity of Bhabatoshbabu's teaching served as a model for Tapasda, I did not doubt, as it would serve as a model for many of us as well.

[2] Tapas Majumdar's Ph.D. thesis, completed in 1957, was called 'Measurement

More than two decades later, in his illuminating and highly original monograph, *Investment in Education and Social Choice*, Tapas Majumdar noted that 'regrettably, it has not yet become common practice in discussions of economic policy to combine the positive macroeconomic argument with the welfare-economic considerations of the underlying social-choice questions.'[3] Those who deal with macroeconomics often opt for criteria of social assessment – in so far as they use any explicit criterion at all – that are remote from human welfare (and also amazingly rudimentary). Yet, as Majumdar points out, macroeconomics deals with problems that are of far-reaching and persistent relevance to welfare economics.

For example, when a decision is taken to accept a certain level of unemployment for the sake of keeping inflation within 'acceptable' limits, a trade-off is made between (1) the interests of the unemployed who could have had employment, and (2) the interests of others who are likely to lose something from an increase in total employment (perhaps through inflationary price rise). The gainers and losers are disparate groups, often coming from quite different classes. The employable unemployed have very divergent interests from that of many others who are a lot richer and in a much better position to influence the decision-making process of governments or of central banks who preside over these matters.

The explanation of the *political* powerlessness of the unemployed and the precariously weak is not hard to seek, but what about its implicit neglect in the discipline of *economic theory?* How are the welfare-economic implications of these policies so radically ignored, in favour of simple 'benchmark' goals, defined without directly referring to any characteristic of human well-being (such as keeping inflation below x per cent per year, or budget deficit below y per cent of the GNP)? What gives so many economists – nice, sympathetic, friendly economists – the intellectual ground for taking such a 'faraway' view? Since these 'benchmark' goals must, presumably, be ultimately justified with reference to individual and

---

of Utility and Welfare Economics,' which was published the following year (under an abbreviated title: *The Measurement of Utility*).

3 Majumdar (1983), p. xii. See also Section 2.6, pp. 34–9.

social welfare, why not bring them into direct consideration? Why not use richer information?

One line of justification for this refusal to 'get into' welfare economics in the 'pragmatic' field of macroeconomics is the widely shared sense that welfare economics is deeply troubled by internal tensions (most notably 'impossibility theorems' beginning with Arrow's), and that there is little hope of getting any 'practical' help from them. That conviction is still quite widespread, but it was in fact beginning to emerge very sharply just at the time that I first met Tapas Majumdar.[4]

I should like to discuss the historical emergence of the impossibility problems and the allegedly 'non-functioning' character of welfare economics (section 2). In the process I shall also present a short — but complete — proof of Arrow's impossibility theorem. A sketch of this proof was presented in Sen (1995), but I might as well put a full demonstration on record, especially since it is quite short and economic, even when wholly spelt out (section 3). It turns out that the crucial part played by informational scarcity is both responsible for Arrow's impossibility result, and for the unsuitability of the unmodified Arrow framework for even considering substantive distributional judgements (section 4). In the last section, I shall go on to discuss the *theoretical* resolution of Arrow's impossibility problem by broadening the 'informational basis of welfare economics' (on which I have tried to write earlier, particularly in Sen 1970, 1977b), and then consider briefly some alternative approaches that have *practical* relevance and promise.

2 THE TROUBLES OF TRADITIONAL WELFARE ECONOMICS

Welfare economics had been dominated for a long time by one special approach, viz. utilitarianism, and even in its heyday (with

[4] It was, in fact, Sukhamoy Chakravarty who was the first amongst us, as he so frequently was, to spot the new book, Arrow (1951a), in a College Street book shop, in what must have been December of 1951, and absolutely startled us all by his account of the impossibility theorem.

great contributions coming from Jevons, Edgeworth, Sidgwick, Marshall, Wicksell, and Pigou), traditional welfare economics was never more robust than utilitarianism itself. Welfare economists merrily constructed magnificent structures right over the intersection of at least three distinct 'fault lines':

(1) the arbitrariness of seeing people only as 'locations' of their utilities (ignoring their freedoms, rights, etc.);

(2) the lack of interest in interpersonal distribution of the real advantages of different people (including the specific indifference of utilitarianism to the distribution of utilities); and

(3) the difficulty of getting hold of utility information, especially in an interpersonally comparable cardinal form (as needed by the utilitarian formula).

In the event, the 'fault line' that actually led to the quake that ravaged traditional welfare economics was the last of the three. In a couple of powerful methodological attacks, Lionel Robbins (1932, 1938) argued that the epistemological foundations of utilitarian welfare economics were incurably defective. Interpersonal comparison of utilities cannot, it was argued, be scientifically made.[5] Indeed, Robbins invoked Jevons himself, in a 'confessional' mood, noting that there were 'no means whereby such comparisons can be accomplished'. 'Every mind is inscrutable to every other mind and no common denominator of feelings is possible.'[6] By the end of the 1930s, economists seemed to be, in general, fairly persuaded that interpersonal comparisons of utilities had no scientific basis, and that there was, therefore, a need to change course from traditional welfare economics.[7] Arrow's work on social-choice theory

---

[5] It is of some interest to note, in the present context, that Tapas Majumdar worked with Lionel Robbins for his PhD thesis at the London School of Economics, on a closely related subject, to wit, the measurement of utility; the thesis was later published as Majumdar (1958). While his approach was distinctly less sceptical than that of Robbins, Majumdar did not go on to explore, in that book, the social-choice implications of his analysis.

[6] See Robbins (1938), p. 636. See also Robbins (1932).

[7] Harsanyi (1955) was one of the few dissidents, in his presentation of a utilitarian welfare economics based on choice behaviour under risk.

came at a point of particular rethinking in the history of welfare economics.

Perhaps more insight into this rejection can be obtained through factorizing utilitarianism into its distinct components. The three distinct components that characterize utilitarian calculus consist of:

1. Consequentialism: All selection of decisional variables (such as actions, practices, institutions, etc.) must be guided exclusively by the merit of consequent states of affairs.
2. Welfarism: The merit of states of affairs must be judged exclusively by the individual utilities in the respective states.
3. Sum-ranking: The assessment of individual utilities in any state of affairs must be done simply by summing the utilities together (i.e., by arithmetic addition).

Utilitarianism invokes *consequentialist* norms that judge consequent states of affairs through *welfarism* and *sum-ranking*.

Of the three factors, it is only *sum-ranking* that is directly vulnerable to the absence of interpersonal comparison of utilities. There was, thus, a strong temptation to reconstruct a different foundation for welfare economics eschewing sum-ranking, but without rejecting the other two demands. This kind of motivation led to a modification of the utilitarian tradition into a form of 'muted' welfarism. This approach went under the somewhat ephemeral name: 'the new welfare economics'. The exclusive reliance on utility information (that is, welfarism) remained, and so did the tradition of judging all policies and choices by consequent states of affairs (that is, consequentialism). But sum-ranking was resoundingly dropped, to dispense with the need for interpersonal comparisons altogether.

In fact, an important part of the so-called new welfare economics had explicit use for only one criterion of social improvement, viz., the Pareto criterion: state x is to be judged better than social state y if at least one person has more utility in x than in y and everyone has at least as much utility in x as in y. A state is 'Pareto efficient' if there is no other feasible state that is superior to it in terms of the Pareto criterion. A good deal of subsequent welfare economics confines attention to Pareto efficiency only, which does not require any interpersonal comparison. That practice is fairly common even today.

Pareto efficiency is totally silent on *distributional* issues (on any space — utilities, incomes, or whatever).[8] A Pareto efficient state can indeed be deeply unequal and iniquitous with some people in deep misery while others are terribly well-off, provided the deprivation of the miserable cannot be reduced without cutting into the welfare of the privileged. However, if welfarism is still accepted (as it was in new welfare economics), it could be claimed that even when we incorporate some criterion of distributional comparisons, the best (or maximal) social outcomes would be among the set of Pareto efficient states.[9]

But it was not entirely clear how distributional judgements would be incorporated into a Paretian system. Also, there was need to deal with the tendency of actual policy judgements to be sensitive to variables *other than* utilities (such as personal rights or freedoms, or the distribution of general-purpose means — such as incomes — on which the ability to promote people's respective ends depend). There was recognition that it would help to get some *further* criteria to be able to incorporate judgments about aspects of choice neglected under the 'muted' welfarism of new welfare economics.

The possibility of systematic procedures for this supplementation was discussed by Abram Bergson (1938), and extensively

[8] As was noted earlier, utilitarianism too is indifferent to the distribution of *utilities*, but when different people share the same strictly concave utility function over income (with shared diminishing marginal utilities), utilitarianism function is *pro*-equality in distributing a given total *income*. To stop with Pareto criterion only, eliminates even this element of implicit concern with distributions.

[9] Some satisfaction was, therefore, appropriately taken in the 'converse' part of the Arrow-Debreu 'fundamental theorem of welfare economics' which indicated that — under some specified conditions (chiefly the absence of externalities and serious non-convexities) — even the best (or maximal) social outcomes would be reachable through a competitive market equilibrium (Arrow 1951b, Debreu 1959).

explored by Paul Samuelson (1947) in his classic treatise *Founda-tions of Economic Analysis*. What was needed for decisions, it was agreed, was an acceptable ordering of alternative social states, and if this could not be done by adding utilities (for Robbinsian reasons, or any other), then such a 'social welfare function' must be derived from other principles (including — but going beyond — the need for Pareto efficiency).

It was at this point that Arrow formulated this task as a 'social choice' problem. This led directly to Arrow's famous 'General Possibility Theorem' (the name that he gave to his 'impossibility theorem'). It also led, incidentally, to the birth of 'social choice theory' as a subject (or, in one sense, a *rebirth* after a lapse of two centuries since the days of vigorous discussion on formal social-choice problems by Borda, Condorcet and other French mathe-maticians, flourishing in the grand days of the 'Enlightenment').

Arrow considered a set of very mild-looking conditions relating social choices or social judgments to the set of individual preferen-ces, and showed that it is impossible to satisfy those conditions simultaneously. Oddly enough, the impossibility surfaced even before any strictly 'distributional' judgement was incorporated (with the mild exception of non-dictatorship), so that the task of adding some demanding distributional criterion was rendered impossible even before it was taken up.

In an n-person society, a social welfare function F determines a social ordering R over the set S of alternative social states (descriptions of states of affairs) as a function of the set (or n-tuple) of individual preference orderings (or non-comparable ordinal utilities) over those states, that is, as a function of $\{R_1, \ldots, R_n\}$, or $\{R_i\}$ for short. Notationally, xR_iy stands for its being the case that person i weakly prefers x to y (that is for him or her, x is at least as good as y); similarly, xRy stands for x being judged to be at least as good as y for the society. (The corresponding *strict* pref-erences are P_i and P respectively.) A social welfare function F is given by: $R = F(\{R_i\})$.[10] Structurally, it is assumed that there are at least three alternatives and a finite set of individuals.

[10] This is the 'relational' form of the social welfare function, and even though

The conditions used by Arrow (in the later and neater version, Arrow 1963) included the unrestricted domain, weak Pareto principle, non-dictatorship, and a requirement called the independence of irrelevant alternatives.[11] *Unrestricted domain* (U) demands that the domain of F includes all possible n-tuples of individual preferences $\{R_i\}$. The *weak Pareto principle* (P) only requires that if all persons prefer any x to any y, then x is socially preferred to y. *Non-dictatorship* (D) excludes the possibility that some individual j could be so powerful that whenever, over the domain of F, he or she prefers any x to any y, society too strictly prefers x to y. And *independence of irrelevant alternatives* (I) can be seen as demanding that the social ranking of any pair $\{x, y\}$ must not depend on anything other than the individual preferences over x and y.

The Arrow 'impossibility theorem' states that there does not exist any social welfare function F that simultaneously fulfills U, P, D and I. What began as an ambitious programme of having a systematic framework, to be based on generally agreed democratic values, for judging social welfare based on individual preferences, ended up in an impasse. In fact, significantly for the distributional issue, that quandary emerged even before any demanding condition of distributional equity (other than the very mild condition of non-dictatorship) had been included in the list of requirements. To be sure, there could be possible social welfare functions over limited domains (Tapas Majumdar [1968]), himself provided an elegant alternative proof of one such result), and some little room can be made for modifications when the requirements of social preference are reduced from the demanding conditions of a social *ordering*.[12] But basically there was not

---

it can be stated in a choice-functional form, there is a clear correspondence between the two; on this see Sen (1977a, 1986a).

[11] I am following here the 'revised' version of the theorem presented in Arrow (1963), and the terminology used in Sen (1970).

[12] In fact, the scope of getting positive possibility results out of relaxing the ordering property of social preference is very limited; on this see Sen (1977a, 1993).

much 'go' anywhere, *within the informational framework* used by Arrow (that is, working on the n-tuple of interpersonally non-comparable individual utilities or preference rankings). The possibility of broadening that informational framework is discussed in Section 4, but before that a short but complete proof of the Arrow impossibility theorem is presented in the next section. It is considerably easier and more economic than the proofs in Arrow (1951a, 1963) and Sen (1970).

3 ON THE PROOF OF ARROW'S IMPOSSIBILITY THEOREM

A set G of individuals is 'decisive' over the ordered pair $\{x, y\}$, denoted $D_G(x, y)$, if and only if whenever everyone in G prefers x to y, we must have xPy no matter what others prefer. If G is decisive over every ordered pair, then G is simply decisive, denoted D_G. The proof of the Arrow theorem can be made to go via two lemmas.

(L.1) If $D_G(x, y)$ for any ordered pair (x, y), then D_G.

Proof: Take an alternative state b different from x and y. To show that $D_G(x, y) \rightarrow D_G(x, b)$, assume that for all persons j in G, $xP_j y$ and $yP_j b$, and for all i not in G, $yP_i b$. Clearly, xPy by $D_G(x, y)$, and yPb by the weak Pareto principle. Thus xPb. Since the preferences of anyone i not in G over (x, b) can be anything, and since the preferences over y, b must not influence the social ranking of x and b (by the independence condition I), clearly $D_G(x, b)$.

In the same way, by taking an alternative a different from x and y, and assuming that for all j in G, $aP_j x$ and $xP_j y$, and for all i not in G, $aP_i x$, it is shown that aPx and xPy, and thus aPy. Hence $D(x, y) \rightarrow D(a, y)$.

To show that $D_G(x, y) \rightarrow D_G$, we need show that $D_G(a, b)$ holds for all a, b. The cases in which we have respectively $x = a$ and $y = b$ are already covered in the preceding demonstrations. Similarly, if $x = b$ and the others distinct, then: $D_G(x, y) \rightarrow D_G(a, y) \rightarrow D_G(a, x)$. Also, if $y = a$ and the others distinct, then:

$D_G(x, y) \rightarrow D_G(x, b) \rightarrow D_G(y, b)$. If, on the other hand, $x = b$ as well as $y = a$, then for some distinct $z: D_G(x, y) \rightarrow D_G(x, z) \rightarrow D_G(y, z) \rightarrow D_G(y, x)$. Finally, if x, y, a, b are all distinct, then: $D_G(x, y) \rightarrow D_G(x, b) \rightarrow D_G(a, b)$. Hence D_G.

($L.2$) For any G, if D_G, and if G has more than one person in it, then for some proper subset G^* of G, we have D_{G^*}.

Proof: Partition G into G_1 and G_2. Assume that for all i in G_1: $xP_i y$, and $xP_i z$, with any possible ranking of y, z, and that for all j in G_2: $xP_j y$, and $zP_j y$, with any possible ranking of x, z. Those not in G can prefer anything. If, now, xPz, then group G_1 would be decisive over this pair, since they alone definitely prefer x and z (the others can rank this pair in any way). If G_1 is not to be decisive, we must have zRx for *some* set of individual preferences over x, z of non-members of G_1. Take that case, but note that it still leaves non-members of G_1 free to have any preference over y, z, along with continuing to prefer x to y, unanimously. Combining the social ranking zRx with xPy (a consequence of the decisiveness of G and the fact that everyone in G prefers x to y), we have zPy. Since only G_2 members definitely prefer z to y, this entails that G_2 is decisive over this pair $\{z, y\}$. But, then, by ($L.1$), G_2 is decisive. So either G_1 or G_2 must be decisive.

Proof of Arrow's Impossibility Theorem: By the weak Pareto principle, the group of all individuals is decisive. It is, by assumption, finite. By successive two-fold partitioning, and each time picking the decisive part (which exists, guaranteed by ($L.2$)), we arrive at a decisive individual, who must, thus, be a dictator.[13]

In the next section the role of informational scarcity in generating

---

[13] Since I have given several different proofs of Arrow's theorem, let me note here that this is the most economic complete proof I know. A sketch of this demonstration was presented, as was noted earlier, in Sen (1995). The first proof, given in Sen (1970) is essentially Arrow's own (1963 version), with some minor blemishes removed. The second proof (Sen 1979) uses the successive elimination argument used here as the last step. The present proof drops the need to introduce the intermediate concept of 'almost decisiveness' (used in Arrow 1963, Sen 1970, 1979), since it is redundant.

the impossibility result is discussed. The informational inputs that are ruled out make it impossible, on one side, to formulate distributional judgements, and on the other side, they make non-dictatorial decision procedures effectively non-usable. Thus, the informational lacuna incorporated in the Arrow framework is both central to its unsuitability for distributional issues, and crucial for the impossibility result itself.

4 INFORMATIONAL SCARCITY, DISTRIBUTIONAL JUDGEMENTS AND ARROW'S IMPOSSIBILITY

It is not hard to demonstrate that Arrow's impossibility result and its many variations are extremely sensitive to the non-use of interpersonal comparison of utilities. Indeed, one way of thinking of that impossibility problem is to see it as the result of combining welfarism (thereby using only utility information) with terribly poor utility data (thereby making it hard to use utility information), while still insisting on a complete and regular structure of social choice (on this see Sen 1970, 1982).

When presenting his formulation of the problem of social choice based on individual preferences, Arrow (1951a, p. 9), followed the viewpoint, then dominant, that 'interpersonal comparison of utilities has no meaning'. The social choices are to be determined just by the set of individual preferences, that is by the utility *orderings* of the respective individuals given separately. Even though welfarism was not explicitly invoked as a condition, in fact it is part of the informational foundation of the Arrovian social welfare function. Formally, a kind of welfarism follows from Arrow's unrestricted domain, independence of irrelevant alternatives, and the Pareto principle.[14] Indeed, lemma $(L.1)$ used to derive Arrow's theorem, presented earlier, is precisely a demonstration that welfarism of a kind is entailed by Arrow's conditions taken together (more particularly, by U, P and I). The result, identified by $(L.1)$, that the decisiveness of any group over *any*

[14] On this, see Sen (1982), essays 11 and 15.

pair of social states amounts to the decisiveness of that group over *all* pairs of social states (no matter what states they are) reflects the disregard of *all information* about the nature of the alternative social states *except the individual preferences* (or utility rankings) over them.

The result of combining welfarism (at least as far as decisiveness is concerned) and very limited utility information (in particular the absence of interpersonal comparability and also of cardinality) is to make the informational basis of the framework of Arrovian social welfare function very poorly discriminating. To illustrate, consider the problem of choosing between different distributions of a given cake between three persons: a distribution problem par excellence. To pursue distributional equity, it would be necessary to identify how well off the three respectively are *vis-à-vis* each other. But can this be done in this informational framework?

Surely not in terms of utilities (that is, in the form of identifying the relation of being 'better off' or 'worse off' as having higher or lower utility), since that would require interpersonal comparison of utilities, which is ruled out. On the other hand, if being 'better off' or 'worse off' is defined in terms of *income or commodity holdings* (or by any other non-utility characteristic incorporated in the descriptions of the states of affairs), then we run into the problem that the use of that information is ruled out by the welfarism of the Arrow framework. Even though two pairs of states $\{a, b\}$ and $\{x, y\}$ differ in actual distributions of incomes or wealths or resource holdings or substantive freedoms, decisions of their respective rankings must be determined entirely in the same way, in terms of the individual utility orderings over them (that is, one of the implications of $(L.1)$). So we are totally prevented from taking any direct note of who is better off and who worse off in either utility or non-utility terms in ranking states of affairs, and that makes distributional judgements fairly impossible to make.[15]

---

[15] On this see Sen (1982), and Hammond (1985).

This informational scarcity not only makes it hard to take note of distributional equity, it also pushes us in the direction of the remarkable impossibility result that Arrow identified. Given the limited informational availability (in particular, no interpersonal comparison or cardinality of utilities, and no non-utility information), we are left with a class of decision procedures that are really some variant or other of voting methods (like majority decision). As they do not need any interpersonal comparison, nor anything other than the individual's preference orderings (as expressed by pairwise votes), they do remain accessible in Arrow's informational framework. But these procedures have problems of regularity and consistency, as had been noted more than two hundred years ago by French mathematicians such as Condorcet and Borda; their results can be easily extended to cover all voting rules — not just majority decision — except for the special case of counting only one person's vote and ignoring the votes of others. What is then left is the unattractive possibility of having a dictatorial method of social judgement — handing it all over to one person whose preferences determine everything. This unattractive method of decision making is ruled out directly by one of Arrow's conditions (to wit, non-dictatorship). Hence the impossibility.

In understanding the relation between motivations and formalities, it is useful to note that the informational framework formalized in the unmodified Arrow system (1) is crucial to Arrow's impossibility result, and (2) does not at all serve well the *need* for distributional judgements — going beyond Paretian efficiency — which had played a big part in sending the subject of welfare economics in the direction of Bergson-Samuelson social welfare functions and thus to Arrow's social choice theory. There is a common explanation to both problems. The central question, then, is this: what modification of the Arrow system is called for (1) to avoid the impossibility, and (2) to make systematic social judgements about distributional equity?

5 MORE INFORMATION FOR SOCIAL CHOICE AND FOR DISTRIBUTIONAL JUDGEMENTS

In complaining about the neglect of social-choice issues in the standard macroeconomic analysis, Tapas Majumdar notes that social-choice considerations must 'come to the fore as soon as the question of interpersonal comparability of any kind is raised, or the question of deciding which set of collective-choice rules should hold is discussed.'[16] This argument nicely complements what was discussed in the last two sections. There it was shown that both Arrow's impossibility and the inability to make informed distributional judgements arise from the informational lacuna — in particular the exclusion of interpersonal comparisons — incorporated in the unmodified Arrow framework. The adequacy of social-choice procedures would, thus, seem to demand more information on interpersonal comparisons. Majumdar's point is, in an important way, the *converse* of this. Considering information on interpersonal comparisons would demand adequate social choice procedures.

Majumdar's reasoning is clear enough. Once we can take note of the fact that in a society there are rich and poor (based on 'any kind' of perspicuous comparisons), then — in taking policy decisions — we must systematically decide how to deal with (that is, trade off, or balance against each other) the respective interests of the better off and worse off. Since that exercise is one of social choice, interpersonal comparisons lead to the demand for social choice, just as social-choice demands interpersonal comparisons.

The Arrow informational framework can be easily extended to admit more information, in particular interpersonally comparable and possibly cardinal utilities, and the systematic framework of 'social welfare functionals' (SWFL) can take over the task for which 'social welfare functions' (SWF) proved inadequate (on this see Sen 1970). That informationally rich social choice frameworks (making use, in particular, of interpersonal comparisons) can provide a

---

[16] Majumdar (1983), p. xii. Majumdar indicates how the neglected questions can be appropriately addressed, particularly in dealing with educational policies.

sound and systematic theoretical basis for actual social decisions has been more than adequately demonstrated by explorations over two decades.[17]

Given these theoretical developments, one of the practical questions that arise in this context concerns the actual procedures to be used for making interpersonal comparisons. Even when Robbins's methodological rejection of interpersonal comparisons is resisted, the practical problem of obtaining usable comparisons between the respective advantages of different people remains.

The mathematical framework of social welfare functionals (SWFL) can be used in different ways, depending on what *interpretation* is made of individual rankings and of interpersonal comparisons. This point is worth clarifying, since the formal frameworks of SWFL are all, typically, presented in terms of individual *utilities*, in particular, and utility information (as Robbins had noted) is peculiarly hard to get. But we need not confine the analysis and actual use of these results to the utility interpretation only.

As an example, consider some measure of real income (with given price weights) as the basis of *intra*personal and *inter*personal comparisons. From this we shall get an individual ordering for each person and interpersonal comparisons between the advantages of any pair of persons (for a *given* social state, and *between* different social states). In this sense, a function that specifies the values of respective social welfares for all income distribution vectors is a SWFL.[18] Even though it is, admittedly, a crude kind of a social welfare functional, nevertheless good practical use can be made of such a framework, as has been amply demonstrated by the vast literature that has followed Atkinson's (1970) classic paper on income distributional judgements.

---

[17] See Sen (1970, 1977), Hammond (1976, 1985), d'Aspremont and Gevers (1977), Arrow (1977), Maskin (1978, 1979), Gevers (1979), Roberts (1980a, 1980b), Blackorby, Donaldson and Weymark (1984), d'Aspremont (1985), among many other contributions.

[18] Indeed the invariance condition would be particularly strong in this case, making social judgements easier to derive.

Recent attempts to get usable indicators of individual advantage in fields other than income have also tended to use — albeit implicitly — the framework of SWFLs. Comparisons can be made of various types of advantages, for example in life expectancy, morbidity rates, educational achievements, health facilities, nutritional adequacy, perceptions of well-being and illfare, and so on.[19] It is also possible to combine them in aggregate indicators. The literature on distribution-adjusted indicators is essentially isomorphic to the underlying social welfare exercise defined over that informational base.[20] There are different ways of combining concern with equity in social welfare judgements based on available statistical evidence.[21]

This is not the occasion to try to provide a critical review of the alternative approaches now being explored, but there is little reason to doubt that the lacuna of usable information cannot provide legitimate grounds for ignoring social choice problems in decision-making, whether in macroeconomics or in micro policies. Tapas Majumdar was not only analytically right to emphasize the linkage between the two distinct classes of problems (problems with which he himself has been involved — both as a teacher and as a researcher), but he was also right in thinking that this linkage can be pursued in practically usable ways.

This is all the more true now, as there is presently much greater opportunity of drawing on widely available empirical

---

[19] For examples of different types, see Adelman and Morris (1973), Sen (1973, 1976), Kapteyn and van Praag (1976), Hammond (1978), Deaton and Muellbauer (1980), Kakwani (1980, 1986), Anand and Harris (1990), Dasgupta and Ray (1990), Osmani (1990), UNDP (1990, 1994), Anand and Kanbur (1993), Anand and Ravallion (1993), Floud (1992), Fogel (1991, 1992), Osmani (1992), Dasgupta (1993), Desai (1995), among many other contributions.

[20] On this see particularly Atkinson (1983), Blackorby and Donaldson (1984), Foster (1985). See also, on related issues, Sen (1976), Hammond (1978), Basu (1980), Roberts (1980), Osmani (1982), Chakravarty, Dutta and Weymark (1985), Kakwani (1986).

[21] Distributional concerns may be related to groups (classified according to, say, class or gender) as well as individuals; some methodological and substantive issues have been discussed in Anand and Sen (1995, 1996).

information and on the analytical techniques developed in contemporary social choice theory and applied welfare economics. Many problems remain to be explored, but there is no intellectual reason to stick to the mechanical 'bench-mark' approaches in practical policy making (and to insist on the disregard of equity that follows from it). The politics of ignoring inequality cannot really be based on social choice pessimism.

REFERENCES

Adelman, I. and C.T. Morris (1973), *Economic Growth and Social Equity in Developing Countries*, Stanford: Stanford University Press.

Anand, Sudhir and Christopher Harris (1992), 'Issues in the Measurement of Undernutrition', in Osmani.

Anand, Sudhir and Kanbur, S.M. Ravi (1993), 'Inequality and Development: A Critique', *Journal of Development Economics*, 40.

Anand, Sudhir and Martin Ravallion (1993), 'Human Development in Poor Countries: On the Role of Private Incomes and Public Services', *Journal of Economic Perspectives*, 7.

Anand, Sudhir and Amartya Sen (1995), 'Gender Inequality in Human Development: Theories and Measurement', Occasional Paper 12, New York: UNDP/HDRO.

— (1996), 'The Income Component of the Human Development Index', New York: UNDP/HDRO.

Arrow, Kenneth J. (1951a), *Social Choice and Individual Values*, New York: Wiley.

— (1951b), 'An Extension of the Basic Theorems of Classical Welfare Economics', in J. Neyman (ed.), *Proceedings of the Second Berkeley Symposium of Mathematical Statistics*, Berkeley, CA: University of California Press.

— (1963), *Social Choice and Individual Values*, enlarged 2nd edition, New York: Wiley.

Arrow, K.J. (1977), 'Extended Sympathy and the Possibility of Social Choice', *American Economic Review*, 67.

Atkinson, A.B. (1970), 'On the Measurement of Inequality', *Journal of Economic Theory*, 2; reprinted in Atkinson (1983).

Atkinson, A.B. (1983), *Social Justice and Public Policy*, Brighton: Wheatsheaf and Cambridge; MA: MIT Press.

Basu, Kaushik (1980), *Revealed Preference of Governments*, Cambridge: Cambridge University Press.

Bergson, Abram (1938), 'A Reformulation of Certain Aspects of Welfare Economics', *Quarterly Journal of Economics*, 52.

Blackorby, Charles and David Donaldson (1980), 'Ethically Significant Ordinal Indexes of Relative Inequality', *Advances in Econometrics*, 3.

Blackorby, Charles, David Donaldson and John Weymark (1984), 'Social Choice with Interpersonal Utility Comparisons: A Diagrammatic Introduction', *International Economic Review*, 25.

Chakravarty, S.R., Bhaskar Dutta and John Weymark (1985), 'Ethical Indices of Income Mobility', *Social Choice and Welfare*, 2.

Dasgupta, Partha (1993), *An Inquiry into Well-being and Destitution*, Oxford: Clarendon Press.

Dasgupta, Partha and Debraj Ray (1990), 'Adapting to Undernutrition: Clinical Evidence and its Implications', in Drèze and Sen.

Dasgupta, Partha, Amartya Sen and David Starrett (1973), 'Notes on the Measurement of Inequality', *Journal of Economic Theory*, 6.

d'Aspremont, Claude (1985), 'Axioms for Social Welfare Ordering', in Hurwicz et al.

d'Aspremont, Claude and Louis Gevers (1977), 'Equity and the Informational Basis of Collective Choice', *Review of Economic Studies*, 46.

Desai, Meghnad (1995), *Poverty, Famine and Economic Development*, Aldershot: Elgar.

Deaton, Angus and John Muellbauer (1980), *Economics and Consumer Behaviour*, Cambridge: Cambridge University Press.

Debreu, Gerard (1959), *Theory of Value*, New York: Wiley.

Drèze, Jean and Amartya Sen (eds) (1990), *The Political Economy of Hunger*, Oxford: Clarendon Press.

Floud, Roderick (1992), 'Anthropometric Measures of Nutritional Status in Industrial Societies: Europe and North America since 1750', in Osmani.

Fogel, Robert (1991), 'The Conquest of High Mortality and Hunger in Europe and America: Timing and Mechanism', in *Favorites of Fortune*, Cambridge, MA: Harvard University Press.

—— (1992), 'Second Thoughts on the European Escape from Hunger: Crop Yields, Price Elasticities, Entitlements and Mortality Rates', in Osmani.

Foster, James (1985), 'Inequality Measurement', in H.P. Young, *Fair Allocation*, Providence, RI: American Mathematical Society.

Gevers, Louis (1979), 'On Interpersonal Comparability and Social Welfare Orderings', *Econometrica*, 47.

Hammond, Peter J. (1976), 'Equity, Arrow's Conditions and Rawls' Difference Principle', *Econometrica*, 44.

—— (1978), 'Economic Welfare with Rank Order Price Weighting', *Review of Economic Studies*, 45.

—— (1985), 'Welfare Economics', *Issues in Contemporary Microeconomics and Welfare*, in Feiwel, G. (ed.), Albany, NY: SUNY Press.

Harsanyi, John C. (1955), 'Cardinal Welfare, Individualistic Ethics and Interpersonal Comparisons of Utility', *Journal of Political Economy*, 63.

Hurwicz, Leonid, David Schmeidler and Hugo Sonnenschein (eds) (1985), *Social Goals and Social Organisation: Essays in Memory of Elisha Pazner*, Cambridge: Cambridge University Press.

Kakwani, Nanak (1980), *Income, Inequality and Poverty*, New York: Oxford University Press.

—— (1986), *Analysing Redistribution Policies*, Cambridge: Cambridge University Press.

Kapteyn, Arie and Bernard M.S. van Praag (1976), 'A New Approach to the Construction of Family Equivalent Scales', *European Economic Review*, 7.

Majumdar, Tapas (1958), *The Measurement of Utility*, London: Macmillan.

—— (1968), 'Sen's General Theorem on the Transitivity of Majority Decisions', in T. Majumdar (ed.), *Growth and Choice*, Calcutta: Oxford University Press.

—— (1983), *Investment in Education and Social Choice*, Cambridge: Cambridge University Press.

Maskin, Eric (1978), 'A Theorem on Utilitarianism', *Review of Economic Studies*, 45.

—— (1979), 'Decision-making under Ignorance with Implications for Social Choice', *Theory and Decision*, 11.

Osmani, S.R. (1982), *Economic Inequality and Group Welfare*, Oxford: Clarendon Press.

—— (ed.) (1992), *Nutrition and Poverty*, Oxford: Clarendon Press.

Robbins, Lionel (1932), *An Essay on the Nature and Significance of Economic Science*, London: Allen & Unwin.

Robbins, Lionel (1938), 'Interpersonal Comparisons of Utility', *Economic Journal*, 48.

Roberts, Kevin W.S. (1980a), 'Interpersonal Comparability and Social Choice Theory', *Review of Economic Studies*, 47.

—— (1980b), 'Price Independent Welfare Prescriptions', *Journal of Public Economics*, 13.

Rothschild, Michael and Joseph Stiglitz (1973), 'Some Further Results in the Measurement of Inequality', *Journal of Economic Theory*, 6.

Samuelson, Paul A. (1947), *Foundations of Economic Analysis*, Cambridge: Harvard University Press.

Sen, Amartya K. (1970), *Collective Choice and Social Welfare*, San Francisco: Holden Day; republished Amsterdam: North-Holland, 1979.

—— (1973), 'On the Development of Basic Economic Indicators to Supplement GNP Measures', *United Nations Economic Bulletin for Asia and the Far East*, 24.

—— (1976), 'Real National Income', *Review of Economic Studies*, 43; reprinted in Sen (1982).

—— (1977a), 'Social Choice Theory: A Re-examination', *Econometrica*, 45; reprinted in Sen (1982).

—— (1977b), 'On Weights and Measures: Informational Constraints in Social Welfare Analysis', *Econometrica*, 45; reprinted in Sen (1982).

—— (1979), 'Personal Utilities and Public Judgments: Or What's Wrong with Welfare Economics?', *Economic Journal*, 89; reprinted in Sen (1982).

—— (1982), *Choice, Welfare and Measurement*, Oxford: Basil Blackwell and Cambridge, Mass.: MIT Press, 1982.

—— (1986a), 'Social Choice Theory', in K.J. Arrow and M. Intriligator (eds), *Handbook of Mathematical Economics*, Amsterdam: North-Holland.

—— (1986b), 'Information and Invariance in Normative Choice', in W.P. Heller, R.M. Starr and D.A. Starrett (eds), *Social Choice and Public Decision Making: Essays in Honor of Kenneth J. Arrow*, Cambridge: Cambridge University Press.

—— (1993), 'Internal Consistency of Choice', *Econometrica*, 61.

—— (1995), 'Rationality and Social Choice', *American Economic Review*, 85.

UNDP (1990), *Human Development Report 1990*, New York: UNDP.

—— (1995), *Human Development Report 1995*, New York: UNDP.

2

Interest, Well-being and Advantage[*]

Bhaskar Dutta

D 60

D 71

1 INTRODUCTION

The dominant theme in traditional welfare economics is *welfarism*, which rules out the use of non-utility information in the evaluation of social states. Welfarism implies that the 'social welfare attached to any social state *x* is taken to depend ultimately only on the individual *utilities* or welfares of the people in that state. Hence, social welfare must be identical in social states *x* and *y* if both result in the same distribution of individual utilities.

Welfarism is the culmination of distinct though interrelated premises. First, there is the presumption that there is *one* simple measure — utility — of a person's *interest*. Of course, the term 'utility' itself has various interpretations. Two possible interpretations are in terms of (1) happiness or pleasure and (2) desire fulfilment. With somewhat greater inexactitude, it can also stand for *whatever* an individual is maximizing. Second, Welfarism also assumes that the *process* through which utility is attained has no relevance in so far as the goodness of a social state is concerned. The latter presumption rules out considerations of freedom or liberty associated with different states.

* I am delighted to be able to contribute this paper to the volume in honour of Professor Tapas Majumdar, whose lectures in Presidency College, Calcutta generated my interest in Welfare Economics. An earlier version of this paper was circulated under the title *Interest and Advantage*. I am most grateful to Prasanta Pattanaik and Arunava Sen for comments and discussion.

There is by now a substantial literature criticising these aspects of welfarism.[1] Perhaps the most severe critic of the practice of equating 'utility' with an individual's interest is Sen (1985a), who argues that this practice by identifying widely different concepts of self-interest, motivation, etc., ' . . . has the effect of taking a very narrow view of human beings (and their feelings, ideas and actions), thereby significantly impoverishing the scope and reach of economic theory.[2]

Sen identifies two different ways of viewing a person's interests and their fulfilment, labelled *well-being* and *advantage* respectively. The well-being of a person can be seen in terms of the quality of the person's being or achievement, whereas advantage refers to the opportunities or freedom that a person has to pursue his or her well-being. This is closely related to Dasgupta (1990), who distinguishes between objectives and goals of an individual and commodities, resources or inputs which make such achievements possible. This allows for a distinction between *outcome-based* approaches and *resource-based* approaches to the problem of defining the standard of living.

Of course, there can be many different approaches within the broad categories of well-being and advantage. For example, the various possible interpretations of utility can be viewed as alternative representations of well-being. However, it is important to note that utility, either as desire-fulfilment or happiness, is not the only sensible proxy for well-being. Consider, for instance, a poor and undernourished landless labourer in India. He is *used* to hunger. So, he is happy and his desires are fulfilled even when he gets barely one square meal a day. But, he is not *well-nourished*, which may be considered an important component of well-being.

Sen (1985a) proposes an alternative formulation of a person's well-being in terms of *functioning*. Functioning is an intrinsic part of the person, and is quite distinct both from the commodities which are used to achieve the functioning, as well as the pleasure

---

[1] See Pattanaik (1992) for a discussion of some of these issues.

[2] See also Sen (1977a).

or happiness achieved from the functioning. Of course, in any evaluative exercise, it is important to decide on the *objects of value*. In Sen's approach, a functioning vector represents a state of being, and is the object of value. Different functioning vectors can be compared (in terms of well-being) through a *valuation ranking*. At first sight, it may seen natural to evaluate a person's interest by focusing on the functioning vector actually *achieved*. However, Sen points out that this ignores the person's advantage. In order to incorporate advantage in the evaluation of interest, it is necessary to also consider an individual *capability set*, which is the set of functioning vectors *available* to the individual.

This is related to the more general notion that the freedom to pursue one's objective is an important component of an individual's interest. As Pattanaik and Xu (1990) observe, a major defence of the (competitive) market mechanism as an allocative mechanism is that it affords freedom of choice to individual agents. Consider, for instance, a specific economy in which the market mechanism results in the allocation x^*. Suppose that the market mechanism is replaced by a command mechanism which *enforces* the same allocation x^*. The naive welfarist would declare that social welfare has remained unchanged since individuals are getting the same commodity bundles. However, most of us would argue that individuals are 'better off' when they are allowed to *choose* from their budget set — the fact that they choose the same bundle as in the command mechanism does not affect this sentiment.

It seems natural to rank alternative choice situations in terms of the degree of freedom by comparing the *opportunity sets* available to an individual under the various situations. As in the capabilities approach, this involves ranking alternative opportunity sets, where given an opportunity set, an individual will choose his or her most preferred outcome in the set.

The purpose of this paper is to discuss some of the issues involved in ranking capability sets and opportunity sets. Although capability sets can also be viewed as opportunity sets, a somewhat different treatment is required in the two cases because an individual's valuation ranking over the set of all possible functionings will typically *not* be *complete*, whereas it is normally assumed that an individual's preference ordering over general opportunity sets is a complete ordering. I take up the ranking of capability sets in Section 2, while Section 3 is concerned with the ranking of opportunity sets.[3]

2 RANKING CAPABILITY SETS

Let X be the commodity space, with generic element x. For any individual i, X_i is the *commodity entitlement set*, the set of commodity bundles that i can possess. Given any $x \in X, c(x)$ represents the vector of *characteristics* corresponding to x. The mapping c is impersonal and is invariant with respect to the individual who possesses the bundle x. In particular, it does not give any idea about how *useful* the bundle x is to any specific individual. For example, a book which may be treated as having the characteristic 'reading pleasure' is not of much use to a blind individual. *Functioning* tells us what a person can do with the commodities in his or her possession. Let f_i be a personal *utilization mapping* of individual i, generating a functioning vector out of a characteristic vector of commodities possessed. F_i is the set of utilization functions available to individual i. If individual i chooses the function f_i and possesses commodity bundle x_i, then the *achieved* functioning is given by the vector b_i, where

$$b_i = f_i(c(x_i)) \qquad (2.1)$$

Individual i's *capability set* is given by

$$B_i = \{b_i \mid b_i = f_i(c(x_i)), f_i \in F_i, x_i \in X_i\}. \qquad (2.2)$$

[3] Thus these are special cases of the general problem of extending a preference ordering over a set to its power set. There is a substantial literature which addresses this general issue. See Kannai and Peleg (1984), Barbera and Pattanaik (1984), Fishburn (1984), Heiner and Packard (1984), Holzman (1984), Kreps (1979) amongst others.

The capability set represents an individual's freedom to choose from possible livings. The functioning vectors are the objects of value, and there is a *valuation ranking* υ defined over B, the universal set of all possible functionings. Obviously, B_i, individual i's capability set, is a subset of B. If the valuation ranking is complete and admits a numerical representation, then υ can be thought of as a real-valued function attaching a real number to each state $b \in B$. However, this does *not* imply that $\upsilon(b)$ can be interpreted as the *utility* derived from b, because the utility derived from a given commodity bundle is sensitive to the *conditioning* influenced by an individual's actual state of being, whereas the judgement of interest should be based on more *objective* criteria.

Of course, different individuals may have different valuation rankings. In some exercises, it may make sense to assume that the evaluation is performed in terms of an outside observer's ranking υ which is the intersection ranking of the individual υ_i's. In general, it is sensible not to impose completeness on the valuation ranking. Thus, υ can be assumed to be a *partial* ordering. I will use $P(\upsilon)$ to denote the asymmetric part of υ.

The well-being approach to evaluation of interests declares i to be more 'fortunate' than j if the valuation ranking υ ranks b_i higher than b_j, where b_i and b_j are the *actual* states of being of i and j. However, this approach ignores completely the advantage of i and j. Incorporation of the 'freedom to choose' aspect necessitates a comparison of the *sets* B_i and B_j.

Let $\boldsymbol{B}$ be the power set of B. The ranking of capability sets is to be done in terms of an ordering $\geq$ defined over $\boldsymbol{B}$, $\geq$ being an extension of the valuation ranking υ. Elements of $\boldsymbol{B}$ are capability sets of different individuals. (In order to simplify the notation, I will omit the subscripts i, j, and let X, Y etc. denote elements of $\boldsymbol{B}$).

My purpose here is to focus on the problems created by the fact that υ is *not* complete. In order to do so, the axioms I will impose on the ordering $\geq$ will give primacy to well-being over advantage.

The first axiom is relatively non-controversial.

Axiom D: For all $X, Y \in \boldsymbol{B}$, if for every $y \in Y$, there is $x \in X$ such that $x \upsilon y$ [resp. $xP(\upsilon)y$], then $X \geq Y$ [resp. $X > Y$].

Given any set $X \in B$, let $M(X) = \{x \in X \mid \text{not } yP(\upsilon)x \text{ for any } y \in X\}$. $M(X)$ is the set of maximal elements in X according to υ.

Axiom M: For all $X \in \boldsymbol{B}, M(X) \sim X$.

This axiom is somewhat against the spirit of advantage. Since a larger capability set gives the individual more freedom, X should be ranked higher than $M(X)$. However, the intuition behind this axiom is that pursuit of self-interest will imply that an individual chooses an element out of the maximal set, and is hence indifferent between two sets having the same maximal set. Axiom M gives only *limited* importance to freedom of choice — a set X may be preferred to Y if $M(Y) \subset M(X)$.

I now introduce a class of orderings over B. First, define $\boldsymbol{R} = \{R \mid R \text{ is an } ordering\ extension \text{ of } \upsilon\}$. By Spzilrajn's theorem, $\boldsymbol{R}$ is non-empty. Any $R \in \boldsymbol{R}$ can be extended to $\boldsymbol{B}$ in the following way.

$$\forall\, X, Y \in \boldsymbol{B}, X \geq Y \leftrightarrow \exists x \in X, xRy\ \forall\, y \in Y. \qquad (2.3)$$

If $\geq$ is derived from R via (2.3), then I will say that $\geq$ has been *induced* by R.

Theorem 2.1: Let $\geq$ be an ordering over $\boldsymbol{B}$. Then, $\geq$ satisfies Axioms D and M iff it is induced by some $R \in \boldsymbol{R}$.

Proof: It is trivial to check that any $\geq$ induced by some $R \in \boldsymbol{R}$ is an ordering satisfying D and M. So, I will only prove necessity.

Suppose $\geq$ is an ordering which is not induced by $R \in \boldsymbol{R}$. Thus, for some $X, Y \in B$, one of the two must be true:

(i) $X > Y$ and $Y \geq' X$ for any $\geq'$ induced by some $R \in \boldsymbol{R}$.
(ii) $X \sim Y$ and $Y >' X$ for any $\geq'$ induced by some $R \in \boldsymbol{R}$.

Case (i): Suppose $Y \geq' X$ for any $\geq'$ induced by some $R \in \boldsymbol{R}$. Choose any $x \in M(X)$. Then, we must have some $y \in M(Y)$ such that $y \upsilon x$. For, suppose not. Then, construct R^* such that for all $z \in B$, if not $z \upsilon x$, then xP^*z. Clearly, $R^* \in \boldsymbol{R}$. Let $\geq^*$ be induced by R^*. Then $X >^* Y$ contradicting the hypothesis that $Y >' X$ for all

$>'$ induced by $R \in \boldsymbol{R}$. So, for all $x \in M(X)$, there is $y \in M(Y)$ such that $y \upsilon x$. By Axiom D, this implies $M(Y) \geq M(X)$. By Axiom M, $M(Y) \sim Y$ and $M(X) \sim X$. By transitivity, $Y \geq X$.

Case (ii): If $Y > X$ for all $>$ induced by some $R \in \boldsymbol{R}$, then for any $x \in M(X)$, there is $y \in M(Y)$ such that $yP(\upsilon)x$. Using Axiom D and M, we get $Y > X$ in an analogous way to Case (ii).

This completes the proof of the theorem.

The theorem is not really surprising. Given the assumed primacy of well-being, the problem of ranking capability sets is non-trivial only if υ is a *partial ordering*. It is not difficult, therefore, to come up with reasonable axioms which together imply that capability sets must be ranked according to *some* ordering extension of υ.

But, *which* ordering extension? I do not believe that it is possible to single out any one extension as the most plausible or natural candidate. Consider the following example.

Example 2.1

Let $B = \{x, y, z, w\}$. The valuation ranking is given by $xP(\upsilon)z$, $wP(\upsilon)y$.

Let $X = \{x, y\}$, $Y = \{z, w\}$.

Then, $M(X) = \{x, y\}$, $M(Y) = \{z, w\}$. The reader can check that $X >^1 Y, X \sim^2 Y$ and $Y <^3 X$ are all possible orderings induced by orderings in $\boldsymbol{R}$.

This suggests that the dominance ranking defined in Axiom D is the only acceptable or noncontroversial ranking. Of course, this dominance ranking will be unable to compare 'most' pairs of capability sets. This casts some doubt on the practical usefulness of the capabilities approach.

3 RANKING OPPORTUNITY SETS

In this section, I will discuss the issue of constructing suitable rankings of opportunity sets.

Let X be a non-empty, finite set of alternatives, with $|X| = n \geq 3$. The power set of X is $\Pi(X)$. R denotes an *ordering* over X. The elements of $\Pi(X)$ are to be interpreted as possible opportunity sets that may be available to an individual, while R represents the individual's preference ordering over the set of all possible opportunities. Let R^* denote an ordering over $\Pi(X)$. Clearly, the only formal difference between the framework here and that of ranking capability sets is that the valuation ranking υ is a partial ordering, whereas R is assumed to be a complete ordering.

There are two distinct possible approaches in the ranking of one-element opportunity sets. One possibility is to assume that R^* ranks singleton opportunity sets in the same way as the alternatives themselves are ranked by R. One could argue, for instance, that $\{x\}$ and $\{y\}$ offer the same degree of freedom, so that given xPy, $\{x\}$ is better than $\{y\}$ in so far as an individual's interest is concerned. For ranking of opportunity sets based *solely* on freedom of choice, Pattanaik and Xu (1990) contend that $\{x\}$ and $\{y\}$ are pair-wise indifferent since an individual is offered *no choice* at all when he has to choose from singleton opportunity sets.[4] These different views are formalized by the two axioms below.

Axiom SD (Simple Dominance): $\forall x, y \in X, xPy \rightarrow xP^*y$.

Axiom INS (Indifference between No-Choice Situations): $\forall x, y \in X, \{x\} I^* \{y\}$. Pattanaik and XU (1990) also define the following conditions.

Axiom SM (Strict Monotonicity): $\forall$ distinct $x, y \in X, \{x, y\} P^* \{x\}$

IND (Independence): $\forall A, B \in \Pi(X), \forall x \notin A \cup B, AR^* B \leftrightarrow A \cup \{x\} R^* B \cup \{x\}$.

Axiom SM captures the basic notion that 'freedom matters'. IND has been widely used in the literature on ranking of sets.[5] As Pattanaik and Xu point out, IND ignores any possible interaction between various opportunities. For instance, suppose an individual prefers {red car} to {train}. However, the person may well

---

[4] See, however, Sen (1991) who argues that even in such situations 'preference' must influence freedom rankings.

[5] See Kannai and Peleg (1984), Barbera and Pattanaik (1984).

prefer {train, blue car} to {blue car, red car} since the former offers greater diversity.

Pattanaik and Xu show that the only ranking rule which satisfies, INS, SM and IND is the rather naive cardinality-based rule which declares a set X to be at least as good as Y if $|X| \geq |Y|$. Below, I prove a more general result.

First, I define two binary relations $>_d$ and $\sim_E$ on $\Pi(X)$.

Definition 3.1: Let $A, B \in \Pi(X)$.

(3.1.1) $A >_d B$ iff either (i) $|A| = |B|$ and there exists a $1:1$ mapping $g: A \to B$ such that for all $x \in A$, $\{x\} R^* \{g(x)\}$ and for some $x \in A$, $\{x\} P^* \{g(x)\}$, or (ii) $|A| > |B|$, and for some $B' \subset A$, $|B'| = |B|$ and there exists a $1:1$ mapping $g: B' \to B$ such that for all $x \in B'$, $\{x\} R^* \{g(x)\}$.

(3.1.2) $A \sim_E B$ iff $|A| = |B|$ and for some $1:1$ mapping $g: A \to B$, $\{x\} I^* \{g(x)\}$ for all $x \in A$.

Thus, $>_d$ is a dominance relation, whereas $\sim_E$ stands for 'is equivalent to'.

Theorem 3.1: Suppose R^* satisfies SM and IND. Then,

$$A >_d B \Rightarrow AP^* B. \tag{3.1}$$

$$A \sim_E B \Rightarrow AI^* B \tag{3.2}$$

Proof: (3.1) Take any $A, B \in \Pi(X)$ such that $A >_d B$. Let $C = (A - B)$ and $D = (B - A)$. Then, $C >_d D$. Also, by repeated use of IND, $AP^* B \leftrightarrow CP^* B$.

First, consider the case where $|C| = |D|$. Let $x^* \in C$ be such that $\{x^*\} P^* \{g(x^*)\}$. Note that the existence of such x^* follows from the fact that $C >_d D$. Now, let $C = \{x_1, \ldots, x_k, x^*\}$ and $D = \{g(x_1), \ldots, g(x_k), g(x^*)\}$.

By IND, we have $\{x_1, x^*\} P^* \{x_1, g(x^*)\}$. Moreover, $\{x_1\} R^* \{g(x_1)\}$ and IND imply $\{x_1, g(x^*)\} R^* \{g(x_1), g(x^*)\}$. Hence, $\{x_1, x^*\} P^* \{g(x_1), g(x^*)\}$ by transitivity. Repeated application of IND, transitivity and the fact that $\{x_i\} R^* \{g(x_i)\}$ give CP^*D. Hence, AP^*B.

Now, suppose $|C| > |D| = k$. Let the first k elements of C (in terms of R) be $C' = \{x_1, \ldots, x_k\}$. So, for each $x_i \in C'$, there is

$g(x_i) \in D$ such that $\{x_i\}\, R^*\, \{g(x_i)\}$. Repeated application of IND and transitivity ensure $C'R^*D$. Moreover repeated use of SM ensures CP^*C'. Hence, CP^*D from transitivity.

(3.2) Suppose $A \sim_E B$. If $A = B$, then we have AI^*B. Suppose $A = \{x_1, \ldots, x_k\}$, $B = \{\sigma(x_1), \ldots, \sigma(x_k)\}$, and $\{x_i\}\, I^*\, \{\sigma(x_i)\}$ for all $i = 1, \ldots, k$. By IND, we have $\{x_1, x_2\}\, I^*\, \{\sigma(x_1), x_2\}$. Using IND again, $\{\sigma(x_1), x_2\}\, I^*\, \{\sigma(x_1), \sigma(x_2)\}$. So, $\{x_1, x_2\}\, I^*\, \{\sigma(x_1), \sigma(x_2)\}$. Repeating this argument, one arrives at AI^*B.

Remark: Note that INS implies that $A \sim_E B \leftrightarrow |A| = |B|$, and $A >_d B \leftrightarrow |A| > |B|$. Hence, (3.1) and (3.2) imply the central result of Pattanaik and Xu (1990).

Of course, the well-being aspect can be incorporated if INS is dropped. However, one may feel that only the R-maximal element in an opportunity set is relevant in so far as an individual is going to choose this element out of his or her opportunity set — the existence of other opportunities only influence advantage.

This is modelled by Bossert, Pattanaik and Xu (1992), who characterize other ranking rules. Two crucial axioms used by them are the following.

Axiom WIND (Weak Independence): $\forall A, B \in \Pi(X), \forall x \notin A \cup B$, $[\max(A)Px$ and $\max(B)Px] \rightarrow [A \cup \{x\}\, P^*\, B \cup \{x\}] \leftrightarrow A \cup B$.[6, 7]

Axiom SIIP (Simple Indirect Indifference Principle): $\forall$ distinct $x, y, z \in X$,

$$xPyPz \rightarrow \{x, y\} \sim \{x, z\}.$$

Bossert, Pattanaik and Xu prove the important result that any ordering over $\Pi(X)$ satisfying Axioms WIND and SIIP must declare sets A and B to be indifferent if $\max(A) = \max(B)$ and $|A| = |B|$. In other words, the only characteristics which matter in the ranking of opportunity sets are the best element and cardinality of the sets, representing the well-being and advantage aspects respectively of an individual's interest. Additional axioms

---

[6] In order to simplify the proofs, they assumed that R was a *linear* ordering.

[7] $\max(A) = \{x \in A \mid xRy \text{ for all } y \in A - \{x\}\}$.

were used to characterise two *lexicographic* orderings R_C^* and R_p^*. These are defined below,

$$\forall\, A, B \in \Pi(X), AR_C^* B \leftrightarrow [\,|A\,| > |B\,|\,] \text{ or } [\,|A\,| = |B\,| \tag{3.3}$$
$$\text{and } \max(A) P \max(B)]$$

$$\forall\, A, B \in \Pi(X), AR_p^* B \leftrightarrow [\max(A) P \max(B)] \text{ or }$$
$$[\max(A) = \max(B) \text{ and } |A\,| > |B\,|\,]. \tag{3.4}$$

Thus, R_C^* gives overwhelming primacy to advantage, whereas R_p^* allows the well-being aspect to 'dictate', and 'freedom of choice' mattering only if two sets have the *same* maximal element. The common characteristic of R_C^* and R_p^*, is that no trade-off is permitted between the two aspects of well-being and advantage.

Is this inevitable? Consider the following approach to the problem of ranking opportunity sets.[8] In Bossert, Pattanaik and Xu, well-being (represented by $\max(A)$) and advantage (represented by cardinality) were the only relevant characteristics. But, of course, WIND suffers from the same defect as IND since it also neglects interaction between different opportunities. One way of removing this defect is by considering a characteristic such as *diversity* of choice. This can be done by partitioning X into (say) $\{X_1, \ldots, X_K\}$. Opportunities within each X_i, $i = 1, \ldots, K$ belong to the same 'type'. For instance, cars of a different colour may be put into one type. Define the *diversity* of a set $A \in \Pi(X)$ to be equal to $|\{i \mid X_i \cap A \neq \emptyset\}|$.

Clearly, one can define orderings R_w, R_a and R_d over X, representing well-being, advantage and diversity orderings respectively of opportunity sets. These are defined below:
$\forall A, B \in \Pi(X)$,

$$AR_w B \leftrightarrow \max(A) R \max(B) \tag{3.5}$$

$$AR_a B \leftrightarrow |A\,| \geq |B\,| \tag{3.6}$$

$$AR_d B \leftrightarrow |\{i \mid X_i \cap A\}| \geq |\{i \mid X_i \cap B\}|. \tag{3.7}$$

---

[8] See Dutta and Sen (1993) for a formal analysis along these lines.

The overall ranking of opportunity sets can be viewed as an aggregate of these 'individual' rankings. Notice that this exercise is formally identical to the Arrovian problem of constructing a *social ordering* from individual orderings. Of course, in the present context, it does not make sense to impose *interprofile* conditions since there can be only *one* ordering of each type. So, the correct parallel to our present problem is the *single profile*[9] approach to the social aggregation problem.

In view of this analogy, it is appropriate to label the lexicographic rules characterized by Bossert, Pattanaik and Xu as *dictatorial* rules. When translated into the Arrovian framework, their axioms imply the absence of interpersonal comparability. It is well-known that the dictatorship results can be avoided by allowing for interpersonal comparability, that is, by imposing weaker *invariance conditions*.[10] Of course, the same menu of possibilities is available in the construction of orderings of opportunity sets.

As an example, I will describe below the 'utilitarian' type ordering R_u^*. It is convenient to assume that R is a linear ordering. Let $a = \max(A)$, $b = \max(B)$, etc.

The *well-being score* of A is:

$$w_A = |\{x \in X \mid aRx\}| + 1 \qquad (3.8)$$

The *advantage or freedom score* of A is:

$$f_A = |A| \qquad (3.9)$$

The *diversity* score of A is:

$$d_A = |\{i \mid X_i \cap A \neq \emptyset\}| \qquad (3.10)$$

Let α_1, α_2, α_3 be any vector of (strictly) positive real numbers such that $\alpha_1 + \alpha_2 + \alpha_3 = 1$. Then, the *Score* of A is:

$$s_A = \alpha_1 w_A + \alpha_2 f_A + \alpha_3 d_a \qquad (3.11)$$

---

[9] See Sen (1985b) for an illuminating discussion of the distinction between single profile and multiprofile approaches to the social aggregation problem.

[10] See, for instance, Sen (1977b).

Finally, R_u^* is defined as follows:

$$\forall A, B \in \Pi(X), AR_u^* B \leftrightarrow s_A \geq s_B \tag{3.12}$$

Clearly, R_u^* allows for non-trivial trade-off between well-being, advantage and diversity. Moreover, the *relative* desirability of these different aspects of interest can be varied by changing the weights α_i, $i = 1, 2, 3$.

Of course, the utilitarian type ordering R_u^* is only *one* ranking rule which permits a trade-off between various aspects of an individual's interest. Given the formal similarity between this problem and the traditional problem of aggregating individual orderings into a social ordering, one can immediately identify other appealing orderings. The characterization of such rules in terms of axioms which are suitable *given* the context, is an interesting exercise.

4 CONCLUSION

Well-being and advantage are both important components of an individual's interest. Consideration of advantage in the evaluation of interest involves the comparison of alternative opportunity sets. This involves the *extension* of an ordering over a set to its power set. In this paper, I have discussed some aspects of this problem. It turns out that there is a formal similarity between this problem and the more traditional problem in social choice theory of aggregating individual preferences into a social preference ordering. While this immediately opens up the possibility of characterizing different extension rules, it also implies that the familiar Arrownian impossibility theorems can be reformulated in this framework. The latter casts doubts on the practical applicability of non-welfarism.

REFERENCES

Barbera, S. and P.K. Pattanaik (1984), 'Extending an Order on a Set to the Power Set: Some Remarks on Kannai and Peleg's Approach', *Journal of Economic Theory*, 32, pp. 185–91.

Bossert, W., P.K. Pattanaik and Y. Xu (1992), 'Ranking Opportunity Sets: An Axiomatic Approach', mimeo.

Dasgupta, P. (1990), 'Well-being and the Extent of its Realization in Poor Countries', *Economic Journal*, 100, pp. 1–32.

Dutta, B. and Arunava Sen (1993), 'Ranking Opportunity Sets and Arrow Impossibility Theorems: Correspondence Results', to appear in *Journal of Economic Theory*.

Fishburn, P. (1984), 'Comment on the Kannai-Peleg Impossibility Theorem for Extending Orders', *Journal of Economic Theory*, 33, pp. 176–9.

Heiner, R. and D. Packard (1984), 'A Uniqueness Result for Extending Orders; with Applications to Collective Choice as Inconsistency Resolution', *Journal of Economic Theory*, 32, pp. 180–4.

Holzman, R. (1984), 'An Extension of Fishburn's Theorem on Extending Orders', *Journal of Economic Theory*, 32, pp. 192–6.

Kannai, Y. and B. Peleg (1984), 'A Note on the Extension of an Order on a Set to the Power Set', *Journal of Economic Theory*, 32, pp. 172–5.

Kreps, D.M. (1979), 'A Representation Theorem for "Preference for Flexibility" ', *Econometrica*, 47, pp. 565–77.

Pattanaik, P.K. (1992), 'Some Non-welfarist Issues in Welfare Economics', to appear in B. Dutta (ed.), *Welfare Economics*, New Delhi: Oxford University Press (in press).

Pattanaik, P.K. and Y. Xu (1990), 'On Ranking Opportunity Sets in Terms of Freedom of Choice', *Recherches Economiques de Louvain*, 56, pp. 383–90.

Sen, A.K. (1977a), 'Rational Fools: A Critique of the Behavioural Foundations of Economic Theory', *Philosophy and Public Affairs*, 6, pp. 317–44.

—— (1977b), 'On Weights and Measures: Informational Constraints in Social Welfare Analysis', *Econometrica*, 45, pp. 1539–72.

—— (1985a), *Commodities and Capabilities*, Amsterdam: North Holland.

—— (1985b), 'Social Choice Theory', in K.J. Arrow and M. Intriligator (eds), *Handbook of Mathematical Economics*, vol. 3, Amsterdam: North Holland.

—— (1991), 'Welfare, Preference and Freedom', *Journal of Econometrics*, 50, pp. 15–29.

II

Working of the Market Economy

A large part of economics is about how a modern market economy works and what its achievements and failures are. Some of the more important questions here are those related to price adjustments, monetary equilibrium, financial sector reforms, and the transition from a centrally planned to a market oriented economy. The four papers in this section deal with these issues.

Complexities of Concrete Walrasian Systems

There is a notion that the inconclusiveness of comparative static analysis in abstract general equilibrium theory arises from the multiplicity and heterogeneity of commodities and agents. This inconclusiveness is in sharp contrast to the transparency and definitiveness of miniature general equilibrium models, e.g. Heckscher-Ohlin trade models. Actually it is quite misleading to conclude that a higher level of aggregation invariably makes the analysis simple. The Mukul Majumdar–Tapan Mitra chapter in fact demonstrates how enormously complicated even a two-good, two-agent framework can be despite strong assumptions such as monotonicity and strict convexity.

Majumdar and Mitra pursue a very standard question: what is the outcome of a Walrasian tatonnement? This is a question that any beginner will want to ask, but attempts at answering it run into a surprising level of complexity. The first problem arises from the possibility of an unbounded number of equilibria, (theorems of Debreau and Kirman and Koch are revealing). Second, the price paths could be hypersensitive to initial conditions: paths starting very close to each other could behave in widely disparate ways. Third, there could be no convergence to an equilibrium or a cycle, the result might end up in 'chaos'. Much of the literature on Walrasian general equilibrium appears preoccupied with convergence to an equilibrium, with little interest shown in what happens to paths that do not converge.

Rational Choice and the Price of Money

Modern approaches to modelling money in macroeconomic models are marked by an explicit concern with micro-foundations and behaviour guided by rational choice. The chapter by Amitava Bose is an expository essay that seeks to bring this out. Two interrelated themes are pursued. The first theme sets out the link in a monetary economy between 'rationality' and two associated concepts, 'money illusion' and 'homogeneity of demand in absolute prices'. Next, the usefulness of money is taken up. The usefulness of paper money to an individual, derives from money having a positive market price in terms of goods. The problem of establishing an equilibrium with a positive price of money is expounded with the help of a simple dynamic general equilibrium model of pure exchange, using only the tools of text book consumer behaviour theory. The analysis brings out the relative importance of 'real balance effects', 'intertemporal substitution effects' and the 'elasticity of expectations' and provides alternative sufficient conditions for the existence of a monetary equilibrium.

Money, Credit and Government Finance in a Developing Economy

Financial markets in all economies, and more so in developing economies, exhibit features that have remained unincorporated in conventional macroeconomic models (such as ISLM models). Assumptions such as interest rates being market clearing rather than administered, widespread existence of secondary markets, etc., make these models rather inappropriate for handling numerous important analytical and policy issues relating to the financial sector. The chapter by Mihir Rakshit is an attempt to remodel the macroeconomics of money, credit and finance, so that these issues can be addressed properly.

The issues clarified include some that are especially relevant for contemporary problems of the Indian economy, such as (i) the relationship between the supply of money and the supply of credit; (ii) financial crowding-in or crowding-out resulting from government borrowing; (iii) implications of administered interest rates for the credit market; and (iv) the effects of financial liberalization, and the operation of mutual funds and other financial intermediaries. However, the chapter also sheds light on the controversy between Keynsians and monetarists on the endogeneity of money supply, the transmission mechanism and the stability of the velocity of circulation.

Three Aspects of Transforming Former Centrally Planned Economies

The transition from a planned to a market economy involves a rough ride, made rougher still by widespread use of inappropriate IMF-monetarist style stabilization policies. Amit Bhaduri contends that these policies are flawed in some major respects on questions of demand management, inflation control and the role of the state.

Conventional stabilization emphasizes the need to reduce aggregate demand through contractionary monetary and fiscal policies. However, these measures often have the effect of reducing aggregate supply as well. Secondly, to the extent that prices of numerous products are cost determined, contractionary measures will simply reduce output and not prices. Moreover, overriding concern with fiscal deficit targets (rather than the level and composition of expenditure) tend to encourage the use of administered price hikes as an escape route. At the same time, the fall in output that accompanies restrictive policies, automatically raises unit fixed cost thereby having a built-in tendency to push prices up. Finally, Bhaduri points to the fallacy of the prescription for a minimalist state, arguing that there is an essential complementarity between state-produced output and private sector output.

3

Complexities of
Concrete Walrasian Systems[*]

Mukul Majumdar and Tapan Mitra

Mathematical form powerfully contributes to defining a philosophy of
economic analysis whose major tenets include rigor, generality and simplicity. It commands the long search for the most direct routes from
assumptions to conclusions. It directs its aesthetic code, and it imposes
its terse language. Another tenet of that philosophy is recognition, and
acceptance, of the limits of economic theory, which cannot achieve a
grand unified explanation of economic phenomena.

Gerard Debreu[1]

1 INTRODUCTION

The rigorous elaboration of the Walras-Pareto 'theory of value'
has often been hailed as 'one of the most notable intellectual
achievements' of economic theory. The volume of research on
the refinements of the Arrow-Debreu-McKenzie model, the axiomatic style of exposition, and the growing use of a variety of
mathematical techniques have led to appraisals of the area by

* Mukul Majumdar wishes to thank the Institute of Economic Research at
Kyoto University for research support. The authors are indebted to Professors
Amitava Bose, Venkatesh Bala, Kaushik Basu, Valerie Bencivenga, and Kazuo
Nishimura for their comments on earlier drafts of this paper and dedicate this
paper with affection and respect to Professor Tapas Majumdar.

[1] See 'Random Walk and Life Philosophy', in *Eminent Economists*, p. 114.

methodologists, philosophers, historians of economic thought as well as by well-known economic theorists.[2] Some of the appraisals, not surprisingly, have been quite negative, characterizing the state of axiomatic general equilibrium theory as 'a wealth of mathematics but no proper object of study' (Jolink 1993, p. 1311). But more balanced assessments have also raised serious questions about the direction of future developments. To take a recent example, one might turn to Morishima's article (1991) on general equilibrium theory ('GET'). Morishima feels that 'unlike physics, economics has unfortunately developed in a direction far removed from its empirical source, and GET in particular, as the core of economic theory, has become a mathematical social philosophy'. Morishima emphasizes that the *price taking behaviour* that underlies the Walrasian model is applicable to only a small part of the modern industrialized economies. Moreover, the axioms of utility and profit maximization are inadequate to capture the motivations behind economic decisions, and may well be irrelevant in understanding the institutions of the highly productive economies of the Far East. On the whole, Morishima's article reflects unhappiness over the 'inadequate concern for actuality' reflected by the research efforts in GET.

Whether a model should be judged by the realism or empirical content of its *assumptions* has been a prominent issue in many a methodological debate. A somewhat extreme view (Friedman 1946) emphasized *predictive power* of the ultimate propositions as opposed to the realism of the assumptions as the key test. Others look for an *explanatory power* or more broadly, an 'understanding' of economic phenomena and institutions from a model, with due recognition that simplifications (in choosing assumptions) are inevitable for making significant progress in economic theory. A prominent theme in Samuelson's *Foundations* was the need to derive 'meaningful' (in principle refutable by empirical evidence)

---

[2] A survey of some of the appraisals is in Weintraub (1985). This book also contains a fascinating discussion of the developments in research leading to the landmarks of the early fifties. See also Radner (1991).

results on comparative statics and dynamics from formal mathematical models. In *Causality in Economics* (1979), Hicks mentioned five reasons for pursuing economic theory, but stressed: 'When theory is applied, it is being used as a means of explanation: we ask not merely what happened, but why it happened'.

If one recognizes that economic theory has its limits, and it 'cannot achieve a grand explanation of economic phenomena', one ought not to be surprised that a *particular* formal model is inadequate for explaining or understanding the forces behind the evolution of market prices in different economies and in different periods of history. It is better to interpret some of Morishima's criticisms as items on the agenda for future research. In this article, our focus is the difficulty of prediction in a Walrasian framework. In Section 1, we consider a Walrasian exchange economy. The *price-taking* agents have well behaved indifference curves, and maximize utility subject to the budget constraint. But, it turns out that maximizing behaviour and the standard assumptions on preferences (including strong convexity and monotonicity) do not impose any special restriction on the excess demand function of the economy. In the absence of special structures on the excess demand function, there is no bound on the number of Walrasian equilibria, and the scope of comparative statics or qualitative economics appears quite limited. Next, we go on to more 'concrete' models, namely, those with only two goods, and examine a Walrasian tatonnement cast in the form of a non-linear difference equation (following the tradition of 'period analysis' in economic dynamics). Even with two goods, one can construct examples of 'chaotic' tatonnement. The price path or trajectory over time may turn out to display *sensitive dependence on initial conditions:* trajectories emanating from nearby initial conditions exhibit remarkably different qualitative behaviour. Also, there may be an uncountable set of initial conditions from which the trajectories do not converge to an equilibrium or a periodic trajectory. At the same time, periodic or cyclical trajectories of *all* periods may be present (see Theorem 4.1 for a precise statement).

One way to look at the examples is to recognize the very limited possibility of predicting long run behaviour. From another perspective, since the initial condition crucially affects the dynamic behaviour, we are reminded of the importance of historical evolutions that presumably start the process from a particular initial condition. And, finally, we see that to 'explain' complicated dynamics, we do *not* have to invoke 'external shocks' (although these may be of importance in a particular context) or to develop complicated models with many variables (see May 1976).

2 THE BASIC MODEL

2.1 Notation

If $x = (x_k)$ is any vector in R^l, we say that x is *non-negative* ($x \geq 0$) if $x_k \geq 0$ for all k; x is *positive* ($x > 0$) if x is non-negative and $x_k > 0$ for some k, x is *strictly positive* ($x \gg 0$) if $x_k > 0$ for all k. For any two vectors x, y in R^l, we write $x \geq y$ (respectively, $x > y$; $x \gg y$) if $x - y \geq 0$ (resp. $x - y \geq 0$, $x - y \gg 0$). The set of all non-negative (resp. strictly positive) vectors in R^l is denoted by R^l_+ (resp. R^l_{++}).

By a preference preorder $\lesssim$ on R^l_+, we mean a binary relation on R^l_+ that is reflexive, transitive and complete (i.e., '$x \lesssim x$' for all x in R^l_+, '$x \lesssim y$, $y \lesssim z$' implies '$x \lesssim z$' for any x, y, z in R^l_+; for any pair x, y in R^l_+ either $x \lesssim y$ or $y \lesssim x$ (or both)). We write $x \sim y$ if $x \lesssim y$ *and* $y \lesssim x$; and $x < y$ if $x \lesssim y$ holds but $y \lesssim x$ does not hold. We interpret '$x \lesssim y$' as 'the commodity bundle x is no better than the commodity bundle y;' $x \sim y$ means that the consumer is indifferent between x and y, $x < y$ means that 'y is preferred to x.'

2.2 Excess Demand Functions

Consider first a Walrasian exchange economy with $l \geq 2$ goods, the prices of which are represented by strictly positive vectors with unit Euclidean norm, i.e., the set of prices is given by

$$S = \{p \in R^l: p \gg 0, ||p|| = 1\} \qquad (2.1)$$

$$\text{where } ||p|| = \left[\sum_{k=1}^{l} P_k^2\right]^{1/2}.$$

We shall restrict our attention mostly to prices bounded away from zero: for a sufficiently small positive ε, let

$$S_\varepsilon = \{p \in S: p_k \geq \varepsilon > 0, k = 1, \ldots, l\} \qquad (2.2)$$

A *consumer* is defined by a pair $(\leq, e)$ where $\leq$ represents his preferences and e is his endowment vector. We assume:

(C.1) $\leq$ *is a strictly convex, monotone, continuous preference preorder on R_+^l and the endowment e is an element of R_+^l.*

Recall that $\leq$ is *strictly convex* if the convex combination with weights different from 0 and 1 of two distinct indifferent consumption vectors is strictly preferred to both.

We say that $\leq$ is *monotone* if for any two vectors x, y in R_+^l with $x > y$, it is true that $y < x$. The preference preorder $\leq$ is *continuous* if for any x in R_+^l, both the sets:

$$\{y \in R_+^l: y \leq x\} \text{ and } \{z \in R_+^l: x \leq z\}$$

are closed in R_+^l.

Given our assumptions, it is known that '$\leq$' can be 'represented' by a *utility function u;* in other words, there is some $u: R_+^l \to R$ such that:

$$u(x) \geq u(y) \text{ if and only if } y \leq x.$$

For the sake of completeness, we recall a simple method of constructing such a utility function. Define

$$M = \{x \in R_+^l: x = (\lambda, \ldots, \lambda), \lambda \geq 0\}$$

When $l = 2$, M is just the 'forty-five degree line' from the origin. For any $x = (\lambda, \ldots, \lambda)$ in M, define $u(x) = \lambda$. Next, since '$\leq$' is continuous as well as monotone, corresponding to any $\hat{y}$ in R^l_+, there is a *unique* $\hat{x} = (\hat{\lambda}, \ldots, \hat{\lambda})$ in M such that $\hat{y} \sim \bar{x}$. Hence, define $u(\hat{y}) = u(\hat{x}) = \hat{\lambda}$. Again, when $l = 2$, it is helpful to visualize the construction by drawing the indifference curve through $\hat{y}$ which intersects the forty-five degree line at a unique $\hat{x}$.

Now, given a price system p in S, a consumer i, represented by $(\lesssim_i, e_i)$, chooses the best element d_i for $\lesssim_i$ in his *budget set*

$$B_i = \{x \in R^l_+ : p\,x \leq p\,e_i\}.$$

The monotonicity assumption on $\lesssim_i$ ensures that d_i will be on the 'budget hyperplane', i.e., $pd_i = pe_i$ (the expenditure on d_i will be equal to the income pe_i). The excess demand of consumer i is the vector $z_i = d_i - e_i$. Thus, the *value* of excess demand of consumer i is necessarily zero, i.e., $pz_i = 0$. Hence, the aggregate excess demand of the economy with n agents defined as

$$z = z_1 + \ldots + z_n$$

also satisfies 'Walras' law':

$$pz = 0 \qquad\qquad (2.3)$$

The motivation behind the next two definitions should now be clear.

A function $f\colon S \to R^l$ is the *individual excess demand function* of consumer $(\lesssim, e)$ if for every p in S, $e + f(p)$ is the best element for $\lesssim$ of $B = \{x \in R^l : p\,x \leq p\,e\}$, i.e., any x in B satisfies $x \lesssim (e + f(p))$.

A continuous function $f\colon S \to R^l$ is an *excess demand function* (for the economy) if for every p in S, $p\,f(p) = 0$.

The basic result of Debreu (1974) can now be stated. Recall that l is the number of commodities.

Theorem 2.1 Let f be an excess demand function. For every $\varepsilon > 0$, there are l consumers whose individual excess demand functions sum to f on S_ε.

Any continuous function satisfying Walras' law can be viewed as an excess demand function (on S_ε) of an appropriately constructed exchange economy with l consumers. Thus, the utility maximization hypothesis in the context of the Walrasian economy imposes no special structure on the excess demand function of the economy (besides Walras' law) *even when the preferences are required to be monotone, strictly convex and continuous*, i.e., the 'indifference curves' look like those appearing in Hicks' *Value and Capital*.

Debreu's theorem has been extended in many directions. In particular, there is no hope of getting any special property of excess demand functions by restricting the *dispersion* of endowments and income. Also of interest is the following result due to Kirman and Koch (1986):

Theorem 2.2 Let n be a positive integer greater than or equal to l, and $\upsilon_1, \ldots, \upsilon_n$ be distinct positive real numbers with $\upsilon_1 + \ldots + \upsilon_n = 1$. Let $f: S \to R^l$ be an excess demand function. Then for every $\varepsilon > 0$, there exists a continuous, monotone, strictly convex preference preorder $\leq$ on R^l_+ and an endowment vector e in R^l_+, such that the individual excess demand functions of agents $i (= 1, \ldots, n)$ represented by $(\leq, \upsilon_i e)$ sum up to f on S_ε.

We see that even when we impose the additional *restriction* that all agents have the *same* preference preordering and that their endowments are of the type $\upsilon_i e$ (so that the distribution of relative income is fixed and price independent) there is still no special restriction on the class of excess demand functions for the economy.

Let us spell out some implications of these results for qualitative economics. The set of Walrasian equilibrium prices is formally given by

$$W = \{p \in S: f(p) = 0\} \tag{2.4}$$

Clearly, for 'explaining' some observed prices perceived as equilibrium prices, or predicting equilibrium prices from appropriate information on excess demand functions, it is essential to have as detailed a knowledge of W as possible. The first task, of course, is to understand conditions on f such that W is *non-empty*. Here, in addition to Walras law, some continuity, desirability and boundedness conditions on f certainly suffice to assure that W is non-empty.[3] However, the existence of an equilibrium price system (mathematically, a 'fixed point' problem) does not imply that W consists of a *single* element: indeed, examples of non-uniqueness cannot be dismissed as pathological. A programme of research initiated by Debreu aimed at studying the properties of W for 'typical' or 'generic' models of exchange economies. The literature is understandably technical, and leads to the conclusion that a 'typical' or 'regular' economy has a *finite* number of equilibria (i.e., the set W is *discrete*). Furthermore, it was also proved that in a 'neighborhood' of a regular economy (i.e., for small 'local' variations around a typical model) the set of equilibrium prices will change continuously with variations in the parameters (preferences/endowments). The importance of such continuity was stressed by Debreu (1975) along these lines: [in the absence of such continuity] 'the slightest error of observation on the data of the economy might lead to an entirely different set of predicted equilibria. This consideration, which is common in the study of physical systems, applies with even greater force to the study of social systems'.

But it is *not* possible to put any upper bound on the number of elements of W, and our Theorem 2.1 indicates why it is difficult to make 'general' qualitative predictions on W.

There are two other routes that have been explored. The first possibility (pioneered by H. Scarf) is to rely on explicit computation of W by assuming particular forms of excess demand functions. The functional forms presumably have to be chosen on the basis of estimates from the relevant data (and practical considerations of computational feasibility will be relevant). 'Computable' general equilibrium models will bring the theory closer to the empirical world (as often urged) and will be used more effectively as researchers gain experience with more sophisticated machines that have a vast memory and exceptional speed.

---

[3] Formally, assume that f is continuous at any $p \gg 0$, and for any sequence p^n in S converging to some p in the boundary of S, $||f(p^n)|| \to \infty$; also f is bounded below. See Arrow and Hahn (1971).

Yet another route has been to develop 'concrete' Walrasian models. Here, drastic assumptions on the number of goods and/or the nature of technology and preferences are usually made in order to derive insightful comparative static or dynamic results. The literature on 'pure' theory of international trade is probably the best example of successful efforts in this direction.

It is of interest to note that in assessing Paul Samuelson's contributions to economics, Lindbeck (1970) observed that Samuelson's 'most important contributions in general equilibrium theory is probably a "concretization" of the Walrasian system, implying a simplification of general equilibrium theory. This makes it possible to analyse concrete problems and to reach operationally meaningful theorems, rather than limiting the analysis to counting of equations and unknowns and saying that "everything depends on everything else".'

In what follows, we look at such a 'concrete' model with only two commodities. It turns out that even with such an extreme simplification, we face complex problems if we want to develop the dynamic processes that underlie comparative static exercises.

3 WALRASIAN TATONNEMENT

What can we say about the behavior of markets when the price system is *not* an equilibrium? Walras himself discussed a market-by-market adjustment process through which an equilibrium can be attained. He emphasized that the *direct pressure* of excess demand in a market on its prevailing (non-equilibrium) price will push it towards an equilibrium level at which the equality of demand and supply will prevail. He recognized that such a change in one market would disturb other markets, but these 'indirect influences, some in the direction of equality and others in the opposite direction' . . . 'up to a point cancelled each other out' (Walras, *Elements of Pure Economics*, 1954 Jaffee translation from the 1926 edition).

A mathematical formulation of the Walrasian tatonnement was

presented by Samuelson in his *Foundations*. We know now
that unless one has some special features (see Arrow and Hahn
(1971) on sufficient conditions for local and global stability of
tatonnement), a dynamic price process in which the price in one
market increases (decreases) if there is positive (negative) excess
demand need not converge to an equilibrium. In a model with
two commodities, however, a particularly interesting result was
obtained by Arrow and Hurwicz (1958), a result which indicates
the possibility of using the tatonnement to approach an equilibrium. We shall first describe a similar situation somewhat
informally.

3.1 Adjustments in a Two Commodity Model

We can conveniently represent a two commodity economy (given
(W)) by a single *excess demand function*

$$\zeta_1(p) \equiv z_1(p_1, 1 - p_1), 0 < p_1 < 1 \qquad (3.1)$$

In this section we shall drop the subscript for the commodity
in order to simplify notation.

Now suppose that we have a family of economies E_θ each
described by an excess demand function of the type (3.1). Formally, the family of economies E_θ is described by a family of
functions $\{\zeta_\theta(p)\}$ where the parameter θ belongs to some (non-
empty) set C. Assume that *for each θ in C, $\zeta_\theta(p)$ is continuous on*
(0,1), *and has finitely many zeros* (i.e., $\zeta_\theta(p) = 0$ has finitely many
solutions). Also, assume the following *boundary condition:*

'*For each $\theta \in C$, $\zeta_\theta(p) > 0$ (resp. < 0) for all p sufficiently close to* 0.
(resp. 1).'

Consider any equilibrium $\bar{p}_\theta$ of the economy E_θ, i.e.,
$\zeta_\theta(\bar{p}_\theta) = 0$; next, we change the value of θ to some other θ'. For
concreteness, assume that $\zeta_{\theta'}(\bar{p}_\theta) > 0$. In other words, we imagine
that the economy E_θ is initially in equilibrium at price $\bar{p}_\theta$ and
then there is a shift of the excess demand function generating
positive excess demand at the price $\bar{p}_\theta$. Now, suppose that the

price adjustment in disequilibrium is modelled as a *continuous time* tatonnement process

$$\frac{dp}{dt} = \alpha \, \zeta_{\theta'}(p(t)), \, \alpha > 0 \qquad (3.2)$$

where $\alpha > 0$ is the speed of adjustment. In this case a theorem of Arrow and Hurwicz can be invoked to assert that $p(t)$ starting from $\bar{p}_\theta$ will converge to *some* equilibrium of the economy $E_{\theta'}$. Since at $\bar{p}_\theta$, excess demand of the economy $E_{\theta'}$ is assumed to be positive (i.e., $\zeta_{\theta'}(\bar{p}_\theta) > 0$), and, by our boundary condition, $\zeta_{\theta'}(p) < 0$ when p is sufficiently close to one, we can use the intermediate value theorem and assert that there is *some* $\bar{p}$ in $(\bar{p}_\theta, 1)$ such that $\zeta_{\theta'}(\bar{p}) = 0$. Clearly, if we take the *smallest* such $\bar{p}$ in $(\bar{p}_\theta, 1)$, say $\bar{p}_{\theta'}$, the process (3.2) starting from $\bar{p}_\theta$ will increase to $\bar{p}_{\theta'}$. Hence, a shift from ζ_θ to $\zeta_{\theta'}$ that generates a positive [respectively, negative] excess demand at the initial equilibrium $\bar{p}_\theta$ leads to an increasing [resp. decreasing] $p(t)$ that will converge to a new equilibrium $\bar{p}_{\theta'} > \bar{p}_\theta$. A formal proof of convergence is spelled out in Arrow and Hahn (1971), and convergence does *not* imply that 'markets will settle down to the new equilibrium $\bar{p}_{\theta'}$ in finite time', but the special structure of the model yields an unambiguous prediction as to the direction of change from the old equilibrium $\bar{p}_\theta$ to the new equilibrium $\bar{p}_{\theta'}$.

But economic theory has a tradition of 'period' analysis in which time is treated as a discrete variable. Whether a continuous time formulation is adequate or well-suited for depicting the evolution of an economic process has been discussed extensively (see Baumol 1971). When we think of the Walrasian auctioneer whose role is to announce prices and then to make the appropriate revisions in the light of responses from the agents in various markets, we feel that Saari's remarks (1985, p. 119) on period analysis are quite persuasive. 'It can be argued', he said, 'that the correct dynamical process associated with the tatonnement process is an iterative one. Just one supporting argument is that the differential dynamic process requires a continuum of information. At each instant of time the information must be updated; so a continuous mechanism is far beyond the capability of any "auctioneer".'

In the tradition of 'period analysis' an adjustment process may also be cast in terms of a discrete-time difference equation. For example, we might write

$$p_{t+1} = p_t + \alpha \, \zeta_{\theta'}(p_t) \text{ where } p_0 = \bar{p}_\theta$$

or simply

$$p_{t+1} \equiv G_{\theta'}(p_t) \tag{3.3}$$

The global behaviour of (3.3) may be in sharp contrast with that of (3.2). It is remarkable that even a simple 'one dimensional' system (3.3) may display extremely complicated behaviour. In the next section we elaborate on this point.

4 A DIGRESSION ON CHAOTIC DYNAMICS

4.1 Abundance of Cycles

It is useful to recall some mathematical definitions. Consider a first order difference equation

$$x_{t+1} = F(x_t) \tag{4.1}$$

where F is a continuous map from some interval X of real numbers into itself. The set X is the *state space* and F is the *law of motion* of the *dynamical system* defined as the pair (X, F). To set the notation, write $F^0(x) \equiv x$, and for each $j \geq 1, F^j(x) \equiv F[F^{j-1}(x)]$. Starting from an initial x in X, the rule (4.1) provides us with the *trajectory* $(F^j(x))_{j=0}^\infty$. Once the initial state x is specified, the law of motion unambiguously specifies x_t, the state of the system in period t. A point x is a *fixed point* of F if $F(x) = x$. A point x is *periodic* if there is some $k \geq 1$ such that $F^k(x) = x$; the smallest such k is the *period* of F. In particular, a fixed point of F is a periodic point of period one. If X is a (non-empty) compact interval and F

is continuous, then F has at least one fixed point. A fixed point x is *locally stable* if we can find an open interval V containing x such that for each $y \in V$, the trajectory $\{F^j(y)\}_{j=0}^{\infty}$ converges to x (approaches x).

Generations of undergraduate students are introduced to difference equations by the linear 'cobweb' models. Recall that if we have a first order, linear, homogeneous difference equation:

$$x_{t+1} = \lambda x_t \tag{4.L}$$

We know that the solution

$$x_t = \lambda^t x_0 \tag{4.LS}$$

displays 'oscillatory' behaviour when $\lambda < 0$. But if $|\lambda| > 1$, it is 'explosive'; and, if $|\lambda| < 1$, it is 'damped'. A *persistent* oscillation or cycle is produced when $\lambda = -1$, and in this case the solution is *periodic* with period 2. When $\lambda > 0$, the solution is monotone (increasing if $\lambda > 1$, constant if $\lambda = 1$, and decreasing to zero if $\lambda < 1$). Thus, the periodic behaviour is somewhat of an accidental feature, a knife-edge possibility in this linear world (4.L). Turning to the solution of a *non-linear* first order equation (4.1), Samuelson observed in his *Foundations:*

'It could no doubt be shown that it must do one of the following: (a) go off to infinity; (b) approach an equilibrium level; or (c) approach a periodic motion of some finite period.'

Of course, if we choose in (4.1) a function F from a bounded set X into X, the possibility (a) that Samuelson alluded to is ruled out. We are then left with possibilities (b) and (c). As far as we recall, in our student days no other systematic analysis of non-linear first-order systems (4.1) that was accessible to us challenged Samuelson's conjecture. But we are now in a position to appreciate the spectrum of possibilities much better.

To gain some insights into the possible complexities of trajectories of (4.1), consider the *tent map* $\hat{F}$ defined as:

$$\hat{F}(x) = \begin{cases} 2x & \text{for } x \in [0, 1/2] \\ 2(1-x) & \text{for } x \in [1/2, 1] \end{cases} \tag{4.2}$$

$\hat{F}$ is 'piece-wise' linear. It has two fixed points, namely, $x = 0$ and $x = 2/3$. Neither, however, is locally stable (by drawing the graph of $\hat{F}$ and looking at the iterates of points close to the fixed points, this can be easily seen).

The map (4.2) is admittedly just a step away from the linear case (4.L) and is simple to describe; yet, it is quite useful for illustrating some general results and capturing some subtle arguments. Let us recall some well-known results from real analysis. In what follows by an *interval* we shall always mean a *non-degenerate* interval, and if X is an interval, a *subinterval*, X_1 of X is an interval X_1 contained in X (for example, $H \equiv [0, 1/2]$ and $T \equiv [1/2, 1]$ are both subintervals of the interval $X = [0, 1]$). An interval is *compact* if it is both closed and bounded (i.e., contains both the end points and does not stretch out into infinity in either direction!). If X is an interval and F is a continuous real valued function on X, $F(X)$ is an interval; moreover, if X is a compact interval, so is $F(X)$. Observe that $\hat{F}$ maps the subintervals H and T of $[0, 1]$ *onto* $[0, 1]$ i.e., $\hat{F}(H) = \hat{F}(T) = [0, 1]$. Thus, T is a subinterval of $\hat{F}(H)$ and H is a subinterval of $\hat{F}(T)$.

We shall characterize a family of dynamical systems (of which the dynamical system with state space $X = [0,1]$ and the law of motion $\hat{F}$ defined by the tent map (4.2) is a member) in which there is an abundance of periodic points. The main theorem, due to Li and Yorke (1975), is one of the most striking results in the literature on dynamical systems. On the way, we pick up some propositions that throw light on the difficulties of predicting the long run qualitative properties of dynamical systems. To avoid misunderstanding we shall state the results somewhat formally.

Lemma 4.1 Let G be a real-valued continuous function on an interval I. For any compact subinterval I_1, of $G(I)$, there is a compact subinterval Q of I such that $G(Q) = I_1$.

One can figure out the subinterval Q directly as follows. Let $I_1 = [G(p), G(q)]$ where p and q are in I. Assume that $p < q$. Let r be the last point of the interval $[p, q]$ such that $G(r) = G(p)$; let s be the first point after r such that $G(s) = G(q)$. Then the subinterval

$Q = [r, s]$ is mapped *onto* I_1 under G. The case $p > q$ is similarly dealt with.

The next lemma has some fairly deep implications regarding the complexity of a class of dynamical systems. Fortunately, the 'proof' based on an induction argument is short and entirely elementary.

Lemma 4.2 Let J be an interval and let $F: J \rightarrow J$ be continuous. Suppose that $(I_n)_{n=0}^{\infty}$ is a sequence of compact subintervals of J and, for all n,

$$I_{n+1} \subset F(I_n). \tag{4.3}$$

Then there is a sequence of compact subintervals (Q_n) of J such that, for all n,

$$Q_{n+1} \subset Q_n \subset I_0$$

and $\tag{4.4}$

$$F^n(Q_n) = I_n$$

Hence, for any $x \, \varepsilon \, Q = \cap_n Q_n$, we have $F^n(x) \in I_n$.

The proof 'by induction' is constructed as follows: $Q_0 = I_0$. Then $F^0(Q_0) = I_0$ and $I_1 \subset F(I_0)$. If Q_{n-1} is defined as a compact subinterval such that $F^{n-1}(Q_{n-1}) = I_{n-1}$ then $I_n \subset F(I_{n-1}) = F^n(Q_{n-1})$. Apply our previous Lemma, 4.1 to the map $G \equiv F^n$ on Q_{n-1} to get a compact subinterval Q_n of Q_{n-1} such that $F^n(Q_n) = I_n$. This completes the induction argument.

A fundamental characterization of compactness implies that the intersection $Q \equiv \cap_n Q_n$ of the 'nested' compact intervals $\{Q_n\}$ must be non-empty. Hence, there is surely *some x* in Q, for which we have $F^n(x) \, \varepsilon \, I_n$ for all n.

Let us reflect on some implications of Lemma 4.2 using our tent map (4.2) for the sake of concreteness. Let Λ be the uncountable set of all sequences with two symbols $\{H, T\}$. Choose an *arbitrary* element s of Λ. By identifying H with the subinterval $[0, 1/2]$ and T with $[1/2, 1]$ as before, we see that the chosen s corresponds to an 'arrangement' or a sequence of compact intervals $(I_n)_{n=0}^{\infty}$ where each I_n is either H or T. Let us stress that the sequence s is *completely arbitrary*: it could even be viewed as a record of the outcomes of an infinite sequence of coin-tossing; the order in which H and T appears is not 'controlled' in any way whatsoever! Now, we have already noted that T is a subinterval of $\hat{F}(H)$ and H is a subinterval of $\hat{F}(T)$; thus, for this sequence $(I_n)_{n=0}^{\infty}$, it is certainly true that I_{n+1} is always a subinterval of $\hat{F}(I_n)$. The last statement of Lemma 4.2 now applies; there is *some* initial x in $[0, 1]$ which generates a trajectory $\{\hat{F}^n(x)\}_{n=0}^{\infty}$ with the property that $\hat{F}^n(x)$ is in I_n. Thus, however 'randomly' we arrange H and T, the dynamical system $(X, \hat{F})$ where $X = [0, 1]$ and $\hat{F}$ is the tent map (4.2), is capable of generating a trajectory that will bounce from I_n into I_{n+1} over time according to this arrangement. Among other things, this means that we can think of 'repeating' or 'cyclical' arrangements like

$$(H\,H\,H\ldots)$$

$$(T\,T\,T\ldots)$$

$$(HT\,HT\,HT\ldots)$$

$$(TH\,TH\,TH\ldots)$$

$$(HHT\,HHT\ldots)$$

$$(HTT\,HTT\ldots)$$

$$(HTH\,HTH\ldots)$$

No matter which 'cyclical' arrangement is contemplated, we can generate a trajectory that will provide an exact 'match'. Now, the set of all such cyclical arrangements (sequences with repeating finite 'blocks') is countable. But, as we said earlier, the set Λ is uncountable. Hence, there is an uncountable number of aperiodic arrangements. And, our simple dynamical system following the law of motion (4.2) on the state space $[0, 1]$ is also capable of producing a trajectory matching *any* such aperiodic arrangement!

By using the two results discussed above, and the 'intermediate value theorem' we can prove the first part [$T.1$] of the following theorem of Li and Yorke (1975); [$T.1$] is also a special case of a deep theorem of Sarkowskii (see Devaney (1989)).

Theorem 4.1 Let J be an interval and $F: J \to J$ be continuous. Assume that there is some point a in J for which there are points $b = F(a)$, $c = F^2(a)$ and $d = F^3(a)$ satisfying:

$$d \le a < b < c \text{ (or, } d \ge a > b > c)$$

Then:

[$T.1$]   For every positive integer $k = 1, 2, \ldots$, there is a periodic point of period k.

[$T.2$] (i) There is an uncountable set W containing no periodic points such that for all

$$x, y \, \varepsilon \, W, x \ne y$$

$$\limsup_{n \to \infty} |F^n(x) - F^n(y)| > 0; \liminf_{n \to \infty} |F^n(x) - F^n(y)| = 0$$

(ii) If x is any periodic point, then for all y in W,

$$\limsup_{n \to \infty} |F^n(x) - F^n(y)| > 0.$$

Of course, by considering (4.2) and the point $x = 1/4$, one notes that $\hat{F}(1/4) = 1/2$, $\hat{F}(1/2) = 1$ and $\hat{F}(1) = 0$. Hence, with $[0, 1]$ as the state space and the tent map (4.2) as the law of motion $\hat{F}$ we get an example where Theorem 4.1 readily applies.

The fact that the existence of a periodic point of period three implies the existence of periodic points of *all* periods is surely bewildering. In particular, it means that by 'observing' a computer print out of a million terms of a trajectory it may not be possible to predict whether we have an aperiodic sequence of numbers, or the first million terms of a periodic orbit of, say, two million periods. But the second part [$T.2$] of the Li-Yorke theorem enables us to challenge Samuelson's conjecture that we quoted above. There is an uncountable set of initial points such that the emanating trajectories will *not* converge to *any* periodic orbit, and these trajectories will 'approach' and 'turn away' from one another along different subsequences of time periods. For brevity, any dynamical system satisfying $(T.1)$ and $(T.2)$ is often called 'chaotic' (there are other definitions). Taking $X = [0, 1]$, $(X, \hat{F})$ is chaotic; so is $X, F^*)$ where F^* is a 'quadratic map' defined by:

$$F^*(x) = 4x(1 - x) \tag{4.5}$$

5 EXCESS DEMAND FUNCTIONS ONCE AGAIN

The long digression of the last section was intended to emphasize the point that there are easily verifiable conditions to identify 'chaotic' behavior. A second point is that chaos may be present in quite simple non-linear (even piecewise linear) dynamical systems. Our task now is to combine the Li-Yorke results (Lemma 4.2 and Theorem 4.1) with the earlier propositions on excess demand functions. What emerges is the striking conclusion that even in a 'concrete' economy of two commodities and (by Debreu's theorem) two agents, the Walrasian adjustment process cast in discrete time may display chaotic behaviour.[4] We shall proceed somewhat heuristically to keep the computational details at a minimal level.

Let us define a function $\hat{G}$ from $X = [0, 1]$ into itself by the formula:

$$\hat{G}(x) = \begin{cases} 1.95x & \text{when } 0 \leq x \leq 1/2 \\ 1.95(1-x) & \text{when } 1/2 \leq x \leq 1 \end{cases} \tag{5.1}$$

We can easily see that $\hat{G}$ is a piecewise linear continuous function that attains its maximum at $x = 1/2$. The maximum value $\hat{G}(1/2)$ is 0.975. We can verify that $\hat{G}$ maps the compact subinterval

---

[4] We should mention an alternative approach followed by Day and Pianigiani (1991). Consider an exchange economy with two goods and two agents. Both have the same utility functions $u(x_1, x_2) = x_1^{1/2} x_2^{1/2}$. The endowments are specified as $(1, 0)$ and $(0, 1)$ respectively. Let $\zeta(p)$ be the excess demand vector for the economy at $p \gg 0$. If we consider $p_{t+1} = p_t + \alpha \, \zeta(p_t)$, we can, for a 'high' value of the speed of adjustment parameter α, verify the Li-Yorke conditions.

$X_1 = [0.02, 0.98]$ into itself. Now, going back to (3.3), we can define a price adjustment process

$$p_{t+1} = \hat{G}(p_t) \tag{5.2}$$

starting from some initial price in X. We can compute that if we set the speed of adjustment parameter $\alpha = 1$, the map

$$\hat{\zeta}(p) = \begin{cases} 0.95p & \text{when } 0 \le p \le 1/2 \\ 1.95 - 2.95p & \text{when } 1/2 \le p \le 1 \end{cases} \tag{5.3}$$

satisfies

$$\hat{G}(p) \equiv p + \hat{\zeta}(p) \qquad \text{for } p \text{ in } [0, 1] \tag{5.4}$$

Note that $\hat{\zeta}(p)$ is positive for all positive p less than $1/2$; and, for all p (in X) greater than $\bar{p} \approx 0.661$, $\hat{\zeta}(p)$ is negative. There is a unique positive $\bar{p}$ at which $\hat{\zeta}(\bar{p})$ equals zero. Now, using Debreu's theorem, we can assert that there is a 'well behaved' Walrasian economy, whose excess demand function agrees with our $\hat{\zeta}(p)$ on, say, $X_1 = [0.02, 0.98]$. Thus, for this economy

$$p_{t+1} = \hat{G}(p_t)$$

or,

$$p_{t+1} = p_t + \hat{\zeta}(p_t) \tag{5.5}$$

provides an example of a tatonnement.

We should point out that there *are* points (other than $\bar{p}$ itself!) from which we can get to the equilibrium $\bar{p}$ in a finite number of steps by following (5.5). For example, if the initial $p_0' = \bar{p}/0.95$ then we can get to $\bar{p}$ in just one period. Then, there are surely points from which we can arrive at p_0' in one period, so that the equilibrium $\bar{p}$ is attained in two periods, and so on. A look at the graph of $\hat{G}$ [defined by (5.1)] is useful to see how these points are generated. But all such points belong to a 'small' countable set (hence, to a set of Lebesgue measure zero).

For this dynamical system $(X_1, \hat{G})$, we can select

$$a = 0.246;$$

hence, $$b = \hat{G}(a) = 0.4797;$$

and, $$c = \hat{G}(b) = 0.935415;$$

and, $$d = \hat{G}(c) = 0.1259407.$$

We can apply Theorem 2.1, and assert that (5.5) gives an example of a chaotic tatonnement. It should be stressed that the example is by no means a 'rare' or knife-edge phenomenon. Saari (1985) and Bala and Majumdar (1992) have investigated in detail the question of 'robustness' of chaos, and have demonstrated that models of chaotic tatonnement are 'non-negligible' in a precise sense. Since the arguments are quite technical we do not pursue this issue here.

The 'tent map' we use leads to particularly simple calculations. But there are more complicated functional forms which are better suited to reveal other types of complexities in dynamics. Again, taking $X = [0, 1]$ consider the map $G: X \to X$ defined as:

$$G(p) = 7.86\, p - 23.31\, p^2 + 28.75\, p^3 - 13.30\, p^4 \qquad (5.6)$$

For this dynamical system (X, G), G has a unique, positive fixed point $\bar{p}^* = 0.72$ [and this $\bar{p}^*$ is also 'locally stable': $|G'(\bar{p}^*)| = 0.89 < 1$]. But G also has a (locally stable) periodic point of period two, the trajectory $(0.3217, 0.93, 0.3217, 0.93, \ldots)$ from 0.3217 [as well as the trajectory from 0.93] is periodic.

Let us contrast a comparative static approach with a dynamic one with the help of the map G in (5.6). First, consider *any* economy (with two goods and two agents) such that $p_0 = 0.3217$ is a unique equilibrium price of the first good. As before (subject to the 'ε-qualification' of Theorem 2.1), we can think of the map $G(p)$ of (5.6) as an excess demand function for the first good, and let us view it as a 'new' excess demand function. Of course, if we are *just* interested in comparing the old equilibrium with the 'new' equilibrium ($\bar{p}^* = 0.72$ where $G(\bar{p}^*) = 0$) we can say that the 'equilibrium price will change from p_0 to $\bar{p}^*$ as a result of the shift to the new excess demand function G.' However, if we consider a dynamic process

$$p_{t+1} = G(p_t) \qquad (5.7)$$

with $p_0 = 0.3217$, (and G given by (5.6)), we note that the trajectory from p_0 will be periodic (with a two period cycle). There will be no 'movement' towards the 'new' equilibrium price.

6 Concluding Comments

'Concrete' Walrasian models are now an integral part of the basic box of tools that economic theorists draw upon. Using such models to derive insights has been, and hopefully will continue to be, an attractive direction of research. Whether 'simple' models can provide a firm foundation for advocating policy measures has been the subject of lively debates and, we are sure, will continue to be a controversial methodological issue. As Frank Hahn (1983) observed: 'the notion of *simple* is not simple' and 'sometimes the uselessness of the general model is simply a frank statement of ignorance'.

Our purpose has been to use such models to get a glimpse of the complex dynamics and to appreciate the programme of research that started in the thirties and has continued ever since, a programme that aims at explaining the nature of dynamic processes that drive a market which is not in equilibrium. It is now clear that even the simplest model with two goods and two agents can generate 'robust' chaotic behavior. This, of course, raises questions about the predictive power of economic models. But, to us, 'it seems satisfactory that we should have detailed empirical knowledge before we can go into the prediction business. This circumstance in no way reduces the importance of theory' Hahn (1983).

Appendix

Proof of T.1 in Theorem 4.1
In addition to Lemma 4.1–4.2, we need

Lemma 4.3 Let J be an interval and $G: J \to R$ be continuous. Let I be a compact subinterval of J. Assume $I \subset G(I)$. Then there is some p in I such that $G(p) = p$.

Proof: Let $I = [\beta_0, B_1]$. Choose $\alpha_i (i = 0, 1)$ in I such that $G(\alpha_i) = \beta_i$. It follows that $\alpha_0 - G(\alpha_0) \geq 0$ and $\alpha_1 - G(\alpha_1) \leq 0$. So continuity of G implies that $G(x) - x$ must be zero for some $x = p$ in I. To complete the proof of $[T.1]$, assume that $d \leq a < b < c$ as in the theorem. The proof for the case $d \geq a > b > c$ is similar. Write $K = [a, b]$ and $L = [b, c]$.

Now, let k be any positive integer. For $k > 1$, let $\{I_n\}$ be a sequence of intervals where $I_n = L$ for $n = 0, \ldots, k - 2$; $I_{n-1} = K$ and define I_n to be periodic inductively: $I_{n+k} = I_n$ for $n = 0, 1, 2, \ldots$. If $k = 1$, let $I_n = L$ for all n. Let Q_n be the sets in Lemma 4.2. Notice that $Q_k \subset Q_0$ and $F^k(Q_k) = Q_0$. Apply Lemma 4.3 to the map $G \equiv F^k$ to get a fixed point p_k of F^k in Q_k. It is clear that p_k cannot have period less than k for F. Otherwise, we need to have $F^{k-1}(p_k) = b$, contrary to $F^{k+1}(p_k) \in L$. The point p_k is thus a periodic point of period k for F.

REFERENCES

Arrow, K.J. and F. Hahn (1971), *General Competitive Analysis*, San Francisco: Holden Day.

Arrow, K.J. and L. Hurwicz (1958), 'On the Stability of Competitive Equilibrium', *Econometrica*, 26, pp. 522–52.

Bala, V. and M. Majumdar (1992), 'Chaotic Tatonnement', *Economic Theory*, 2, pp. 437–46.

Baumol, W.J. (1971), *Economic Dynamics*, 3rd Edition, London: MacMillan.

Day, R.H. and G. Pianigiani (1991), 'Statistical Dynamics and Economics', *Journal of Economic Behavior and Organization*, 16, pp. 37–86.

Debreu, G. (1974), 'Excess Demand Functions', *Journal of Mathematical Economics*, 1, pp. 15–21.

—— (1975), 'Four Aspects of the Mathematical Theory of Economic Equilibrium', in *Proceedings of the International Congress of Mathematicians*,

Vancouver, 1974, pp. 65–77; reprinted in *Mathematical Economics, Twenty Papers of Gerard Debreu, 1983*, Cambridge: Cambridge University Press, pp. 217–31.

Devaney, R.L. (1989), *An Introduction to Chaotic Dynamical Systems*, Menlo Park, CA: Benjamin-Cummings Publishing.

Friedman, M. (1946), 'Lange on Price Flexibility and Employment', *American Economic Review*, 36, pp. 613–31.

Hahn, F. (1983), 'On General Equilibrium and Stability', in E.C. Brown and R.M. Solow (eds), *Paul Samuelson and Modern Economic Theory*, New York: McGraw Hill.

Jolink, A. (1993), 'Economic Equilibrium in the History of Science: Reviewing the Invisible Hand', *Economic Journal*, 103, pp. 1303–13.

Kirman, A.P. and K.J. Koch (1986), 'Market Excess Demand in Exchange Economies with Identical Preferences and Collinear Endowments', *Review of Economic Studies*, 53, pp. 457–63.

Li, T. and J.A. Yorke (1975), 'Period Three Implies Chaos', *American Mathematical Monthly*, pp. 985–92.

Lindbeck, A. (1970), 'Paul Anthony Samuelson's Contribution to Economics', *Swedish Journal of Economics*, 72, pp. 342–54.

May, R. (1976), 'Simple Mathematical Models with Very Complicated Dynamics', *Nature*, 261, pp. 459–67.

Morishima, M. (1991), 'General Equilibrium Theory in the Twenty-first Century', *Economic Journal*, 101, pp. 69–74.

Radner, R. (1991), 'Intertemporal General Equilibrium Theory', in L.W. McKenzie and S. Zamagni (eds), *Value and Capital: Fifty Years Later*, London: MacMillan, pp. 423–68.

Saari, D.G. (1985), 'Iterative Price Mechanisms', *Econometrica*, 53, pp. 1117–32.

Samuelson, P.A. (1947), *Foundations of Economic Analysis*, Cambridge, MA: Harvard University Press.

Szenberg, M. (1992), *Eminent Economists*, Cambridge, MA: Cambridge University Press.

Weintraub, E.R. (1985), *General Equilibrium Analysis: Studies in Appraisals*, Cambridge, MA: Cambridge University Press.

4

Rational Choice
and the Price of Money[*]

Amitava Bose

The macroeconomics of money is not what it used to be. Increasingly, modern approaches to money have come to emphasize microeconomic foundations based on rational choice, revealing a preference for discarding anything that is not shown as being derived from neoclassical consumer behaviour theory. A good representative modern approach is the general equilibrium approach elucidated by Hicks (1935), Patinkin (1965) and Grandmont (1983).[1]

The purpose of this expository chapter is to bring out the essentials of the general equilibrium approach without exhibiting its complexity or potential generality. The themes that will be taken up have been around for a long time. The intention is to 'modernize' some 'classical' questions about money and to demonstrate how these can be expounded with the help of elementary consumer behaviour theory against the backdrop of the simplest possible general equilibrium model of pure exchange.

[*] This paper has been written for Professor Tapas Majumdar, whose lectures on consumer behaviour theory in Presidency College opened up for me the fascinating world of economic reasoning. For my introduction to temporary monetary equilibrium theory, I am very grateful to Dipankar Dasgupta.

[1] The analytical framework is that of Hicks (1946).

1 RATIONALITY, HOMOGENEITY AND MONEY ILLUSION

The issue of rationality will keep cropping up in the course of this essay. Specifically, the following question will be explored: How much bite does the assumption of agent rationality possess in probing the basic concerns of monetary economics? It will be seen that the rationality axiom can be an extremely powerful analytical tool. However, the claims made on behalf of the axiom have sometimes been exaggerated.

There was a lively debate in the nineteen fifties, sometimes referred to as the Patinkin controversy, about how to model a monetary economy. That debate — on the dichotomy between the 'real' sector and the 'monetary' sector, the determinateness of the nominal price level, the consistency between the homogeneity postulate and the Quantity Theory of Money — is now firmly part of history.[2] But certain aspects of that debate are still interesting when viewed through modern spectacles. One such aspect relates to the operational consequences of rationality for a modern money-using economy. In particular, is violation of the 'homogeneity postulate' a signal of 'money illusion' and irrationality in the context of such an economy?[3]

In a modern society, money circulates as pieces of paper that are neither desirable *per se* nor redeemable into something that is. The *homogeneity postulate* is one implication of this property of paper money. According to the homogeneity postulate, the excess demand functions of *rational* agents — those who do not suffer from *money illusion* — should be homogeneous of degree zero in absolute prices and money income.[4] This is one of the first lessons of consumer behaviour theory. The argument proceeds in two short steps. First, a doubling of all prices and money income leaves the consumer's budget constraint unaffected. Second, if the

[2] See Patinkin (1965) and the references cited therein.

[3] The homogeneity postulate was extensively used in debating what determines the price level; in particular, whether the price level can be determined from goods market equilibrium.

[4] Here all prices are expressed in terms of money.

consumer's preference map is undisturbed by the change, then his utility maximizing demands would be left unchanged as well and the consumer could be confirmed to be free from money illusion. The crucial step is the second one, the requirement that the rational consumer's preferences be uniquely defined on the space of real goods so that there is no reason for these preferences to change when the quantity of money or some other equally 'irrelevant' nominal variable changes. This is another way of saying that the consumer regards money to be intrinsically useless, i.e. money is a *non*-good.

It is misleading to link the validity of the homogeneity postulate to freedom from 'money illusion', a term which suggests 'irrationality'. In a general way, agents could be described as irrational if their behaviour cannot be explained as the outcome of systematically maximizing a well-defined objective subject to operative constraints. Of course, if agents *are* irrational then the homogeneity postulate would fail, but the point is that the postulate could fail for quite a different reason. This other reason has nothing to do with irrationality at all. It has to do with the *form* that money takes, viz. whether it is commodity money that we are dealing with or paper money.

The homogeneity postulate would fail if agents regard the quantity of money as an intrinsically useful commodity and post it on one of the axes when drawing indifference curves. The matter can be clarified as follows.

Suppose there are three goods, quantities demanded of which are denoted by x, y and μ, the last variable referring to 'money'. Consider a consumer who possesses an initial endowment consisting solely of money, the supply of which to the consumer is $\bar{M}$. The consumer's 'money income' is then $\bar{M} - \mu$, i.e. the excess supply or 'offer' of money to the market in exchange for the other goods, of which the consumer has no initial supply. Holding constant the quantity demanded of money, we can draw a family of indifference curves in two dimensions between x and y. On the same supposition, we can also draw a budget line in the same diagram, enabling us to portray optimal choices of x and y subject to the restriction that μ is given. While this is not a complete picture of consumer choice, it is a useful slice of that picture (Fig. 4.1).

Now suppose that there is a doubling of the two money prices (of x and y) and the level of money income. Certainly, the budget line remains unaltered, but can we be equally certain that the indifference curves remain unchanged? Suppose that the doubling of money income is the result of a doubling of both the endowment as well as the demand for money. If money and either of the other goods are 'related' goods, i.e. either substitutes or complements, then the doubling of μ will affect the marginal rate of substitution between x and y at the original consumption point (x, y). However, by hypothesis, the relative price between these goods has remained unchanged. So the optimal x and y will be affected whenever μ changes.

On the other hand, if μ does not change, it is the budget line in Fig. 4.1 which will be affected since the level of money income

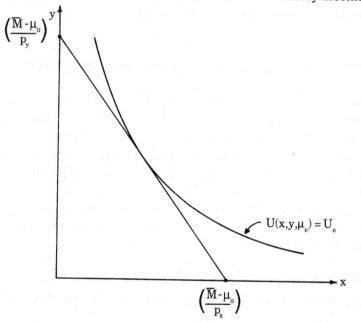

Figure 4.1 Commodity money

will then not change in the same proportion as the endowment of money. In either case, therefore, the original consumptions of the non-money goods cannot continue to be utility maximizing after a proportional change in money income and all money prices. Therefore if money is a good, there are problems with the homogeneity postulate.

As against this, consider the case where money does not enter the utility function. This is like setting $\mu = 0$ both before and after the change and obtaining zero-degree-homogeneity in the usual classroom manner.

The distinction between commodity money and paper money is exactly captured in the contrast between the above two cases. The homogeneity postulate derives validity from the way in which consumers look at money. If money is regarded as intrinsically useful then it is essentially commodity money and homogeneity cannot be assumed. If money is intrinsically useless, it is paper money and homogeneity prevails. It can hardly be correct to label the former case as one of 'money illusion'.

2 EQUILIBRIUM AS A SEQUENCE AND OUTSIDE MONEY

We now come to the second implication of the fact that money is a non-good. This is analytically a more significant implication, though it is only in recent literature that this has been made explicit.[5] The argument is an example of how a good deal of mileage can be extracted from a relatively simple application of the rationality assumption. There is no reason why anyone who regards money to be a non-good would hold on to positively priced money, sacrificing an equivalent amount in goods, except in anticipation of a further round of exchanges. In a finite horizon model, there comes a point beyond which there is nothing, not even exchange! Therefore, in the last period everyone will try to dispose of whatever money they possess and this will drive the

---

[5] See, e.g., Cass and Shell (1980).

price of money down to zero. Anticipating that money will be useless in the terminal year, no one would wish to hold money in the penultimate year, so the price of money will be driven to zero in the penultimate year as well. Clearly, we may work our way back and conclude that money will be useless at each date. To avoid this embarrassing possibility, at every date some transactions must be kept uncompleted. So, rather than a single equilibrium or a complete set of markets at a given date, a money-using economy must be seen as travelling across a *sequence* of equilibria that stretches out without end.

It is easier to model the now-defunct institution of commodity money, both because static methods suffice and also because a positive price for the money good can be obtained directly from its marginal utility. It might appear that static methods would also suffice for obtaining a positive price of paper money provided it is backed up (is *redeemable*), since in that case there is at least one agent with a positive final demand for money. It is, however, crucial to properly model the behaviour of this special, and somewhat deviant, agent in order to avoid problems of indeterminacy and arbitrariness.

To illustrate, consider the following artificial example involving a static economy. Let us imagine that there is an agency — call it the 'bank' — that issues paper money and is institutionally committed, for unexplained reasons, to hold paper money at the completion of all transactions. Suppose that agents are initially endowed with (non-money) goods and only the bank is endowed with money. No other agent has a final demand for money but suppose that the bank has a final demand for money equal to its initial endowment. Then such a bank can be used as a clearing house and one can define a static — and very complete — Walras equilibrium that determines relative commodity prices in the usual manner.

This example has a bearing on several issues of importance. First, it is clear that the above Walras equilibrium can be supported by a positive price of money in terms of any one of the traded goods. Second, money here is *inside* money. This is so not because the issuing agency has been named 'bank' but because redeemability implies that the aggregate *net liability* of money summed up over *all* agents cancels out to zero. That would clearly continue to be the case even if, in the above example, the issuing agency were to be named 'government' instead. The distinguishing trait of *outside money* is its non-redeemability and not its issuance by the government. Third, while in certain cases inside paper money is just a special case of commodity money — since someone has a final demand for it — this is not invariably the case as is explained below. In the micro approach, commodity money is something that, by definition, yields direct utility. The behaviour of the supplier of money can therefore be obtained from utility maximization. Consequently, there is a well-defined demand-supply theory of money that can be applied to obtain a determinate, positive price of money. But in the above example with the 'bank', it is immediate from the homogeneity postulate that neither the quantity of money nor the price level is of any consequence in defining the goods market equilibrium or in shaping its character. The price of money is clearly indeterminate and this is an example of the goods-money dichotomy against which Patinkin launched his celebrated attack.

What is wrong in the example is that the final demand for money is not obtained from utility maximization. The bank is a strangely passive and shockingly naive non-economic animal. The initial money supply and the terminal demand for money are simply given and neither is affected by any economic variable. Thus both the quantity of money as well as the nominal prices are irrelevant magnitudes. No wonder the price of money is indeterminate. The trouble with dichotomous constructions such as these is that they fail to face up to the fact that non-good money and static equilibrium just will not mix. While such models implicitly acknowledge the fact that money has no intrinsic worth — by emphasizing the homogeneity postulate — in using them one is obliged to impose an unexplained end-of-the-period demand for money from outside in order to prevent the price of money from being driven to zero.

3 AN INTERPRETATION AND EXPOSITION
OF THE PATINKIN CONSTRUCTION

If the time horizon is kept open-ended, the problem of specifying a terminal demand for paper money is obviated and there is little reason for engaging in artificial and *ad hoc* constructions such as in the example just provided. What we have to do instead is hold on fast to the principle enunciated earlier that monetary equilibrium is best seen as an infinite sequence: *Every equilibrium is followed by another.* Because of this, at the close of any particular round of transactions (a period or a 'week'), there will be a final demand for money *even if it is a non-good.* Money does not directly provide utility, true, but there is still a natural enough explanation for the demand for money in terms of utility maximization. The value of money to the individual holding it is nothing but the value of goods that money will buy in the future. There is a simple case in which it is easy to give shape to this suggestion. This is the case in which the future relative prices between different goods are fixed. It is possible then to invoke the Hicksian device of 'composite goods' (Hicks 1946). Money, in a manner reminiscent of Marshall, can be seen as a composite good that stands proxy for all future consumptions and that can be contraposed against current goods in the indifference map of a typical agent. It is revealing to develop Patinkin's model starting from this composite good idea.[6] The real quantity of money is an *as if* good.

Patinkin's work is an elaborate excursion over a wide terrain of questions. Our concern is with the modelling of time and money. Given this, we choose to convey only the essence of Patinkin's equilibrium and accordingly employ a much chiselled down version of his model, described heuristically in what follows. There is a representative individual, with preferences defined over (c, d), where c is current consumption and where $d = L/P^e$, with L being the terminal holding of money at the end of the current

---

[6] Patinkin of course deals also with the transactions demand, in addition to the store of value demand being emphasized here.

period and P^e the expected price level of future goods in units of money. The agent's initial endowments are expressed as a bundle (x, M) where x is the endowment of the current good and M is an endowment of money (in nominal units) for the current period. Let P be the current price level and let $R^e = P/P^e$ be well-defined and finite. In units of the future good, the agent's life-time budget constraint is

$$R^e c + d = R^e(x + M/P) \qquad (1)$$

From utility maximization, his demand function for c, i.e. his consumption function, can be written as follows

$$c = c(R^e, m) \qquad (2)$$

Here R^e is an intertemporal relative price, reflecting the *real return factor*, and $m \equiv M/P$ stands for the agent's real cash balances. Note that the 'price' and 'income' terms of text book consumer theory are easily identified as R^e and $R^e(x + M/P)$ respectively.

The agent is, by hypothesis, 'representative'. What this means is that the market clearing condition for the goods market boils down to

$$c = x \qquad (3)$$

The model implied by (2) and (3) has one unknown too many, the unknowns being c, m, and R^e. One has to say something about expectations formation and the determination of R^e. Patinkin focussed on a Hicksian temporary equilibrium. The future is there, casting its shadow on the present, but Patinkin's concern was with equilibrium in the current period only. In particular he was not interested in checking if the expectations now held about the future will in fact materialize subsequently. Thus the features observed of the current market clearing outcome may or may not persist, they may only be *temporary*.

Patinkin made a rather special assumption in regard to the formation of expectations. He took $P^e = E(P)$, where E is a given function, and then he followed Hicks of Value and Capital in assuming that $E(P)$ is increasing in P and that the 'elasticity of expectations' was unity, i.e., $E'(P) > 0$ with $PE'(P) = E(P)$. This implies that in (2) and (3), we can take R^e to be fixed:

$$R^e = \hat{R} > 0 \tag{4}$$

where $\hat{R}$ is simply given. Thus the onus of inducing equilibrating changes in demand — in (3), c adjusts to a given x — falls entirely on real balances, m. This explains the importance, in Patinkin's analysis, of the *real balance effect*. It also explains the need, in his analysis, for assuming that the price level is flexible since it is this that makes real balances variable.

Price flexibility and real balance variability are no doubt necessary, but these properties are in themselves not sufficient for the existence of a meaningful equilibrium. It appears that Patinkin overestimated the potency of the real balance effect on this score.

4 IS PRICE FLEXIBILITY ENOUGH?

Let us combine (2) and (4) and write $c(\hat{R}, m) \equiv h(m)$. Equilibrium requires $h(m) - x = 0$ for arbitrary x. Equilibrium is assured, thanks to the continuity of h, if large values of m induce excess demands for current consumption and low values of m induce excess supplies (Fig 4.2). Since the effect of changes in m on demand is exactly an income effect, the first requirement can be met by assuming that current consumption is asymptotically strictly noninferior: $c \to \infty$ as $m \to \infty$. This would rule out the possibility of a permanent excess supply in the goods market. That can only happen at a zero price of goods. But then the value of real balances would be infinity and, given our assumption about asymptotic noninferiority, that would induce an infinitely large excess *demand* for current consumption, not an excess supply. This is essentially the manner in which Haberler (1941, 1952) and Patinkin (1948) used the real balance effect to question the Keynesian claim that excess supply of goods and labour could persist despite price flexibility. (The assumption that the expected rate of return is fixed is analogous to the Keynesian one of a

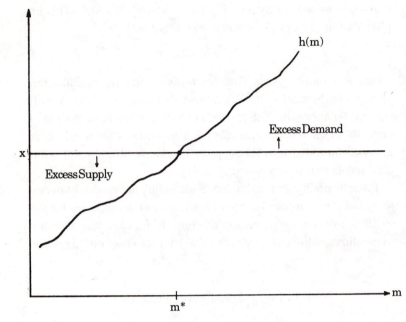

Figure 4.2 Money is valuable

'liquidity trap'; the Haberler-Patinkin argument doubts that the liquidity trap is sufficient to produce excess supply).

But this is only half the distance covered. For a meaningful equilibrium, there is one other possibility to rule out and that is the case of a permanent excess supply of money, leading to a zero price of money. Should that happen, money would not buy goods and would cease to function as a medium of exchange. Even with full upward flexibility of the price level (i.e. downward flexibility of the price of money), the ability of the real balance effect to eliminate *this* possibility is questionable.

First consider a condition that does work in a technical sense: $c \to 0$ as $m \to 0$, in symmetry with the previous case. Then $c = x > 0$ can occur only at a strictly positive m, say $m^* > 0$, and money must be valuable. However, the existence question is not that easily disposed of. This kind of consumption vanishing condition though sufficient, is not economically sensible. The reason is simple. While infinite real cash balances imply infinite wealth, zero cash balances do not imply zero wealth! A zero value of money need not pauperize consumers since these people could be endowed also with real goods.[7]

The failure of the consumption vanishing condition can be illustrated in the Patinkin model. Revert to the budget constraint (1) and use (4) to freeze the intertemporal terms of trade at $\hat{R}$.

$$\hat{R}c + d = \hat{R}(x + m) \tag{5}$$

Treating m as a parameter, we can generate a family of parallel budget lines, one for each m. The poorest such budget is that for which $m = 0$, and it is the one that satisfies

$$\hat{R}c + d = \hat{R}x \tag{6}$$

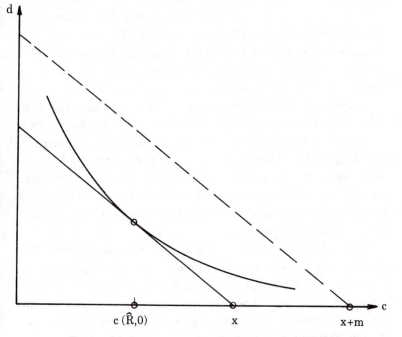

Figure 4.3 Excess supply when money is free

[7] For examples of this from a more general context, think of the situation in which there is perfect indexation of wages, or one in which wages are paid in kind.

With 'well-behaved' preferences — indifference curves do not hit the d-axis at least — there *must* exist an interior solution for c whenever (6) holds for $x > 0$ (Fig 4.3). Thus consumption does not vanish even if real balances do.

This shows that price flexibility does not make the real balance effect automatically strong enough in the downward direction. Additional conditions are required to ensure a positive price of money. Patinkin does make use of an additional condition but he does not make it explicit and does not emphasize its importance for his model. It is a somewhat restrictive condition on the endowment bundle.

Moving back to (6) and Fig 4.3, it is clear that with x positive and $\hat{R}$ finite, and with future consumption considered essential (indifference curves do not hit the c-axis), $m = 0$ must imply $c(\hat{R}, m) < x$, i.e. $h(0) - x < 0$. This shows that a monetary equilibrium is indeed assured in Patinkin's model. However, the question is: to what extent can one thank price flexibility for that? After all, price flexibility merely makes $m = 0$ a feasible state of affairs; the effect of that on consumption is another matter.

As a matter of fact, there are two other assumptions that contribute to making money valuable in the Patinkin framework. One of these is the assumption that future consumption is essential. This helps rule out the degenerate case depicted in Fig 4.4(a) of an equilibrium with a zero price of money. This kind of survival condition is obviously economically a most reasonable assumption to impose. But there is another much less acceptable assumption that had been slipped in.

Suppose the endowment bundle also holds a provision for goods in the future, say to the tune of $y > 0$. This immediately raises the possibility that such an endowment bundle is located, not to the right, but to the *left* of the consumption tangency point on the non-monetary budget constraint (Fig 4.4(b)). In that case the equilibrium would be one with a permanent excess supply of money, rendering money useless. Thus the location of the endowment point is important and the assumption that there is no endowment of goods in the future is not a harmless simplification;

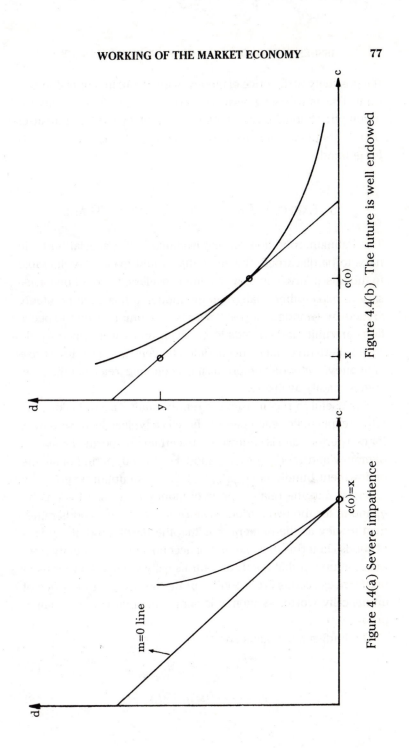

Figure 4.4(b) The future is well endowed

Figure 4.4(a) Severe impatience

the positivity of the price of money in the Patinkin model depends on it. This is worrying because there is no good reason why the assumption should be true for the typical agent. It is this that raises doubts about the habit of taking the potency of real balance effects for granted.

5 EXPECTATIONS AND THE TERMS OF TRADE

The Patinkin condition on endowments is too special and will have to be discarded. But since that would make us vulnerable to the possibility of money becoming useless, it would be necessary to make other changes in the model. It has been pointedly argued by Grandmont (1983) that the assumption that expectations are unit elastic needs to be given up as well. Once we do so, an alternative sufficient condition that ensures a positive price of money, without compromising economic reasonability, becomes readily available.

It is useful to reconstruct the representative agent making the future explicit. For each period, there is a typical agent who lives for two periods and is endowed with certain prespecified amounts of money and goods in each period. For the t th period of life the endowment bundle is (x_t, M_t), $t = 1, 2$. Consumption is given by c_1 and c_2 and the relative price of money in terms of goods by q_1 and q_2 for the two periods. The reason for using goods rather than money as the numeraire is that the positivity of the prices of goods (in terms of some unit of account) follows directly from the assumption that goods are intrinsically desirable in terms of preferences (goods are 'good'), but the positivity of the price of intrinsically worthless money is something that surely requires proof.

The budget constraints are

$$c_1 + s = x_1 + q_1 M_1 \tag{7}$$

$$c_2 = x_2 + q_2^e(s/q_1 + M_2) \tag{8}$$

where s stands for the real demand for money in the first period. Note that in the absence of bequests there is no real demand for money from this agent in his terminal year.[8] The above equations can be merged into one in two ways. Everything can be expressed in present values, i.e. in units of the current good. In that case, when $q_t \neq 0$, we would have

$$c_1 + \pi c_2 = (x_1 + \pi x_2) + (m_1 + \pi m_2)$$

where $m_t \equiv q_t M_t$ and $\pi \equiv q_1/q_2^e$ stands for the expected *inflation factor*, the inverse of the expected return factor, R^e, that has already been introduced. In what follows, the life-time budget constraint will continue to be expressed in terms of R^e with an occasional reference to π whenever convenient.

$$R^e c_1 + c_2 = (R^e x_1 + x_2) + (R^e m_1 + m_2) \tag{9}$$

In temporary equilibrium, expectations are formed on the basis of current realizations. Let $f: \boldsymbol{R} \to \boldsymbol{R}$ be an expectations function:

$$q_2^e = f(q_1) \tag{10}$$

It turns out that elasticity assumptions on f are crucial for the existence of a monetary equilibrium, although the point is blurred in the Patinkin model by his unit elasticity assumption. The importance of the elasticity of expectations for the present discussion is a matter that has been clarified by Grandmont (1983).

Consider a change in q_1, equivalently an opposite change in the current 'price level'. A straightforward effect of this is to change the present real value of the endowment of money, $q_1(M_1 + M_2)$ and thereby generate an income effect, a generalized real balance effect. But another effect is of relevance. This effect results from the expectations-induced change in q_2 and thereby, possibly, in R^e as well. This *terms of trade* effect, which depends

---

[8] The market demand for money in the next period comes wholly from individuals who are not as yet born and who are therefore not represented by the 'representative' agent of the current period.

on the elasticity of expectations, plays an important role in arguments about the price of money.[9]

To tackle the existence issue, consider the demand for and the supply of money in real terms. The real supply is $q_1 M_1$ or m_1. In this model, the real demand for money is nothing but a saving function: money being the sole store of value, the real value of money held is equal to the amount of consumption foregone. The saving function may be denoted $s(R^e, m)$ where $s = x_1 + m - c$. Equilibria with free money will be ruled out if there is a positive demand for saving when money is free, i.e. if $s(R^e, 0) > 0$. Then, since at a zero price the real supply will be zero (i.e. $m_1 = 0$), there must be an excess demand for money, contradicting the requirements of equilibrium. Then no equilibrium will be possible at a zero price of money.

It follows from this that whether money will command a positive price or not is something that hinges on the urge to save being strong enough when the price of money is low. It has already been suggested that vanishing real cash balances may not suffice to bring about the reduction in current consumption necessary for this. However, when the price of money goes to zero, it is not merely that real balances go to zero; the intertemporal terms of trade will also be affected. If the asymptotic elasticity of expectations is strictly less than one, then we expect the terms of trade to blow up to infinity as the current price of money crashes to zero. The effect of this kind of an explosion in the terms of trade must be to make saving positive. Hence there will be an excess demand for money if the price of money does indeed fall to zero, showing that it is impossible to have equilibrium with so low a price of money and, therefore, that the equilibrium price of money must be strictly positive. This, in essence, is the argument of Grandmont (1983).

It will be seen from (7) and (8) that c_1 is a function of q_1 and q_2^e,

---

[9] In Grandmont (1983) the terms of trade effect is called the intertemporal substitution effect even though it is not a pure substitution effect. Patinkin (1965), of course, ignores this effect altogether, assuming that the elasticity of expectations is unity.

given the endowments (x_1, M_1) and (x_2, M_2). With (10), c_1 can therefore be reduced to a function of q_1 alone: $c_1 = c(q_1)$. Similarly, the reduced form savings function is given by $s(q_1) \equiv x_1 + q_1 M_1 - c(q_1)$, retaining the earlier notation. We want to demonstrate that with $q_1 = 0$, there will be an excess demand for money. Since $q_1 M_1 = 0$ whenever $q_1 = 0$, we want to check for $s(0) > 0$.[10]

Using (10), write $R^e = R(q_1)$ and assume that $R(0)$ is well-defined and, for the moment, finite. We may refer to $R(0)$ as the *expected barter terms of trade*. Next, consider the *no-trade terms of trade* when $q_1 = 0$ and let it be denoted as $\bar{R}$. This will be the slope of the indifference curve at the endowment point when that point corresponds to $q_1 = 0$, i.e. when there is no real endowment of money initially. Clearly, by definition, $s = 0$ when $R = \bar{R}$. Since $s(0) > 0$ only when $\bar{R} < R(0)$, the problem of ensuring a positive price of money can be reduced to one of ensuring that this condition is met (Fig 4.5).

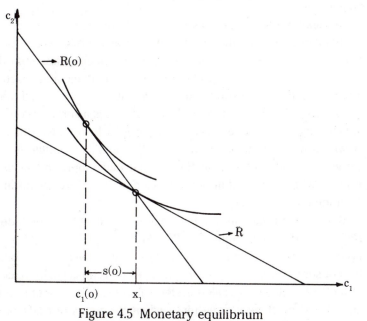

Figure 4.5 Monetary equilibrium

[10] This is only sufficient. A nominal excess demand for money can exist with $s(0) = 0$.

Starting with this condition, essentially two approaches can be distinguished. In one of these the condition is ensured by making $\bar{R}$ as small as possible by appropriate choice of the endowment point while postulating a lower bound on $R(0)$. This is the approach of Patinkin (1965), at least implicitly. In the other approach, one tries to make $R(0)$ as large as possible by appropriate assumptions on expectations; this is the approach of Grandmont (1983).

6   Avoiding Uselessness of Money: A Condition

Under fairly general assumptions, the condition $\bar{R} < R(0)$ ensures that a temporary equilibrium, if it exists, must be a temporary *monetary* equilibrium, i.e. one with $q_1 > 0$. The Patinkin and Grandmont conditions referred to earlier can be seen as alternative special cases.

We shall sketch the proofs using plenty of heuristics that can be tightened up in familiar ways. The main assumptions are those on the preferences of the representative consumer. As is standard, preferences are assumed to be continuous, convex, and strictly increasing in the two goods. Additionally it will be assumed that consumption in both periods is essential; this is a survival condition that makes indifference curves asymptotic to the axes. Finally, it will assumed that preferences are 'smooth', i.e. indifference curves are differentiable, at least in the neighbourhood of the endowment point. This important assumption ensures a unique no-trade terms of trade, $\bar{R}$.

Begin with the case in which the expected barter terms of trade, $R(0)$ is positive and finite. For $R^e = R(0)$, the pair $(c_1(0), s(0))$ is chosen though, since the option not to save is always available, the consumption point (x_1, x_2) might have been chosen in its place. Thus $(c_1(0), c_2(0))$ is 'revealed preferred' to the endowment point (x_1, x_2) and must be costing more when the terms of trade are given by $\bar{R}$. (Note that use of smoothness of preferences has been used). Therefore,

$$(R(0) - \bar{R})(c_1(0) - x_1) < 0 \qquad (11)$$

From this it follows that if the expression $(R(0) - \bar{R})$ is positive and finite then it must be the case that $(x_1 - c_1(0)) = s(0) - m_1 > 0$, a positive real excess demand for money will exist when money is free; so money will not be free.

To apply this condition to the Patinkin case, note that in Patinkin $x_2 = 0$. From the fact that second period consumption is essential, this implies $\bar{R} = 0$. Regarding elasticity of expectations, generalize Patinkin's unitary elasticity by simply requiring the elasticity of expectations to lie between finite and positive bounds. Then the above proposition applies and if the lower bound is given by r, then $R(0) \geq r > 0$. Thus the condition $R(0) > \bar{R}$ is met in the Patinkin model.

However, in general the endowment condition may or may not be met; we have already given an illustration of such a possibility. It would be nice to have a condition that ensures a positive price of money *regardless of the location of the endowment point*. A generic condition is now provided in terms of the elasticity of expectations.

Let us simply assume that $f(0)$ is finite and remove the restriction that $R(0)$ is bounded above. Indeed, what we wish to demonstrate is that the following simple condition is sufficient for the existence of a positive price of money:

$$R(0) = +\infty$$

Note that if $R(0) = +\infty$ then from nonsatiability in second period consumption, $c_2(0) = +\infty$. Let D stand for the *nominal* demand for money, so that $s = q_1 D$. Now the second period budget constraint is (refer to (8))

$$c_2(0) = (x_2 + m_2(0)) + f(0) D$$

Given the assumption that $f(0)$ is finite, all the terms on the right side of the above equation except D are finite. Hence if $c_2(0) = +\infty$, then $D = +\infty$ as well. But the endowment of money, M_1, is finite. Thus there will be excess demand for money if its price falls to zero, proving that equilibrium with free money is an impossibility.

REFERENCES

Cass, D. and K. Shell (1980), 'In Defence of a Basic Approach', in J.H. Kareken and Neil Wallace (eds), *Models of Monetary Economics*, Federal Reserve Bank of Minneapolis, pp. 251-60.

Grandmont, J-M (1983), *Money and Value. A Reconsideration of Classical and Neoclassical Monetary Theories*, Cambridge University Press.

Haberler, G. (1941), *Prosperity and Depression*, Third edition, Geneva.

—— (1952), 'The Pigou Effect Once More', *Journal of Political Economy* LX, 240-6.

Hicks, J.R. (1935), 'A Suggestion for Simplifying the Theory of Money', *Economica* II (February).

—— (1946), *Value and Capital*, Second edition, Oxford University Press.

Patinkin, D. (1948), 'Price Flexibility and Full Employment', *American Economic Review* XXXVIII, 543-64; ibid., XXXIX (1949), 726-8.

—— (1965), *Money, Interest and Prices*, Second edition, Harper & Row.

5

Money, Credit and Government Finance in a Developing Economy[*]

Mihir Rakshit

The purpose of the paper is to examine the behaviour of the financial sector in a developing economy with special reference to issues like

(i)   relationship between the supply of money and supply of credit under alternative institutional systems;

(ii)   financial crowding-in or crowding-out effects of government borrowing;

(iii) implications of administered interest rates for the credit market; and

(iv)   effects of financial liberalization and operation of mutual funds and other financial intermediaries.

While the issues under investigation are of immediate relevance to LDCs where problems associated with fiscal deficit and financial repression or liberalization loom large, some of our results are of a more general nature and throw light on the controversy between monetarists and neo-Keynesians on the exogeneity or endogeneity of money supply, the transmission mechanism and stability of the income velocity of circulation. Section I draws attention to some crucial characteristics of mainstream models that make them ill-suited for analysing the behaviour of financial markets in general

* Written in grateful remembrance of my initiation to Macroeconomics by Professor Tapas Majumdar at Presidency College, Calcutta. Some of the results were derived in an earlier paper presented at WIDER (Rakshit 1986).

and those of developing economies in particular. Models of money and credit markets are constructed in Sections II through V taking explicit account of distinguishing features of institutional arrangements and rules prevailing in LDCs like India. The focus in all these models is on factors governing the supply of credit and its allocation, and the demand side of financial markets is brought in only to the extent it has an important bearing on the formation of credit. The final section summarizes the main conclusions and suggests areas of further research.

1 MONEY MARKET IN MAINSTREAM MACRO MODELS

In order to appreciate the basic features of and problems attended with mainstream analysis of the financial sector, consider the IS-LM money market equilibrium relation used extensively in almost all macro models of the Keynesian and monetarist variety. In all these models there are only two financial assets, viz., money and bonds, and the latter include not only fixed interest bearing securities, but also equities and loans of all kinds. The short run equilibrium is characterized by market clearing interest rates, given the stock of money and bond in the economy. It is primarily through the impact of the interest rate on investment-saving decisions that the link between the real and the financial sector is forged and the transmission mechanism operates.

The difficulty, however, is that financial markets in almost all economies exhibit features that make models of the IS-LM variety largely inappropriate for analytical or policy purposes.[1] There are significant differences between various instruments of credit and abstraction from these differences in the IS-LM model, it is felt, makes the results highly suspect. Attention has also been drawn to the serious difficulty of economic interpretation of stock equilibrium in one market juxtaposed with flow equilibrium in the other. Financial stocks like bond or money change over time through capital accumulation or budget deficit and implications

---

[1] Hicks (1981, 1991) himself was acutely aware of some of these issues.

of these changes for the money market are not captured in the IS-LM framework. What is more damaging for the model, financing of investment requires *new* loans and it is not clear how people's willingness to hold *existing* stocks of bonds at some rate of interest ensures that at that interest rate investors are also able to get necessary funds for carrying out their plans. To be more specific, even if income and the interest rate are such that (a) existing quantities of money and bond are willingly held and (b) *ex ante* investment equals *ex ante* saving, the demand for new bonds may fall short of their supply. The implication is that *ex ante* investment cannot be financed and hence the commodity market equilibrium at the IS-LM cross cannot obtain.

There have been, to be sure, several attempts at extension and modification of the IS-LM framework. Recognizing that investment implies changes in stocks over time, Blinder and Solow (1973, 1974) as also Tobin and Buiter (1976) examine the medium and long run behaviour of the economy under specified fiscal and monetary policies. There have been attempts at generalization of the two-asset framework along the lines suggested by Friedman (1956). The most important examples in this regard are Tobin (1969), Brunner and Meltzer (1972) and Modigliani and Papademos (1987). Also of interest is Bernanke and Blinder's (1988) extention of the IS-LM model by considering banks' choice among three assets — free reserves, bonds and loans. However, these extensions do not resolve satisfactorily some of the basic problems relating to modelling of the financial sector.

Consider first the relative speed of adjustment of prices and quantities in the financial market. Not only in LDCs, but in industrialized countries also, returns on most financial assets, unlike bond prices, do not adjust immediately to eliminate excess demand or excess supply. This happens when (i) returns are administered by the central bank or by an oligopolistic association of financial intermediaries; (ii) there is credit rationing of the Stiglitz-Weiss (1981) variety due to asymmetric information; or (iii) financial assets are not readily marketable and economic agents require time to adjust their portfolio or find prospective borrowers. Under these conditions adjustments in the quantity of credit or financial assets can be faster than interest rates. In a developing economy the major constituents of the portfolio of households are not bonds, but bank deposits, provident funds, life insurance and various instruments of government borrowing.[2] Since almost all of these assets are non-negotiable and their returns quite sticky, the transmission mechanism generally works through quantity adjustments in the financial sector rather than changes in rates of interest.

The second and more important problem relates to the relative speed of quantity adjustments in commodity and financial markets. It is assumed in both Keynesian and monetarist models that adjustment of financial stocks in the economy is much slower than (short-run) adjustments in production and employment. However, the operation of the money multiplier in both its text-book and 'structural' forms involves a process of lending and creation of deposits in successive rounds and the time required for the major part of this multiplier to work itself out need not be shorter than the Keynesian short run.[3] Again, certain types of financing government expenditure initiate, as we shall see, a process of lending and borrowing and this process overlaps and interacts with that of spending and generation of income. The stock-flow equilibrium analysis *a la* IS-LM does not under these conditions capture the

[2] In India, for example, more than 90 per cent of financial savings of households are held in the form of assets which do not have a secondary market.

[3] This is partially recognized by Hicks (1948) in his dynamic version of the IS-LM model; but the solution suggested is far from satisfactory. Bernanke and Blinder (1988) gloss over the problem in an otherwise interesting extension of the IS-LM model. In this model commercial banks' choice lies among bonds, free reserves and loans. However, unlike the bond market, the market for bank loans does not adjust immediately. Again, free reserves at the disposal of an individual commercial bank depends not only on its own loan, but also on the credit extended by other banks and the portfolio choice of the public. Hence adjustment to equilibrium in the loan market involves a process similar to that of the money multiplier. The implication is that the equilibrium has to allow for adjustments in the asset and liability sides of banks and producers and hence in the amount of borrowing and accumulation of assets by firms. See also Section 4.

essence of the interaction between the financial and real sectors of the economy even in the short run.

Finally, the behaviour of economic agents is influenced significantly by institutional arrangements and rules under which the financial sector operates. In almost all developing countries, specialized development institutions and banks provide the major part of finance to investors; government borrowings from households and banks are quite substantial; and the state plays an important role in regulating the operation of the capital market, extending the coverage of commercial banks and changing the structure of the financial system. An examination of the impact of alternative financial regimes or structures on the formation of credit thus acquires special significance in any modelling of money and finance in a developing economy.

2 FINANCE IN A FIXED INTEREST REGIME

In order to isolate the basic mechanism behind the formation of credit we consider first the simplest case where all interest rates are administered, the economy is closed, investment is financed entirely through credit, saving is undertaken only by households and there are no financial intermediaries other than commercial banks. The asset liability structure of the economy, consisting of the government, the central bank, commercial banks, firms and households, may then be represented by the following table:

TABLE 1
SECTORAL ASSETS AND LIABILITIES

	Asset	Liability
Government	$V_g + E_g$	$L_m + L_{gb} + L_{g1} + L_{g2} \; (= L_g)$
Central Bank	L_m	H
Commercial Banks	$H_b + L_{gb} + L_{fb}$	$D_{1h} + D_{1f} + D_2 \; (= D)$
Firms	$V_f + D_{1f}$	$L_{fb} + L_{fh} \; (= L_f)$
Households	$H_h + D_{1h} + D_2 + L_{fh} + L_{g1} + L_{g2}$	W

where V_g = value of asset in the government sector; E_g = excess of liability over asset in the government sector; L_m = government debt to the central bank; L_{gb} = government borrowing from commercial banks; L_{g1} = government borrowing (Type 1) from households; L_{g2} = government borrowing (Type 2) from households; H= high power money; H_b = cash reserves held by commercial banks; L_{fb} = bank loans to firms; D_{1h} = demand deposit held by households; D_{1f} = demand deposits held by firms; D_2 = time deposits; V_f = value of real assets held by firms; L_{fh} = loans to firms by households; H_h = currency holding of households; W = household wealth. E_g and W are included as balancing items.

We assume without any loss of generality that the government and firms are the ultimate users of credit and that firms do not hold cash balances or time deposits. Before examining factors affecting the supply of money and credit and their distribution, it is useful to focus on some accounting relations obtained from the sectoral asset — liability structure of the economy.

Narrow Money : $M_1 = H_h + D_1$ where $D_1 = D_{1h} + D_{1f}$ (1)

Broad Money : $M_2 = H_h + D_1 + D_2$

$$= L_m + L_{gb} + L_{fb} \qquad (2)$$

Total Credit : $L = L_g + L_f$

$$= M_2 + (L_{fh} + L_{g1} + L_{g2}) \qquad (3)$$

Household Wealth : $W = V_f + V_g + E_g = L_g + L_f - D_{1f}$ (4)

National Wealth : $W_h = V_f + V_g$

$$= (L_f + L_g) - (D_{1f} + E_g) \qquad (5)$$

Relation (2) shows that while concepts of money and credit are indeed distinct, the aggregate supply of money in the broad sense identically equals aggregate lending by central and commercial banks. L denotes total credit extended to final users, viz., the government and firms, and does not include loans given to financial intermediaries in the system (viz., commercial banks). R.h.s. of (3) also distinguishes between bank and non-bank credit — a distinction that, as we shall see, is of crucial importance in analysing the working of the financial sector. (4) and (5) indicate relations between household wealth, national wealth, total credit and its use by the government and firms. Since our focus is on the supply side of financial markets, all magnitudes are expressed in nominal terms.

Credit within and outside banking system

Relations (1) to (5) are accounting identities and do not suggest any causal link relating to the formation of credit. For examining the behaviour of the financial sector we need to know the rules imposed by monetary authorities and behaviour of economic agents. We consider first the implications of rules prevailing in India in the pre-liberalization era (with one or two minor simplifications).

Interest rates on different types of loans and financial assets, $D_1, D_2, L_{fh}, L_{g1}, L_{g2}, L_{fb}$ and L_{gb}, are assumed to be fixed[4] and denoted respectively by $i_{d1}, i_{d2}, i_{fh}, i_{g1}, i_{g2}, i_{fb}$ and i_{gb}. Given the degree of liquidity, riskiness and convenience of holding alternative financial assets by households, it is assumed that

$$i_{d1} < i_{d2} < i_{g1} < i_{fh}.$$

There are also some financial assets issued by the government (e.g., National Savings Certificates, Public Provident Fund, etc.) on which effective returns (inclusive of income tax or other benefits) are very high. But for individuals there are quantitative limits beyond which purchase of these assets is not permitted or effective returns on them fall drastically. In respect of these assets, denoted here by L_{g2}, households may be regarded as quantity constrained. So far as banks are concerned, their cash reserve ratio is fixed at r. In India, as in other developing countries, the government appropriates a significant part of bank credit at fairly low rates of interest through instruments like the Statutory

---

[4] We have taken i_{d1} to be positive since variation in i_{d1} is often considered an important instrument at the disposal of monetary authorities. We have also assumed interest on all government securities held by the central bank to be zero.

Liquidity Ratio (SLR) indicating the fraction of deposits, say V, banks have to hold in the form of excess reserves or low yield government securities.

Since we are concerned with the maximum amount of loan the financial sector can generate we assume that (expect for L_{g2}) lenders are not quantity constrained at given rates of interest. Banks will hold neither excess reserves[5] nor any L_{gb} in excess of the SLR requirement. D_{1f} represents transactions demand for money balances by firms and can be regarded as proportional to nominal GDP, Y, given the production and payments structure of the economy:

$$D_{1f} = k_{df} Y \tag{6}$$

For households we distinguish between two components of transactions demand, viz. currency and demand deposits, since not only are they not perfect substitutes in effecting transactions in developing countries, but their role in the generation of money and credit are quite different. We admit of the possibility that there can be some substitution between H_h and D_{1h} in response to changes in i_{d1}, but assume that $H_h + D_{1h}$ is proportional to money income:[6]

$$D_{1h} = k_{d1} (i_{d1}) Y \qquad k'_{d1} \geq 0 \tag{7}$$

$$H_h = k_c Y \text{ where } k_c = k_h - k_{d1}(.) \tag{8}$$

and k_h is the fraction of Y, households want to hold in the form of

---

[5] We take r to be the minimum stipulated by the central bank plus what is required for day-to-day operation of commercial banks. The latter will depend upon relative magnitudes of D_1 and D_2, a point we ignore for simplicity. See, however, Section V.

[6] It is interesting to note that in spite of significant changes in the structure of the economy, the M_1/Y ratio in India has shown remarkable stability over the last forty years. During this period there has been a substantial increase in time deposits to GDP. This supports the Keynes–Hicks thesis (Hicks 1991) relating to the essential distinction between the transactions and asset demand for money balances.

money balances. (7) and (8) incorporate the assumption that i_{d1} is not large enough to affect the choice in respect of L_{fh}, L_{g1}, etc.

We have already noted that given its high return in relation to other financial assets, households hold whatever the government chooses to borrow in the form of L_{g2}. Let W_a denote households' free wealth, i.e., the total asset at the disposal of households after meeting the transactions demand for money balances and holding the available amount of L_{g2}:

$$W_a = W - (k_h Y + L_{g2})$$

W_a is distributed between D_2, L_{fh} and L_{g1} on the basis of returns on these three types of assets:

$$\frac{L_{fh}}{W_a} = \alpha_{fh} \underset{(-)\ (+)\ (-)}{(i_{d2},\ i_{fh},\ i_{g1})} \tag{9}$$

$$\frac{L_{g1}}{W_a} = \alpha_{g1} \underset{(-)\ (-)\ (+)}{(i_{d2},\ i_{fh},\ i_{g1})} \tag{10}$$

$$\frac{D_2}{W_a} (= \alpha_d) = 1 - \alpha_{fh} - \alpha_{g1} \tag{11}$$

So far as the government and the central bank are concerned we assume L_{g2}, L_m and hence H to be policy parameters. Our problem is to analyse the determination of other entries in Table 1, given the structure of interest rates and the demand for various financial assets on the part of economic agents.

Given the level of income and the cash reserve ratio, M_2, i.e. the maximum possible credit generated by the banking system, is obtained from (2), (6), (7), (8) and

$$H_b = H - k_c Y = r (D_1 + D_2): \tag{12}$$

$$M_2 = \frac{1}{r} \left[H - (1 - r) k_c Y \right]. \tag{13}$$

The difference between (13) and the usual relation in the money multiplier analysis lies in explicit incorporation in the former of the cash drain from the banking system.

While M_2 gives the supply of what can be called monetized credit, the aggregate supply of loan is obtained from (3), (4), (8) to (11) and (13):

$$L = \frac{H}{r\alpha_d} - Y\left[\frac{1}{\alpha_d}\left(\frac{k_c}{r} + k_{dd}\right) - k\right] + L_{g2} \tag{14}$$

where $k_{dd} = k_{d1} + k_{df}$; $k = k_c + k_{d1} + k_{df}$ (the Cambridge k).

The amount of non-bank credit L_n is the difference between L and M_2:

$$L_n = \frac{1 - \alpha_d}{\alpha_d}\left[\frac{H}{r} - Y\left(\frac{k_c}{r} + k_{dd}\right)\right] + L_{g2} \tag{15}$$

3 SOME ECONOMIC IMPLICATIONS

Money and Credit Multipliers

Relations (13), (14) and (15) indicate the nature of interrelation between money and credit, and the way they are governed by (i) high power money; (ii) structure of interest rates; (iii) preference of the public among alternative financial assets; (iv) amount of 'high yield' instruments of borrowing in respect of which households are quantity constrained; and (v) level of money income. In examining the significance of these factors we consider in some detail effects of changes in high power money and note the main similarities and differences between the present model and that underlying the usual money multiplier analysis.

The money and credit multipliers in the system, $\partial M_2/\partial H$ and $\partial L/\partial H$ respectively, are immediate from (13) and (14):

$$\frac{\partial M_2}{\partial H} = \frac{1}{r} \tag{16}$$

$$\frac{\partial L}{\partial H} = \frac{1}{r\alpha_d} \qquad (17)$$

Demand deposits in the model are treated as part of transactions demand for money and do not compete with other financial assets like D_2, L_{fh} or L_{g1} (see fn. 6). Hence at a given income level any addition to reserve money finds its way into the coffers of commercial banks and raises the aggregate money supply by $\Delta H/r$.

With no changes in M_1, the entire rise in M_2 has to be in the form of an increase in D_2. However, given Y and L_{g2}, out of a unit increase in additional loan given by households, only α_d is held in the form of time deposits. Hence with D_2 rising to the tune of $1/r$, the increase in total lending will be $(1/r\ \alpha_d)$. In other words, the credit multiplier is a multiple of money multiplier and the former varies inversely with the proportion of 'free wealth' (W_a) households decide to hold in the form of time deposits.

The role of the relative preference for non-monetary financial assets over D_2 in the generation of credit is clearly indicated by (13) and (15). This relative preference does not affect M_2, but has a significant impact on the supply of loans extended outside the banking system. It is useful to distinguish between two parts of non-monetized loans: (i) the part, comprising the first component of (15), is related to the operation of the banking system; and (ii) autonomous component (L_{g2}) in respect of which households are quantity constrained. It is evident from (13), (14) and (15) that an increase in the second component generates an equivalent increase in L and L_n, and has no effect on M_2. The explanation is not far to seek. When L_{g2} goes up, there is initially some withdrawal from D_2, L_{fh} and L_{g1}. But since the additional holding of L_{g2} does not cause a permanent decline in the quantity of reserve money in the system, bank deposit and credit, and hence L_{fh} and L_{g1} remain unaffected in equilibrium.[7] (This should be true not only

---

[7] When in the 80s the Government of India introduced National Savings Certificates, Public Provident Fund and some other financial assets carrying high interest rates and substantial tax concessions, banking circles were apprehensive

for L_{g2}, but also for high yield term deposits with reputed companies which are obliged to keep such borrowings within stipulated limits.)

The first component on r.h.s. of (15) shows the relation between monetary mechanism and the supply of non-bank credit. Since

$$\frac{H}{r} - Y\left(\frac{k_c}{r} + k_{dd}\right) = D_2$$

the supply of non-bank credit may more conveniently be expressed as

$$L_n = \frac{\alpha_{fh} + \alpha_{g1}}{\alpha_d} D_2 + L_{g2} \tag{15a}$$

Thus while an increase in H raises L_n by $(\alpha_{fh} + \alpha_{g1})/\alpha_d$ $(\Delta H)/r$, equations (15) and (15a) suggest that (i) with unchanged asset preference, any factor causing a change in D_2 effects a proportionate chance in L_n; and (ii) the importance of non-bank credit relatively to D_2, as already noted, varies inversely with α_d (or directly with $\alpha_{fh} + \alpha_{g1}$).

Interest Rate Policy

In an administered interest regime changes in the level or structure of interest rates can play an important role in regulating the supply of credit and its distribution. Our analysis of the formation of credit suggests that effects of changes in various rates of interest do not operate in the same direction. Consider first the impact of changes in interest rates on demand deposits. An increase in i_{d1} may conceivably induce households[8] to substitute D_{1h} for H_h and

---

of a sharp decline in the growth of bank deposits. Our analysis suggests why the fear proved unfounded and why there was no financial crowding-out effect of government borrowing in this period. (Rakshit 1986).

[8] Our assumption that firms do not hold cash balances precludes such substitution.

hence generate additional supply of credit both within and outside the banking system. The quantitative results in this regard follow directly from (13), (14), and (15):

$$\frac{\partial M_2}{\partial i_{d1}} = \frac{1-r}{r} k'_{d1} Y \tag{18}$$

$$\frac{\partial L_n}{\partial i_{d1}} = \frac{(1-r)(1-\alpha_d)}{r\,\alpha_d} k'_{d1} Y \tag{19}$$

$$\frac{\partial L}{\partial i_{d1}} = \frac{1-r}{r\,\alpha_d} k'_{d1} Y \tag{20}$$

The economic interpretation of (18) to (20) is fairly obvious from our earlier analysis and need not detain us here. Also, the impact of small changes in i_{d1} is unlikely to be of much quantitative significance because of the differences in the nature of transactions that currency and demand deposits help to effect in developing countries (Rakshit 1982). Our reading of the situation is that relative values of k_h and k_{d1} depend more on structural characteristics of the economy than on i_{d1}.

In view of the sensitivity in the composition of W_a to relative returns on different financial assets,[9] changes in i_{d2}, i_{fh} or i_{g1} will have important effects on the credit market. However, since these rates do not influence the cash drain from commercial banks, total bank credit as also D_2 remain unchanged and the entire effect operates, as may be checked from (13), (14), and (15), through the generation of non-bank credit:

$$\frac{\partial L}{\partial i_j} = \frac{\partial L_n}{\partial i_j} = -\left[\frac{H}{r} - \left(\frac{k_c}{r} + k_{dd}\right) Y\right] \left(\frac{\partial \alpha_d / \partial i_j}{\alpha_d^2}\right)$$

$$= -D_2 \left(\frac{\partial \alpha_d / \partial i_j}{\alpha_d^2}\right) j = d2,\, fh,\, g1 \tag{21}$$

[9] Empirical evidence suggests that while aggregate savings are not interest elastic in LDCs, savings in particular types of financial assets are fairly sensitive to their relative yields.

where $(-\partial \alpha_d / \partial i_j)$ gives the change in non-bank credit per unit of W_a due to a unit increase in i_j. Since D_2 remains unchanged in equilibrium, an increase in i_{d2} reduces total credit through an attempt on the part of households to hold more of time deposits at the expense of L_{fh} and L_{g1}. Similarly, hikes in i_{fh} or i_{g1} raise the supply for non-bank credit through a fall in α_d or an increase in the credit multiplier.[10] Quite clearly, the credit multiplier will be more sensitive to interest rate changes, the larger the availability of close substitutes of D_2 outside the banking system.

Crowding-in and Crowding-out Effects of Government Borrowing

The model of credit formation considered above helps to resolve the controversy concerning the crowding-in and crowding-out effects of various types of public borrowings. Consider first the distribution of total credit between the government and firms. Recalling that

$$L_{gb} = V(D_1 + D_2)$$

where V = statutory liquidity ratio (SLR), equilibrium quantities of L_g and L_f are given by following relations:[11]

$$L_g = \left(1 + \frac{V}{r} + \frac{\alpha_{g1}}{r\alpha_d}\right)H - Y\left[V\frac{k_c}{r} + \alpha_{g1}\left(\frac{k_c}{r\alpha_d} + k_{dd}\right)\right] + L_{g2} \quad (22)$$

$$L_f = \frac{H}{r\alpha_d}\left[\alpha_{fh} + \alpha_d(1 - \overline{V+r})\right]$$

$$- Y\left[\frac{k_c}{r\alpha_d}\left\{\alpha_{fh} + \alpha_d(1 - \overline{V+r})\right\} + \frac{k_{dd}}{\alpha_d}\cdot\alpha_{fh}\right] \quad (23)$$

[10] Though the framework used here is somewhat different from that of neo-structuralists like Wijnbergen (1983) and Taylor (1983), our analysis lends support to their conclusion relating to the contractionary impact of a rise in interest rates on bank deposits. Note however that the effects operate in opposite directions for i_{d1} and i_{d2}. See also Rakshit (1986).

[11] It is assumed without any loss of generality that to banks L_{fb} is superior at the margin to all financial assets supplied by the government.

We have already noted that apart from interest rates, instruments at the disposal of the government and monetary authorities taken together are H, r, V and L_{g2}. Equations (22) and (23) identify major differences among alternative instruments of government borrowing in respect of their crowding-in and crowding-out effects.

Government borrowing from the central bank has significant crowding-in effects on the supply of credit to the public as also the private sector. The effects are generated through the operation of money and credit multipliers and the consequent increase in loans to the government and firms from banks and households. The SLR requirement raises bank credit to government by $V \Delta H/r$, while additional holding of L_{g1} amounts to $\alpha_{g1} \Delta H/r$. It is also clear from (23) and our earlier analysis that the incremental loan to firms consists of $(1 - \overline{V + r}) \Delta H/r$ from banks and $\alpha_{fh} \Delta H/r \, \alpha_d$ from households.

Second, an increase in the cash reserve ratio reduces the supply of bank as well as non-bank credit. There is a reduction in both L_g and L_f, though the decline in the former is relatively less. Thus contrary to the popular view, a rise in r does not cause a diversion of funds from the private to the public sector.

Third, there is a one-to-one crowding-out effect when government borrowing is raised through an increase in V. In this case there is no change in M_2 or L_n and the additional L_{gb} is wholly at the expense of L_{fb}.

Fourth, government borrowing through additional issue of high yield financial assets to households (L_{g2}) has no crowding-in or crowding-out effect whatsoever.

Finally, the impact of an increase in i_{g1} is examined. It is useful in this connection to distinguish between two types of effect, the scale effect and the substitution effect. An increase in i_{g1} tends to raise α_{g1} at the expense of α_d and α_{fh}. A reduction in α_d boosts the aggregate supply of non-bank credit and the scale effect refers to the change in L_g and L_f at the enhanced level of L_n, were there no change in α_{g1}, α_{fh} and α_d. The substitution effect on the other hand is reflected in variation in L_g and L_f, given the augmented supply of non-bank credit, due to changes in α_{g1} etc. and hence in the composition of the households' portfolio. With both the scale and substitution effects operating in the same direction, the supply of loan to the government goes up unambiguously. So far as L_f is concerned, the scale effect is positive, but the substitution effect is negative and the outcome depends on the numerical magnitude of these two effects. To be more specific, write (23) in the following form:

$$L_f = \frac{\alpha_{fh}}{\alpha_d}\left[\frac{1}{r}(H - k_c Y) - k_{dd}\right] + \frac{1 - V + r}{r}(H - k_c Y) \qquad (23a)$$

Evidently, there will be crowding-in or crowding-out according as the (absolute value of the) elasticity of α_d with respect to a change in i_{gl} is larger or smaller than that of α_{fh} — a result that admits of fairly simple economic interpretation.

It thus appears that the conventional notion regarding the financial crowding-out effect of government borrowing in LDCs is somewhat simplistic, if not totally unfounded. Except for the credit generated through instruments like SLR, enhanced government borrowing does not generally induce, in fact it may well raise, the quantity of credit supplied to the private sector.

4 ON ADJUSTMENT AND TRANSMISSION MECHANISM

The model comprising equations (13) to (15), (22) and (23) focusses on stock equilibrium in credit markets at given interest rates, or more specifically, on levels of M_2, L, L_n, etc., that are consistent with the supply of reserve money, interest rates and preferences of economic agents among alternative financial assets. This is in sharp contrast with the conventional approach where equilibrium in the system indicates interest rates that are consistent with historically given quantities of different financial assets and the portfolio choice of economic agents. We have already suggested in Section I, why the conventional model fails to capture some important features of the interaction between the financial and real sectors of the economy. However, it is as yet not clear from our exposition how far the model of credit formation set froth in Section 2 constitutes a more appropriate approach for analysing the role of monetary factors, especially since the model abstracts from the process through which stocks are adjusted and the way these adjustments are intertwined with generation of income and other flows in the system. In order to appreciate the implication of the present approach for the transmission mechanism we present an elementary sketch of the interaction between the financial and commodity markets.

Credit and Commodity Markets

The model we propose to develop can be regarded as an integration of IS-LM and loanable fund approaches to macroeconomic analysis, except that all interest rates are taken to be administered, relations between bank and non-bank credit (as set forth earlier) are explicitly introduced and lenders are assumed not to be quantity constrained (barring the market for L_{g2}). The commodity market is characterized by demand-determined production at fixed prices. Consumption depends only on disposable income and household wealth. Investment is undertaken only by the private sector and equals the quantity of loans available. A part of government expenditure, considered autonomous, is met through taxes while the other part is financed through borrowing. We ignore interest payments on public debt without losing any essential element of the problem.[12] The commodity market equilibrium condition then becomes

$$Y_t = C\,(Y_t - G_{1t},\, W_t,\, A) + I_t + G_{1t} + G_{2t}$$

$$= C\,(Y_t - G_{1t},\, W_t,\, A) + G_{1t} + 1_t \qquad (24)$$

where subscript t stands for the time period t; C = consumption; I = investment; A = autonomous factor; G_{1t} = tax–financed

---

[12] The reason is that when taxes are adjusted to interest payments on public debt to keep G_1 unaffected, (24) remains unchanged under usual assumptions.

government expenditure; G_{2t} = loan – financed government expenditure; and 1_t = the flow of new loans available during t.

The simplest way of examining the impact of financial factors on the commodity market is to assume that

$$I_t = L_t - L_{t-1} = l_t \qquad (25)$$

where L_t is the equilibrium stock of total credit at the end of period t, as given by (14). In other words, we make initially the assumption that the length of time required for (stock) adjustments in the credit market is the same as the (Keynesian) period of income generation.

For notational simplicity, we write

$$L_t = L \ (H_t, \ Y_t, \ L_{g2t}) \qquad (14a)$$
$$+ \quad - \quad +$$

$$l_t = l \ (H_t - H_{t-1}, \ Y_t - Y_{t-1}, \ L_{g2t} - L_{g2t-1}) \qquad (25a)$$
$$+ \qquad\quad - \qquad\qquad +$$

Remembering that

$$W_t = L_t - k_{df} \, Y_t \qquad (26)$$

(14a), (24), (25a), and (26) describe the inter-period dynamics of the credit and commodity markets, given the time profile of government policy parameters G_{1t}, H_t, and L_{2gt}, and initial values of the variables. In order to appreciate the nature of this dynamics and the interaction between the two markets, it is useful to consider first stationary equilibrium values of Y and L (to be denoted by Y^* and L^* respectively) corresponding to some constant quantities of H, G_1, and G_2, and then trace the traverse of the system as the credit market is subjected to some shock. Since the stationary equilibrium is characterized by

$$L_t = L_{t-1} = L^*$$

$$Y_t = Y_{t-1} = Y^*$$

Y^* and L^* are obtained from the relations:

$$Y^* = C(Y^* - G_1, L^* - k_{df} Y^*, A) + G_1 \qquad (27)$$

$$L^* = L(H, Y^*, L_{g2}) \qquad (28)$$

Figure 5.1 gives a diagrammatic characterization of stationary equilibrium with Y^*Y^* and L^*L^* representing (27) and (28) respectively. Verify, that were the consumption independent of wealth, Y^*Y^* would have been vertical and the stationary value of Y (but not of L), independent of factors affecting the supply of credit. The reason is fairly simple. With an unchanged stock of credit, there is no credit-financed expenditure and L^* can affect income only through the wealth effect.

Given the stationary configuration of the system in period 0 at F_0 (Fig 5.1), consider an increase in H in period 1 by ΔH. The credit market equilibrium in 1 is obtained from (14a)

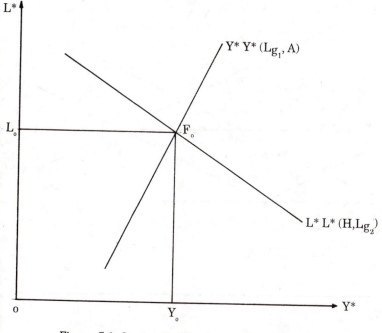

Figure 5.1 Stationary Equilibrium in Credit
and Commodity Markets

$$L_1 = L (H + \Delta H, Y_1, L_{g2}) \tag{29}$$

and may be represented by northward displacement of $L^* L^*$ to the tune of ΔH times the credit multiplier, as given by (17).

Using (24) and (26), the commodity market equilibrium condition in 1 may be written as

$$Y_1 = E (Y_1, G_1, L_1, L_1 - L_0) \tag{30}$$

where $E(\cdot)$ stands for the aggregate demand function. Note that (29) and (30) suitably modified hold not only for period 1, but also for all subsequent periods:

$$L_t = L (H + \Delta H, Y_t, L_{g2}) \tag{29a}$$

$$Y_t = E (Y_t, G_1, L_t, L_t - L_{t-1}) \tag{30a}$$

for $t = 1, 2, \ldots$

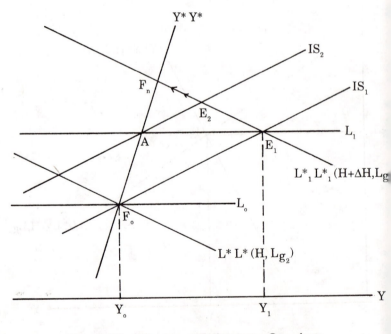

Figure 5.2 Adjustment Following a One-shot
Increase in Reserve Money

Figure 5.2 shows the behaviour of Y and L over time and their movement from the old to the new stationary equilibrium when reserve money remains unchanged from period 1 onwards. F_0 represents the initial stationary configuration at the intersection of L^*L^* and Y^*Y^* (as in Fig 5.1). With H rising by ΔH in period 1, L^*L^* shifts to $L_1^*L_1^*$ and remains in this position in subsequent periods also. Since the commodity market equilibrium relation between L^* and Y^* is still given by Y^*Y^*, the stationary position of the economy moves to F_n where both Y^* and L^* are larger than in the old equilibrium at F_0.

However, for determining income and credit in period 1, the relevant commodity market balance relation is not (27), but (30), represented by IS_1 with 0_1 taken as the origin to measure $L_1 - L_0$. (It may be verified that IS_1 passes through F_0 and is flatter than Y^*Y^*.) The equilibrium in period 1 thus occurs at E_1 with Y and L rising by $Y_0 Y_1$ and $0_1 0_2$ respectively (Fig 5.2).[13] In period 2, the origin for measuring the flow of new credit shifts to 0_2 and the commodity market equilibrium curve moves leftward to IS_2 and passes through A at which $L_2 - L_1 = 0$ and $0_2 A$ equals Y with no credit financed expenditure. It is thus clear that with an initial jump from F_0 to E_1, the economy moves through E_2, E_3, etc. along $L_1^*L_1^*$ as income falls and L rises towards their stationary values at F_n. During this transition from E_1 to F_n the crucial factor generating additional credit and keeping Y above its new stationary value is the gradual decline in Y that reduces currency with the public and permits positive flows of bank and non-bank credit.[14]

---

[13] When consumption does not depend on wealth, *stationary* value of Y does not change with an increase in reserve money, but still Y goes up in period 1 and then declines over time toward its old value Y_0.

[14] One may linearize (14a) and (30a) and solve for Y_t and L_t under alternative assumptions relating to the time profile of H, L_{g2}, G_1, and A. It is not very difficult to see that when H, L_g, G_1, and A grow at a proportionate rate g, both Y and L will grow at the same rate under the steady state, and from any out-of-steady state position the economy moves towards the steady state under usual assumptions concerning households' saving and asset holding behaviour.

Some Economics of Intra-period Adjustment

In order to gain further insight into the nature of credit formation and its interdependence with the generation of income, we suggest some plausible process of adjustment from F_0 to E_1, similar to the operation of investment and money multipliers. With H rising by say ΔH, credit financed government expenditure and hence Y go up by the same amount. However, household wealth at this stage rises only to the extent of household saving; i.e., in round 1

$$(\Delta W)_1 = s (\Delta Y)_1 = s \Delta H$$

where s = marginal rate of household saving.[15] Given the assumptions relating to portfolio choice, $(\Delta W)_1$ is distributed among alternative financial assets in the following manner:

$$(\Delta H_h)_1 = k_c \Delta H; (\Delta D_{1h})_1 = k_{d1} \Delta H; (\Delta D_2)_1 = \alpha_d q \Delta H;$$

$$(\Delta L_{fh})_1 = \alpha_f q \Delta H; (\Delta L_{g1})_1 = \alpha_g q \Delta H$$

where

$$q = s_h - \overline{k_c + k_{d1}} = s_h - k_h$$

Assume that new loans obtained by firms and the government are spent in round 2 and are meanwhile held as deposits with commercial banks and the central bank respectively. In other words, loans obtained by the government will constitute a temporary withdrawal of reserve money. The increase in the cash reserves of commercial banks is hence given by

$$(\Delta H_b)_1 = (1 - k_c) \Delta H - \alpha_g q \Delta H - V [\Delta H (\alpha_d q + k_{dd})$$
$$+ (\Delta L_{fb})_1] \tag{31}$$

where the expression within third brackets on r.h.s. of (31) is total bank deposits including the deposit created while extending loans to firms. With no shortage of demand for bank credit, there is no excess reserves by the end of round 1, i.e.,

---

[15] With no change in G_1, $(\Delta Y)_1$ equals the increase in household disposable income.

$$(\Delta H_b)_1 = r\left[\Delta H\left(\alpha_d q + k_{dd}\right) + (\Delta L_{fb})_1\right] \tag{32}$$

Relations (31) and (32) determine $(\Delta L_{fb})_1$ which together with $(\Delta L_{g1})_1$ and $(\Delta L_{gb})_1$ yield $(\Delta L_g)_1$ and $(\Delta L)_1$:

$$(\Delta L_{fb})_1 = \Delta H\left[\frac{1 - k_c - \alpha_g q}{r + V} - (\alpha_d q + k_{dd})\right] \tag{33}$$

$$(\Delta L_{gb})_1 = \Delta H\frac{V(1 - k_c - \alpha_g q)}{r + V} \tag{34}$$

$$(\Delta L_g)_1 = (\Delta L_{gb})_1 + (\Delta L_{g1})_1 \tag{35}$$

$$(\Delta L)_1 = \frac{\Delta H}{r + V}\left[(1 + V)(1 - k_c) + q\left\{r(1 - 2\alpha_d) + V(\alpha_f - \alpha_d) - \alpha_g\right\}\right]$$

$$\tag{36}$$

In round 2 income generation takes place through consumption out of $(\Delta Y)_1$ and credit-financed expenditure to the tune of $(\Delta L)_1$:

$$(\Delta Y)_2 = (1 - s)(\Delta Y)_1 + (\Delta L)_1 \tag{37}$$

Extra credit supplied by the end of round 2 may be obtained as before. It may be verified that given our assumptions relating to s, k_c, etc., cumulative totals of additional Y and L generated in successive rounds during period 1 (over those in period 0) approximate the comparative static values obtained from short run equilibrium conditions (29) and (30).

An Interim Perspective

It is time we take stock of one or two lessons of the model set forth and indicate their similarities and differences with some important strands of thought in macroeconomic analysis.

First, the model is in consonance with the Schumpetarian idea (Schumpeter 1934) of the crucial role of bank credit in permitting any major expansion of the economy. Not only is non-bank credit relatively unimportant in earlier stages of economic development, but banks (especially of the continental type) and specialized financial institutions[16] supported by central and commercial banks are in a much better position than private individuals both to assess new projects and to reduce risk by relying on the operation of the law of large numbers (Rakshit 1982). Hence extension of bank credit is very often a pre-requisite of investment in general and innovative investment in particular. Again, the expansionary impact of bank credit is larger than that of non-bank credit since bank loans, as we have seen, crowd in non-bank loan, but the former is generally independent of the latter.

Second, our analysis of intra-period adjustment mechanism suggests that extension of credit within and outside the banking system occurs simultaneously. While credit induces injection in the income expenditure stream, income itself, by adding to the demand for financial assets out of household savings, affects adjustments in the supply of credit. If households or banks take time in adjusting their portfolio or extending loans out of excess reserves, the income generation process itself is slowed down. Again, operation of credit multiplier becomes long drawn if output, income and consumption lags are large or α_g and V are high (so that in each round of income generation a relatively large fraction of reserve money is temporarily withdrawn from the system). Hence the operation of the Keynesian and credit multipliers are so intertwined that juxtaposition of stock equilibrium in the financial sector with flow equilibrium in the commodity market, as is done in IS-LM models of the Keynesian and monetarist variety, does not appear quite in order.

Third, even for keeping income at an unchanged level, it is necessary for money supply to grow over time.[17] The reason is similar to that underlying the acceleration principle. When

---

[16] In most developing countries these institutions are largely funded by central and commercial banks so that loans given by such specialized institutions may be clubbed with bank credit for our purpose. We discuss in the next section the role of financial intermediaries.

[17] Except when the economy is in stationary equilibrium.

consumption does not depend on wealth, an unchanged income level requires a constant l and hence a constant increment of high power money per unit of time. This condition is relaxed somewhat when household wealth influences consumption; but in this case also money supply has to grow, though not at a constant absolute rate, in order to arrest the fall in income towards its stationary value.

Fourth, while a rise in the propensity to invest is sterilized[18] through the operation of credit constraint, a higher propensity to save results in a lower level of income in equilibrium.[19] However, we no longer have the Keynesian paradox of thrift: an attempt on the part of households to save more does result in more saving. The reason is enlarged bank and non-bank credit as currency with the public declines with the fall in aggregate demand.

Finally, the model brings into sharp focus the Keynesian perception concerning the unique role of the demand for money balances in causing effective demand failures.[20] It is clear from our description of intra-period adjustment that whether saving constitutes a leakage from the income-expenditure stream or not depends crucially on the portfolio choice of savers. The largest leakage is caused by the acquisition of currency, the leakage being a multiple of the additional currency held. The marginal leakage is unity when saving is held in the form of additional demand or time deposits. The reason is that with no change in cash reserve, (stock of) bank credit remains unaffected. However, when households provide loans to firms and the government[21] out of savings,

---

[18] In the aggregate.

[19] A rise in the propensity to save in period 1 causes an anti-clockwise rotation of IS_1 through F_0 in Fig 5.2. The stationary equilibrium value also shifts north-west with a leftward movement of $Y^* Y^*$.

[20] 'Unemployment develops, that is to say, because people want the moon; — men cannot be employed when the object of desire (i.e. money) is something which cannot be readily choked off. There is no remedy but to persuade the public that green cheese is practically the same thing as to have a green cheese factory (i.e. a central bank) under public control.' (Keynes 1936).

[21] And the government's marginal propensity to spend out of new loans is unity.

the entire amount flows back to the expenditure–income stream. It is thus clear that saving devoted towards extension of credit outside the banking system does not involve any leakage from the income-expenditure stream.

5 Extensions and Generalisations

We have examined implications of the elementary model in some detail since once we have grasped its underlying economics, it is not very difficult to extend and generalize the model by incorporating some features of the financial sector that have so far been left out for simplicity. In order not to lose sight of the main links in the system, these features are considered separately and the focus is only on major modifications in results generated by the elementary model.

Lags in Adjustments in Credit and Income

In the elementary model we have assumed that within the 'short' period income adjusts fully to the flow of credit which in its turn corresponds both to saving (during the period) and to asset preferences of households and banks. However, the time profile of the economy, as our analysis of the adjustment process suggests, should depend crucially (among other factors) on the rapidity of responses of households, firms, banks and the government in respect of their spending, acquisition of financial assets or extension of loans. In other words, apart from the Robertsonian or Lundberg type lags, we also need to consider (investment) implementation lag as also lags in buying or selling financial assets, or negotiation of loans. While the use of household saving that adds to cash balances, demand or time deposits[22] may be regarded as instantaneous, the same cannot be said of loans to firms and

---

[22] There is generally an asymmetry in adding to and reducing time deposits (or company deposits) — an asymmetry that has interesting implications for the nature of the adjustment process, especially when adjustment is cyclical in nature.

the government. This is due in part to inertia, but the more important reasons are (a) preponderance of small savings among the vast majority of households in an LDC and (b) fixed cost of transactions. The result is that households first use their savings to build up bank deposits until they are large enough to make additions to L_{fh} or L_{gl} economical.

So far as banks are concerned, purchase of government securities to satisfy the SLR requirement should not involve any lag. But extension of new production or term loans to firms involves some search, appraisal and screening. Again, in a typical investment project the period over which it is implemented is generally much longer than the time during which the necessary finance is garnered. What is no less important in lengthening the adjustment lag in a credit constrained regime is that most investment projects are taken up only after firms have secured the required fund from alternative sources.

The tendency for the adjustment process to slow down due to the sluggish response of households, firms and banks is countered to a certain extent by the way the Treasury operates in most LDCs. The phasing of government expenditure over a financial year is not strictly tied to actual receipts. The target for monetized deficit relates only to net central bank credit to government over the financial year. Any shortfall (excess) of government expenditure from (over) revenue and capital receipts automatically causes injection (withdrawal) of reserve money. Thus if yearly budgetary targets are consistent, intra-period movements in the supply of reserve money promotes faster adjustment of the system towards equilibrium.

The major implications of lags operating in the generation of credit and income may be summed up as follows. As in standard macro dynamic models, output-income-expenditure lags make current expenditure and income dependent on both present and past incomes. Again, the lumpy nature of most investment projects[23] and their relatively long period of execution imply that investment

---

[23] So that firms need to be assured of a critical minimum amount of credit facility before they execute the investment project.

expenditure in a period is governed by the flow of credit in current as also in previous periods. Ignoring the effect of wealth on expenditure for simplicity, the commodity market equilibrium condition may be summarized as

$$Y_t = E\,(Y_t, Y_{t-1}, \ldots ; L_t - L_{t-1}, L_{t-1} - L_{t-2}, \ldots) \tag{37}$$

Similarly, with slow response of households, firms and banks in the process of credit creation and the impact of saving on adjustment in the loan market, the stock of credit in period t can easily be shown to depend on stocks of high power money and income levels in t, $t{-}1$, etc.:

$$L_t = L\,(H_t, H_{t-1}, \ldots ; Y_t, Y_{t-1}, \ldots) \tag{38}$$

The dynamical system summarized by (37) and (38) would yield the behaviour of income and credit over time, given policy parameters (including H_t, etc.) and (the appropriate number of) initial values of Y and L. From the well-known properties of solutions to dynamical systems it is clear that our conclusions regarding stationary or steady state equilibrium (if there be any) remain unaffected. Also, existence of lags contributes toward stability of the system. However, framing and execution of monetary and fiscal policies now require knowledge of both behavioural parameters and lags operating in markets. Finally, the policy problem is compounded by the fact that when the credit or commodity market is subjected to some shock, the adjustment of income and credit to their new equilibrium values will generally be cyclical with over and under shooting of variables from their equilibrium values.

Non-banking FInancial Intermediaries

While examining the role of financial intermediation outside the banking system it is useful to distinguish between two types of intermediaries operating in LDCs. First, some of these organizations, to be called Financial Institutions, specialize in providing medium and long-term loans to industry or agriculture and are set up with funds from the government as also the central and commercial banks. As Table 2 makes it clear, financing of those institutions by the central Bank and the government amounts to injection of reserve money either directly or indirectly, the consequences of which for the credit market can be analysed along lines suggested in Section 2. However, to the extent that commercial banks contribute toward funding of Financial Institutions there is *ceteris paribus* a decline in net credit extended to firms. Given H and Y (and hence the amount of total deposit), the commercial banks' contribution to the capital base of these institution (F_b) can only be at the expense of an equivalent decrease in L_{fb}. But only a fraction of additional F_b can be lent out to firms by Financial Institutions since they need to keep a part of their total assets as demand deposits in order to meet transactions requirements (D_{1F}).

TABLE 2

SECTORAL ASSETS AND LIABILITIES

	Asset	Liability
Government	$V_g + E_g + F_g$	$L_m + L_{gb} + L_{g1} + L_{g2} + L_{gN}$
Central Bank	$L_m + F_{cb}$	H
Commercial Banks	$H_b + L_{gb} + L_{fb} + F_b$	$D_{1h} + D_{1f} + D_{1F} + D_{1N} + D_2$
Financial Institutions	$L_{fF} + D_{1F}$	$F_g + F_{cb} + F_b$
Financial Intermediaries	$L_{fN} + L_{gN} + D_{1N}$	L_{Nh}
Firms	$V_f + D_{1f}$	$L_{fb} + L_{fh} + L_{fF} + L_{fN}$
Households	$H_h + D_{1h} + D_2 + L_{fh}$ $+ L_{g1} + L_{g2} + L_{Nh}$	W

where F_g = government loan to Financial Institutions; L_{gN} = loan to government from financial intermediaries; F_{cb} = central bank loan to Financial Institutions; F_b = loan from commercial banks to Financial Institutions; D_{1F} = demand deposit held by Financial

Institutions; D_{1N} = demand deposit held by financial intermediaries; L_{fF} = loan from Financial Institutions to firms; L_{fN} = loan
from financial intermediaries to firms; L_{NH} = loan from households
to financial intermediaries.

Second, there are financial institutions like life insurance companies and various types of mutual and pension funds which
attract household savings and finance final users of funds. These
intermediaries are also often required to hold part of their asset
in the form of government securities (L_{gN}). The impact of the
operation of financial intermediaries on the credit market depends
crucially on the degree of substitutability between D_2 and deposits
with these organization (L_{Nh}). If L_{Nh} is a close substitute of L_{fh} or
L_{g1} (rather than of D_2), there would not be a significant effect on
total credit, especially since a part of the asset of finance companies is held as demand deposits (D_{1N}) to carry out their day-to-
day operations. However, given the high cost to households of
gathering reliable information regarding the financial viability of
firms, the small size of asset at the disposal of individual households and their strong risk aversion,[24] only a minor part of household saving is directly lent to firms in LDCs. Hence the setting up
of large mutual funds tends to reduce α_d and causes thereby an
increase in the supply of total credit.

DEMAND-CONSTRAINED CREDIT MARKET

Our analysis so far has been based on the assumption that the
credit market is characterized by excess demand. However, for
given interest rates and other policy parameters, the market can be
constrained on either the demand or the supply side. Since the
behaviour of the system is significantly different in the two cases it
is instructive to consider characteristics of the demand constrained
regime and conditions under which it will be operative.

When demand constraint is in force in the loan market, firms
are able to carry out their plans relating to investment and

---

[24] The last two factors are closely connected.

borrowing[25] (given the amount of loan outstanding at the end of the previous period):

$$I^f = I^{fd} (i_{fh}, i_{fb}, Y) \quad (39)$$
$$(-) \ (-) \ (+)$$

$$L_f = L^{fd} (i_{fh}, i_{fb}, Y) \quad (40)$$
$$(-) \ (-) \ (+)$$

where superscript 'fd' refers to firms' demand and I to investment.

Assuming government expenditure to be autonomously determined at G, total government borrowing at the end of the period (L_g) will be negatively related to Y (with a positive relationship between Y and government revenue from all sources):

$$L_g = L_g (Y) \quad (41)$$
$$(-)$$

With demand determined production in the commodity market, equilibrium income is given by the relation

$$Y = E^d (Y, G, I^{fd}(\cdot)) \quad (42)$$

where the impact of wealth on aggregate demand has been ignored without any loss of generality for the short period analysis.

Let Y^e be the solution to (42). The configuration of the financial sector may now be easily spelt out. The equilibrium W is easily obtained from

$$W = \bar{L}_g + \bar{L}^{fd} - k_{df} Y^e \quad (43)$$

where L_g and $\bar{L}^{fd}$ are values of L_g and L^{fd} respectively at $Y = Y^e$.

Since the credit market is demand constrained, households and firms are not able to lend as much as they would have liked to firms. However, quantity constraint does not generally operate in respect of financial assets supplied by the government (L_{g1} and L_{gb}). The implication is that SLR is no longer operative and

[25] L^{fd} is positively related to Y because of both larger investment and the greater requirement of holding demand deposits.

banks hold their assets in excess of required reserves in the form of government securities (L_{fb}).[26] So far as households are concerned, their choice now relates to D_2 and L_{g1} out of W_a which needs to be redefined in view of quantity constraint on L_{fh}:

$$W_a = W - (k_h Y^e + \bar{L}_{fh} + L_{g2}) \tag{44}$$

where $\bar{L}_{fh}$ is the amount of loans firms take from households.

Let θ and $1 - \theta$ be fractions of firms' borrowings from households and banks respectively:

$$\bar{L}_{fh} = \theta\, (i_{fh}, i_{fb})\, \bar{L}^{fd} \tag{45}$$
$$(-)\ (+)$$

$$\bar{L}_{fb} = (1 - \theta)\, \bar{L}^{fd} \tag{46}$$

Plugging (43) and (45) into (44) we have

$$W_a = \bar{L}_g - L_{g2} - k\, Y^e + (1 - \theta)\, \bar{L}^{fd} \tag{47}$$

where $k = k_c + k_{d1} + k_{df}$

Allocation of W_a between D_2 and L_{g1} is given by

$$D_2 = \beta\, (i_{d2}, i_{g1})\, W_a \tag{48}$$
$$(+)\ (-)$$

$$L_{g1} = (1 - \beta)\, W_a \tag{49}$$

where β is the fraction of W_a held in the form of time deposits. Using (47), (48), and the relations

$$H_h = k_c\, Y^e$$

$$D_1 = (k_{d1} + k_{df})\, Y^e = k_d\, Y^e$$

$$H_b = r\, (D_1 + D_2)$$

the supply of reserve money turns out to be

[26] In India the commercial banks' portfolio exhibited this feature in 1993–94 when credit market was demand constrained (see Rakshit 1994).

$$H = (1 - \beta) (k_c + r k_d) Y^e + r \beta [(1 - \theta) \bar{L}^{df} + \bar{L}_g - L_{g2}] \quad (50)$$

Thus with fixed G, H can be changed only through appropriate adjustments in L_{g2} or r. But what is important to note is that such changes do not affect the aggregate amount of credit or Y.

Finance in a Flexible Interest Regime

Since most LDCs have been engaged for some time in unfreezing interest rates and reducing the coverage of directed credit programmes, our model may perhaps be deemed not very relevant under changed circumstances. However, financial liberalization does not necessarily lead to a fully flexible interest rate regime. In view of the predominance of oligopolistic elements in the credit market quite a few crucial rates of interest remain sticky even when they are not fixed by monetary authorities. It is nevertheless instructive to consider implications of flexible interest rates and examine how far our earlier conclusions need revision in such situations.

In order to come to grips with the essential aspects of the problem and not to violate the space constraint we focus only on the financial sector, ignore government borrowing from banks or households, and abstract from holding of currency and bank deposits by firms. Household wealth now comprises H and L_f:

$$W = H + L_f \quad (51)$$

Let cash reserve ratios for demand and time deposits be r_1 and r_2 respectively (with $r_1 > r_2$). Transactions demand for money balances consists of H_h and D_1 and is given by

$$H_h = k_h (i_{d1}, i_{d2}) Y \quad (52)$$
$$(-) \ (-)$$

$$D_1 = k_{d1} (i_{d1}, i_{d2}) Y \quad (53)$$
$$(-) \ (-)$$

where i_{d1} = interest rate on demand deposit (D_1); i_{d2} = interest rate on time deposit; $k_h = H_h/Y$; and $k_{d1} = D_1/Y$.

With a competitive banking system which does not require any real resources for its operation, relations between interest rates on bank deposits and the lending rate i_{fb} are obtained from the zero-profit rule:

$$i_{d1} = (1 - r_1)\, i_{fb} \tag{54}$$

$$i_{d2} = (1 - r_2)\, i_{fb} \tag{55}$$

With no excess reserves in equilibrium under the flexible interest regime, time deposit and money supply are given by

$$D_2 = \frac{1}{r_2}\,(H - c_d\, Y) \tag{56}$$

$$M_2 = \frac{1}{r_2}\,(H - \delta\, Y) \tag{57}$$

where $c_d = k_h(\cdot) + r_1\, k_{d1}(\cdot)$; $\delta = (1 - r_1)\, k_h(\cdot) + (r_1 - r_2)\, k_{d1}(\cdot)$.

The supply of bank credit to firms, L_{fb}^s, is then immediate:

$$L_{fb}^s = M_2 - H = \frac{1}{r_2}\Big[(1 - r_2)\, H - \delta\, Y\Big] \tag{58}$$

If the two components of transactions demand for money balances are interest insensitive, the supply of money and bank credit, it is clear from (57) and (58), become independent of interest rates (and hence of the demand for credit) at given levels of H and Y. Considerations of empirical relevance[27] and of keeping the algebra relatively uncluttered induce us to stick for the most part to the assumption of insensitivity of k_h and k_{d1} to changes in interest rates. Only at the concluding part of the section do we indicate some consequences of dropping the assumption.

[27] In India both currency with the public and demand deposit as ratios of GDP have remained fairly stable over the last four decades in spite of significant changes in interest rates during this period.

Household wealth after meeting transactions demand is

$$W_a = H + L_f - kY \qquad (59)$$

where $\qquad k = k_h + k_{d1}$

Distribution of W_a between L_{fh} and D_2 will be governed by relative returns on the two assets:

$$\frac{L_{fh}^s}{W_a} = \mu \, (i_{fh}, \, i_{d2}) \qquad (60)$$
$$\qquad\qquad (+) \; (-)$$

$$\frac{D_2^d}{W_a} = 1 - \mu(\cdot) \qquad (61)$$

where superscripts s and d stand for supply and demand respectively.

A simple way of specifying firms' total demand for loan and its composition would be the following (taking the level of income as given):

$$L_f^d = L_f^d \, (i_{fh}, \, i_{fb}) \qquad (62)$$
$$\qquad\qquad (-) \; (-)$$

$$\frac{L_{fd}^d}{L_f^d} = \varphi \, (i_{fh}, \, i_{fh}) \qquad (63)$$
$$\qquad\qquad (+) \; (-)$$

$$\frac{L_{fh}^d}{L_f^d} = 1 - \varphi(\cdot) \qquad (64)$$

Plugging (55) into (60), $\mu(\cdot)$ can be transformed as a function of i_{fh} and i_{fb}. Equilibrium in the loan market may now be characterized by

$$L_f = L_f^d \, (i_{fh}, \, i_{fb}) \qquad (65)$$

$$\varnothing(\cdot) \, L_f^d(\cdot) = \frac{1}{r_2} \left[(1 - r_2) \, H - \delta \, Y \right] \text{ (from (58) and (63))} \qquad (66)$$

$$(1 - \phi(\cdot))\, L_f^d(\cdot) = \mu(\cdot)\,(H + L_f - k\, Y) \quad \text{(from (59), (60) and (66)). (67)}$$

Equations (65) to (67) yield equilibrium values of L_f, i_{fh} and i_{fb} and hence of other variables in the system (from earlier relations). Interaction between the financial and real markets may be examined by linking investment demand to the flow of credit along lines suggested in Section 4. Without going into details of this interactions we propose to indicate some major similarities and difference between results of the flexible interest rate system and that of the models set forth earlier.

First, even with fully flexible interest rates, the quantity of credit may remain relatively unaffected by changes in demand (as in the fixed interest regime with credit rationing). To see why consider an autonomous increase in the demand for credit, L_f^d. With given H and Y, supply of bank credit to firms [as given on r.h.s. of (66)] remains unchanged. Hence total credit can rise only if the increase in i_{fh} is relatively more than that of i_{fb} in order to induce households to hold a larger fraction of their assets in the form of L_{fh}. However, such a change in the interest rate structure prompts firms to substitute L_{fb} for L_{fh}. Household preferences and firms' choice relating to modes of financing thus tend to generate a relatively stable differential between i_{fh} and i_{fb}. If the differential is indeed stable in equilibrium, an increase in L_f^d (with a fixed supply of L_{fb}) will raise both rates of interest until the additional demand for credit is choked off. It is only when the equilibrium interest differential and the ratio of L_{fh} to L_{fb} vary with aggregate credit would the supply of non-bank loan respond to changes in the aggregate demand for credit.

Second, interest insensitivity of demand for cash balances, it follows from above, tends to produce stable values of the money and credit multipliers. The implication is that when there is a change in reserve money, the nature of the credit demand function affects primarily the extent of variation in interest rates rather than the quantity of credit generated in the system.

Third, the supply of both bank and non-bank credit will be responsive to changes in demand when the currency with the public and the demand deposit are interest elastic. The effect is similar when a part of the cash reserves of commercial banks constitutes speculative demand and hence is elastic to interest rate changes. However, the quantitative significance of these effects is somewhat doubtful.

Finally, while in a fixed interest regime a change in the ratio of non-bank to bank credit could be effected through variations in the structure of interest rates, the ratio, as we have seen, tends to be somewhat sticky in a flexible interest regime. The most important factor determining the ratio thus turns out to be the stage of development of the financial sector, or rather of the range and variety of financial assets available outside the banking system and the access of various groups of households to these assets. Thus even when monetary authorities do not take appropriate measures to meet the credit requirements of a growing economy, financial innovation or the introduction of new instruments of borrowing and lending often plays an important role in preventing the emergence of serious credit constraints and prolonged stagnation.

6 CONCLUSION

1. The paper takes the IS-LM framework as its point of departure taking explicit account of (a) absence of secondary markets for major instruments of credit; (b) widespread prevalence of sticky interest rates with or without intervention by monetary authorities; and (c) consistency between commodity market equilibrium and *flow* equilibrium in the credit market (keeping in view the close connection between investment and supply of *new* loans).

2. Supply of credit and its distribution depend crucially on the structure of the financial sector, rules under which it operates and the asset preference of economic agents. These factors influence the relation between bank and non-bank credit as also values of the money and credit multipliers.

3.   Economic expansion generally requires an increase in the supply of reserve money and bank credit since extension of new loans is *prior* to investment while loans from households and non-bank financial intermediaries are available only out of *realized* savings.

4.   The process of credit formation is intertwined with the generation of income. The rapidity with which extension of new credit takes place affects the rate of adjustment in the commodity market. At the same time, production, income and expenditure lags tend to slow down the process of adjustment in the supply of credit by households and financial intermediaries.

5.   Whether government borrowing has a crowding-in or crowding-out effect depends on the nature of instruments used for obtaining credit. In a fixed interest regime borrowing via SLR (Statutory Liquidity Ratio) has a one-to-one crowding-out effect and that through high yield financial instruments no crowding-out effect whatsoever. However, additional credit obtained through an increase in interest rates on financial asset supplied by the government will normally have a crowding-in effect.

6.   Even in a flexible interest regime the aggregate supply of money and credit may fail to respond significantly to changes in demand, at least in the short run. The reason lies in the inelasticity in the supply of bank credit and relative stickiness in the differential between different rates of interest. The most important factors affecting the aggregate supply of credit in relation to reserve money or bank credit are (a) variety/diversity of financial assets outside the banking system; and (b) the extent to which various groups of economic agents have easy access to capital markets. Hence the importance of financial innovation and extension of the coverage of financial intermediaries in preventing the emergence of serious credit constraints in a growing economy.

REFERENCES

Bernanke, B.S. and A.S. Blinder (1988), 'Credit, Money and Aggregate Demand', *American Economic Review*, 78.

Blinder, A.S. and R.M. Solow (1973), 'Does Fiscal Policy Matter', *Journal of Public Economics*, 2, pp. 319–37.

—— (1974), *The Economics of Public Finance*, Washington, D.C.: Brookings Institution.

Brunner, K. and A.H. Meltzer (1972), 'Money, Debt and Economic Activity', *Journal of Political Economy*, 80, pp. 951–77.

Friedman, M. (1956), 'The Quantity Theory of Money: A Restatement', in Friedman, M. (ed.), *Studies in the Quantity Theory of Money*, Chicago: Chicago University Press.

Hicks, J. (1948), *A Contribution to the Theory of Trade Cycles*, London: Oxford University Press.

—— (1981), 'IS-LM: An Explanation', *Journal of Post-Keynesian Economics*, VIII.

—— (1991), *A Market Theory of Money*, London: Oxford University Press.

Keynes, J.M. (1936), *A General Theory of Employment, Interest and Money*, London: Macmillan.

Modigliani, F. and L. Papademos (1987), 'Money, Credit and the Monetary Mechanism', in deCeeco, M. and J.P. Fitoussi (eds), *Monetary Theory and Economic Institutions*, London: Macmillan.

Rakshit, M. (1982), *The Labour Surplus Economy*, Delhi: Macmillan and New Jersey; Humanities Press.

—— (1986), 'Monetary Policy in a Developing Country', Helsinki, WIDER (mimeo).

—— (1994), 'Money and Public Finance under Structural Adjustment: The Indian Experience', *Economic and Political Weekly*, nos 16 and 17.

Schumpeter, J.A. (1934), *The Theory of Economic Development*, Cambridge, MA: Harvard University Press.

Stiglitz, J.E. and A. Weiss (1981), 'Credit Rationing in Markets with Imperfect Information', *American Economic Review*, 71, pp. 393–410.

Taylor, L. (1983), *Structuralist Macroeconomics*, New York: Basic Books.

Tobin, J. (1969), 'A General Equilibrium Approach to Monetary Theory', *Journal of Money, Credit and Banking*, 1, pp. 15–29.

Tobin, J. and W. Buiter (1976), 'Long-run Effects of Fiscal and Monetary

Policy on Aggregate Demand', in Stein, J.L. (ed.), *Monetarism*, Amsterdam: North Holland.

Wijnbergen, S.V. (1983), 'Interest Rate Management in LDCs', *Journal of Monetary Economics*, 12, pp. 433–52.

6

Three Aspects of
Transforming Former
Centrally Planned Economies[*]

Amit Bhaduri

Against the background of accumulating experiences in the former command economies now in the process of transition towards the market system, at least three aspects of the transformation debate deserve special attention, because, in all these three areas conventional wisdom has turned out to be particularly unsatisfactory. For expositional clarity, they are grouped under the following headings:

(a) the significance of *demand management*;
(b) the characterization of the *inflationary process*; and finally,
(c) the *role of the state* during transformation.

1 DEMAND MANAGEMENT

From a broad macroeconomic perspective, the command economies were supply-constrained, shortage economies, where both the level and the pattern of demand continuously kept ahead

[*] This paper was written [at the invitation of the Parliament of Ukraine] during my stay as a fellow (1994–95) in the Wissenschaftskolleg zu Berlin. Later rounds of revision benefited from comments by Jan Kregel, Kazimierz Laski, Egon Matzner and Rune Skarstein.

of supply. As a result, compression of demand was unavoidable at the initial stages, as these economies struggled to move from a supply-determined system to the logic of a demand-determined, market-oriented system. Consequently, the role of aggregate demand assumed importance as an intrinsic part of the process of stabilization. And yet, the role of demand was underestimated in almost every case of 'shock therapy' in so far as demand contraction was an 'overkill' in two respects. The reduction in the *level* of demand went considerably beyond what was necessary, and continues for a longer *time* than is necessary. The underlying theoretical reasons are to be found in the monetarist doctrine which strongly influenced the design of shock therapy. It wrongly postulated that reducing demand through such methods as domestic credit restriction and reduction of government budget deficit affects almost exclusively prices, but not the quantities supplied. Thus, inflation has all along been fought by compressing demand, while almost no attention has been paid to the fact that lower aggregate demand would also reduce aggregate supply in the process. Aggregate demand and aggregate supply are *not* independent variables; indeed, they are highly interdependent and the designs of transformation need to recognize this interdependence. A reduction in 'money' supply not only reduces prices but also quantities, even if the velocity of circulation remains quasi-constant. Indeed, the causation may often run in the opposite direction. A reduction in the supply of money may be brought about endogenously by reducing first the level of economic activity which, in turn, reduces correspondingly the demand for money.

It needs to be mentioned that there has been considerable autonomous disruption of supply as old systems of trade and regional specialization in the former socialist countries broke down. The disruption has been more severe in some economies than in others. However, beyond such autonomous disruptions in supply, it continued to fall even below what could have been its viable level, as the overkill of demand contraction was continued.

This fall in supply is justified typically on grounds of 'efficiency', e.g. by evoking the Schumpeterian image of 'creative destruction'. It is argued, for instance, that total *import liberalization* would weed out the internationally inefficient producers, but would allow the efficient ones to survive. From a macroeconomic standpoint, the argument is usually specious. So long as import liberalization leads to larger autonomous import surplus (or current account deficit) at any given level of investment, it would shrink the size of the domestic market through the chain reaction of the multiplier mechanism. Not only would the inefficient firms lose out to foreign competitors, but as jobs are lost in these firms, the demand for the products of even efficient firms would be reduced through the multiplier. Formally, the essence of the argument can be seen from the national accounting equilibrium condition,

$$I = S + (M - E) = sY + A$$

where I = investment, S = savings, M = import, and E = export. Therefore, a larger *autonomous* import surplus $A = (M-E)$ at any given level of investment I, entails lower domestic saving S which, in turn, is associated with a lower level of domestic income (Y) determined by the smaller size of the domestic market.[1] Hence, import liberalization, in so far as it creates a larger autonomous trade deficit through capital account transfer, may accentuate the problem of falling aggregate demand, *both* for inefficient, and for efficient firms. The typical mistake is to think only in terms of either the supply side or of imports induced through a given marginal propensity, which might suggest that efficient domestic firms would survive despite foreign competition. The demand side repercussions, which in turn affect again the supply side in the manner outlined above, must not be overlooked, particularly by

---

[1] An autonomous rise in import surplus means a *shift* of import as a function of income, exchange rate etc. This may be brought about by higher capital inflow, as in the case of former East Germany, or by higher foreign aid as in the case of some developing countries. See Bhaduri & Skarstein (1996a).

politicians. Therefore, the case for intelligent demand management through selective expansionary policies is stronger when import liberalization proceeds rapidly. Alternatively, the pace of import liberalization needs to be controlled. That is the political choice for economies undergoing transformation.

2 INFLATION

Almost indiscriminate demand contraction has been justified in many transitional economies in the name of fighting inflation. While this method was undoubtedly effective in the early stages of transformation, it is seldom realized that the *persistence* of inflation in some of these economies cannot be countered further through contraction of demand. In countries like Poland and Hungary, a kind of *recessionary inflation* has been at work since about 1993–4, which has been aggravated by policies of continuing demand contraction. Such an inflationary process arises from two sources. First, attempts to reduce the level of government budget deficit have often involved raising the administered prices of essential inputs such as electricity, transport, etc. That has, in turn, raised the unit variable cost of production which has led to higher mark-up prices. Very high nominal interest rates, and higher cost of imported inputs after devaluation have further strengthened this inflationary pressure operating through higher unit costs. Second, recession itself has meant lower capacity utilization for industry. This has required some of the recurring overhead costs (like managerial personnel salaries, interest payments on debt, etc.) of the enterprises to be spread over a smaller amount of output produced. Consequently, the unit overhead cost increases as recession leads to further loss of production. With less subsidy from the government, the enterprises have tried to cover their rising *unit* variable cost by raising prices. In this process of recessionary inflation, the deeper the recession is, the stronger is the pressure on enterprises to raise prices to cover unit variable costs. It is a 'cost-push inflation' but with a difference: it is not led by rising wage cost. Consequently, the more the government tries to combat such inflation through restrictive fiscal policies like cutting the budget deficit or restrictive monetary policies like high nominal interest rate, the more it is likely to fuel the process of recessionary inflation.

The formal essence of the argument can be summarized briefly. For simplicity of exposition, let labour be the only element of cost. Overhead costs of managerial and special technical labour, L_m is given as proportional to normal or full capacity output (Y^*), i.e., $L_m = aY^*$, $a > o$. Variable labour cost is proportional to actual output (Y), i.e. $L_v = bY$.

Thus, at a uniform wage w assumed for both types of labour for simplicity of exposition, unit cost of output is,

$$c = \frac{wL_m + wL_v}{Y}$$

and, with mark-up 'm', the price level for the enterprise is, $p = (1 + m).\ w\ [(a/z) + b]$

where $z = Y/Y^*$ i.e. the degree of industrial capacity utilization. It follows that prices tend to rise with lower z, other factors remaining the same. Thus, z tends to fall under an austerity programme of reducing budget deficit which fuels this process of inflationary recession.

Nevertheless, it must be mentioned that the recent cases of *hyperinflation* in many parts of the former USSR, is a very different one. In a situation of hyperinflation domestic currency as money loses its function as a 'store of value', because of reluctance to hold money for *future* purchases. In this flight away from money to real commodities, money is used almost entirely as an *immediate* medium of exchange for transactions, increasing tremendously, the velocity of circulation. Only when money has almost no role as a store of future value, with the velocity of circulation approaching some maximal institutionally determined level, does the quantity theory of money begin to be an acceptable guide to policy (Kalecki 1991). A reduction in money supply, especially by reducing the high-powered, base money, can be effective in checking hyperinflation. Indeed there is no alternative to drastic restraint on money supply, and even currency reform in these extreme cases. However, it has been an extraordinary folly of IMF-sponsored stabilization to treat all inflation as hyperinflation of this kind! It is essential to recognize that the mechanisms fueling inflationary processes are different in different situations. A recessionary inflation of the type outlined earlier cannot and should not be fought in the same way as a hyperinflation.

3 THE ECONOMIC ROLE OF THE STATE

An assumption implicit in the transition process is the leading role of the private sector in making the economy more market-oriented. Nevertheless, this assumption is in no way contradicted by the fact that the state has to have a supportive role. This supportive role does not imply a minimalist state. From the standpoint of economic theory, it requires the state to create 'external economies' which the private sector can internalize and appropriate, under existing property rights, to increase its profitability.

External economies created by the state for appropriation by the private sector, can come either from a reduction in the production costs of the private sector or from higher revenue earned by the private sector. For instance, better public schooling or communication services may increase private profitability by reducing the latter's cost of training or communication. Indeed, much of the growth of the small private trade and commercial services in east Europe can be looked upon from this angle as internalizing partly the benefits of publicly-owned infrastructure for private profits. However, the controversial issue of protection of specific industries from foreign competition can also be looked upon as a way of creating external economies for these industries by increasing their revenues through protection or generation of demand by the state.

The question of which types of 'external economies' for the private sector are most beneficial cannot be settled in general. It is contextual. Nevertheless, in transitional economies with almost no tradition of private industrial entrepreneurship, there can be little doubt that 'market friendliness' of the state consists largely of systematically creating external economies that can be appropriated relatively easily through private enterprise. Some implications of this deserve emphasis.

First, using a biological analogy, the internalizing of externalities by the private sector would make it somewhat of a 'parasite' living on a 'host' population.[2] Just as a parasite's health and fortune are interlinked with the health of the population which hosts it, this parasitic advantage of benefiting from external economies can continue to grow, only so long as the host population — the state in this case — also grows in some sense. In short, it is difficult to imagine the private sector expanding vigorously in a transitional economy, while the regulatory and other powers of the state are decaying, or even being taken over by mafia-rule. However, this does not mean that the state has to increase continuously *relative* to the private sector. Nor does it imply continuous widening of state activity in the economic sphere. The implications are quite different, and must be understood in the dynamic context of the transformation process. During the course of the transformation, the *nature* of the external economies to be created by the state for private appropriation would continue to change. For instance, at some (initial) stage, it may be usual economic and social infrastructure like education, health and communication or legal infrastructure for enforcement of contracts in economic transactions. At another (later) stage, it may be research and development expenditure for selected industries, their temporary protection, and other elements of industrial policy in general.[3] In the legal sphere, proper functioning of stock exchange markets may require enforcement of different rules at different stages by the state. Thus, the nature of the external economies to be generated by the state, as well as the ways by which they are to be appropriated, partially or totally, by the private sector would evolve as the transitional

[2] Bhaduri (1995), provides mathematical models elaborating this idea.

[3] See Bhaduri (1996b) for a formal analysis of these ideas.

economies undergo structural transformation. It is best to think of the overall relationship between the state and the private sector as one of *adaptive* cooperation which evolves over time. It would be tragic if this supportive, dynamic role of the state is misunderstood or misrepresented for ideological reasons. That would make the task of transformation no easier.

REFERENCES

Bhaduri, A. (1995), 'Dynamic Patterns in Transformation', *Structural Change and Economic Dynamics*.

Bhaduri, A. and Skarstein, R. (1996a), 'Short Period Macroeconomic Aspects of Foreign Aid', *Cambridge Journal of Economics*, vol. 20, pp. 195–206.

Bhaduri, A. (1996b), 'Reflections on the Economic Role of the Transformational State' (in French translation) in R. Delorme (ed.), *'Formes d' Organisation et Transformations Socio-Economiques a l' Est*, Paris: Editions l'Harmattan.

Kalecki, M. (1991, originally written in 1955), 'A Model of Hyperinflation', in *Collected Works of Michal Kalecki*, J. Osiatynski (ed.), Oxford: Clarendon Press, vol. 2, pp. 90–6.

III

Human Capital

The costs of providing education along with the nature of consequent benefits in terms of improving human capital, have held the
interest of economists for a long time. Education provides capabilities, thus acquiring added significance in discussions of well-
being and advantage. The two chapters by Alok Ray, and Amal
Sanyal and Anjan Mukherji, discuss different social costs and
benefits of education.

Brain Drain: A Social Cost Benefit Perspective

Ray analyses the phenomenon of 'brain drain' in terms of a social
cost-benefit approach. Brain drain, at least in the short-run, may
not represent a net social loss to the country exporting educated
persons, if one takes into account, remittances, import of a part
of the value created by the emigrant in the host country, and the
expected gains from a possible future return of the migrant to the
country of origin. Ray also discusses some policy issues relating
to the production and export of skilled personnel, and the implications of stopping the brain drain. His results, as expected, are
sensitive to the institutions prevailing in the migrants' country of
origin. A related issue of significance is the under-utilization and
waste of skilled personnel in many developing countries, independent of any brain drain.

General Versus Specialised Education: An Alternative View

Sanyal and Mukherji analyse the benefits of general education against specialized education, when the aptitude of a student is not known. Early specialization can lead to a mismatch of aptitude and the line of specialization chosen. This entails a social loss as the expenses incurred in providing the education are irreversible. Investment in general education helps in acquiring information about the aptitudes of students. Thus, the authors argue, such investment commands a premium over and above the pure productivity of that investment, in a world of imperfect knowledge about the distribution of aptitudes. An implication of this is to reduce the degree of irreversibility of higher education by making it more flexible. Additional investment, to this purpose, is worthwhile as it induces some extra benefits.

7

Brain Drain:
A Social Cost Benefit Perspective

*Alok Ray**

1 INTRODUCTION

The 'brain drain', as the expression strongly suggests, is considered to be imposing a significant net loss on the country from which the skilled personnel are flowing out. The problem is viewed as a serious one for LDCs like India, which have to bear the enormous costs of training doctors, engineers, scientists and academicians through a heavily subsidized public education system. Many of such trained personnel go abroad and finally settle there. There has been talk, in responsible circles, of 'closing the doors' ('though keeping the windows open').[1]

Academic economists have seized upon the opportunity to investigate the theoretical and empirical aspects of the phenomenon in terms of a variety of models.[2] However, having gone through the literature I could not help feeling that most of the basic issues (which would also be relevant for policy purposes) can conveniently be captured in a simple social cost-benefit (or project evaluation) analytical framework[3] rather than complex

---

* I have substantially benefitted from discussions with Amit Bhaduri and Amitava Bose.

[1] See Dandekar (1968).

[2] See Adams (1968); Bhagwati (1976a, 1976b) for collections of articles on brain drain.

[3] The essential spirit (though not the details or the modifications) of the present

general equilibrium models. This is something which is missing in the literature. The present paper is an attempt to fill this gap.

Specifically, we shall focus on the following questions:

(i)   What are the major components of gains and losses from brain drain for the country of emigration?

(ii) What are the parameters on the values of which the case for or against brain drain crucially hinge?

(iii) In the absence of detailed empirical knowledge about the values of the parameters, can a 'presumption' be established either way?

(iv) What policy guidelines can be derived?

Apart from clarifying the conceptual and the analytical issues, we shall offer some comments on the situation as it obtains in a country like India, in terms of the analytical framework developed in this paper.

2   COMPONENTS OF GAINS AND LOSSES

Let us first have a look, from the standpoint of the country of emigration (call it India), at the major components of gains and losses arising out of a person emigrating abroad (call it USA).

An immediate question arises: should the emigrant's welfare be considered a part of the welfare of India or not? Opinions may differ on this question.[4] However, given the serious concern expressed about brain drain from LDCs and the fact that the emigrant (to the extent he migrates out of his free will and is not expelled or thrown out) gains from the migration, it is but natural that the social gains and losses for India arising out of emigration should refer to the welfare of those left behind or the non-emigrant population of India. This is all the more so if the emigration is permanent but it may not be so clear cut if the migration is of the 'to and fro'

---

framework is derived from the so-called OECD–UNIDO approaches as developed in Little and Mirrlees (1968) and Dasgupta, Marglin and Sen (1972).

[4] See Bhagwati and Rodriguez (1976e) for more discussion on this point.

variety or if there is a possibility that the emigrant will come back after spending some time abroad ('reverse migration'). To avoid taxonomy, we shall measure India's gains and losses in terms of the welfare of the non-emigrant population of India (even after the emigrant returns to India which, however, is not certain, *ex-ante*). We shall, however, take into account the contribution (or, rather the expected value thereof) that the returning emigrant may make to the welfare of the rest of the population by assigning appropriate probabilities to his return.

The basic issue, therefore, is: how is the availability of goods and services (including foreign exchange) for the non-emigrant population affected by emigration?

The main element of social loss from emigration is the social value of output the emigrant could have produced in India had he not gone abroad. This has to be understood in a wide sense as referring to the reduction in the total value of national output (valued at appropriate 'shadow prices'[5]) as a result of a person leaving India along with his human and non-human capital. One has to set this against three components of gain. First, the goods and services the emigrant would have consumed in India are released. This reduction in consumption by the emigrant in India adds to the flow of goods and services available for the non-emigrant population. Second, the foreign exchange earned through the emigrant's remittances and occasional visits as a tourist, valued at the shadow price of foreign exchange, is a source of national gain for India. It is the *net* remittance which is relevant since the person may also take away foreign exchange from India while emigrating. Finally, a part of the output the emigrant would produce in USA may also benefit India. Most obvious is the case where the emigrant is engaged in research abroad, the fruits of which are available to India (a kind of 'public good' or 'international external economies')

---

[5] We are not going into the question of how shadow prices are determined. The interested reader may refer to Little and Mirrlees (1968) and Dasgupta, Marglin and Sen (1972). Needless to say, the exact shadow prices which are the Lagrangeans associated with the optimization exercise would depend upon the specification of the national objective function as well as the constraints.

free of cost.[6] The social usefulness, from India's stand point (which may be quite different from the social usefulness from USA's point of view), of his research output is the relevant consideration here. To take care of the possibility of the emigrant returning to India at a future point of time, we must also include the value of his output contribution minus his consumption in India (after he comes back) in the measurement of the gains to the rest of the population. Since the return of the emigrant is not certain *ex-ante*, we shall have to take the (mathematical) expected value of output minus consumption in this context.

In terms of notations, L, the annual net social loss for India due to the emigration (and possible coming back) of a person[7] to USA (relative to his remaining in India), can, therefore, be written as

$$L = P \cdot X - P \cdot C - (P - M) \cdot \alpha \cdot X^* - R \cdot e_s - E(P \cdot X') + E(P \cdot C') \,(1)$$

where

X =   reduction in national output (vector) in India due to emigration to USA;

P =   price (vector) reflecting the social value, from India's point of view, of goods and services produced and/or consumed in India;

C =   reduction in consumption (vector) of the emigrant in India due to emigration;

X^* =   increase in national output (vector) in USA due to emigration of the person from India into USA;

α =   the vector representing the proportions of X^* that are made available to non-emigrants in India;

M =   the vector representing the cost of importing $\alpha \cdot X^*$, from India's point of view;

R =   net foreign exchange remittance by the emigrant;

e_s =   the shadow price of foreign exchange reflecting the social valuation of a marginal unit of foreign exchange;

[6] Even if India has to pay for this output, there is a net benefit to the extent the value of benefit derived by India from this research in USA exceeds the payment India has to make for it.

[7] The same expression (1) would be applicable for any number of emigrants.

X' = increase in national output (vector) in India due to the emigrant returning to India (relative to his non-return);

$E(P.X')$ = expected value of output obtained by multiplying PX by the probability that the emigrant stays in India in that year after his return;

C' = increase in consumption (vector) of the returning migrant in India (relative to his non-return);

$E(P.C')$ = expected value of consumption obtained by multiplying $P.C'$ by the probability that the emigrant stays in India in that year after his return.

Some clarifications should be provided in order to avoid possible confusions.

First, the value of L as given in (1) is the flow in a given year. To derive the present value of the stream of L over the life span of an emigrant one would have to add up the stream of L (discounted at the proper 'social rate of discount'). Values of some of the variables in L in a given year may well be zero. For example, suppose an otherwise productive person emigrates from India to USA for higher studies in the year 1990, then returns to India permanently in the year 2000 and his projected life span extends to the year 2030. For him, X would be non-zero for each year from 1990 to 2030; $X^* = 0$ from year 2000 to 2030; $X' = 0$ from year 1990 to 1999 and X' from year 2000 to 2030 may well be greater than X for the corresponding years as a result of higher productivity through education and training abroad.

Second, under what situations is $P.C$ likely to be different from $P.X$? Some writers such as Grubel and Scott (1966) emphasized the equality between the value of marginal product and the income of the emigrant at the margin and hence advanced the argument that the departure of the emigrant would not affect the welfare of the non-emigrants. Apart from the fact that this would not be true for *finite* changes,[8] there are other factors such as taxes, savings, externalities, living on transfers from others

---

[8] First pointed out by Berry and Soligo (1969).

(particularly valid for an unemployed person), monopoly fee setting above the value of marginal product (e.g. by doctors and lawyers) which may create a divergence, either way, between the social marginal product and the consumption of a person. Third, should foreign exchange remittances be valued at the shadow price of foreign exchange or at the 'premium' (equal to the gap between the shadow price and the official price) on foreign exchange? Since the *full* social value of the remittance accrues to India (which includes both non-emigrants and the Government of India) and nothing has to be paid to the emigrant for this unilateral transfer, naturally the shadow price of foreign exchange is the relevant parameter. A hypothetical example may be useful at this point. Suppose, the emigrant from India is selling off a plot of land to a member of the non-emigrant population before his departure. If the productivity of land is not affected, X remains unchanged by the transaction. If the emigrant uses the money to increase his consumption, C is affected. But if he takes away a part of the sale proceeds of land in foreign exchange, R would be affected in a negative way.

Fourth, we are assuming that α proportion of the emigrant's output contribution in USA goes to augment the bundle of goods and services available to the non-emigrant population of India. However, there is a price, M, which India has to pay for the import of this good or service and there is a net benefit to India only to the extent P, the social valuation of this good or service in India, exceeds the import price, M. For example, if an Indian agricultural scientist stationed abroad invents a high-yielding variety of rice and the knowledge ('public good') is made available free of cost to India, M would be zero, α would be close to unity and P which reflects the social usefulness of this knowledge in India would be 'high'. If, by contrast, an Indian engineer in USA makes an improvement in the design of an ICBM (inter-continental ballistic missile) and the new design is kept a closely guarded secret in US Defence Department, then $\alpha = 0$ and P, the social valuation of such knowledge in India, may be 'low' (though its valuation in USA may be very high indeed). M can be treated as 'high' if the cost (either in the narrow sense of royalty payment for such knowledge or in the wider sense of political costs in terms of military alliance with USA) of obtaining the knowledge is high.

Fifth, if the probability of an emigrant's return to India in year 2000 when his age is, say, around 40 years, is one-fourth (derived from an empirical observation that, say, 25 per cent of the emigrants return home at around 40 years of age when they face the problem of bringing up their children in an 'alien' culture), then $E(P.X')$ for year 2000 should be one-fourth of the social value of output the man could contribute in India after his return. Of course, such probabilities can be meaningfully assigned only to the behaviour of a group and not to a particular individual within the group. Fortunately for us, in real-life considerations of brain drain we are concerned with the gains and losses from the emigration of a group such as doctors or computer engineers so that trying to compute expected values need not be a meaningless exercise.

Sixth, even if accurate measurement of the values of the variables or the parameters could be a serious problem, the framework suggested above sharpens our conceptual understanding of the issues. It is better to try measuring, even if inaccurately, the right things than to accurately measure the wrong things!

Finally, note that our measure of net loss (or benefit) is solely concerned with the total size of the cake available to the non-emigrant population and not with its distribution. One may object to this and suggest that any change in the distribution of the cake within the non-emigrant population[9] as a result of emigration (e.g. through remittances to relatives in India) should also enter into the benefit-cost calculus of emigration. We have abstracted from the income distribution problem primarily to keep the analysis manageable and strictly within the limits of an economist's domain. However, in principle, one can allow for income distributional considerations in the social welfare index by attaching appropriate welfare weights to different classes of income receivers.

[9] Or between the emigrants and the non-emigrants to the extent the higher level of well-being of emigrants generates 'envy' or 'happiness' to those left behind!

3 SOME POLICY ISSUES

An interesting point emerges immediately. Since the emigrants have been trained at the cost of India, it is often suggested that they (or the recipient country) should reimburse the cost of their training or at least a part of the value of their additional potential earnings. It should be clear from the above analysis that the social cost inflicted by the emigrants on India is *not* the cost of their training which is the same for people who have been similarly trained but decide to stay in India. It is a 'sunk cost' in the short run. The only differential element is the social loss as measured by the capitalized value of L as given in (1) above which does not have any systematic relationship to the cost of their training or the value of earnings either at home or abroad. So a 'compensatory' emigration tax[10] which just compensates for the loss imposed by emigration on the rest of the society should be quite different from the cost of training or additional potential earnings. In fact, $\tilde{L}$,[11] the capitalized value of L, is likely to be less than either of these magnitudes and may even be negative for certain types of migration, calling for *subsidization* of emigration![12] For example, if the marginal emigrant consumes the value of his marginal product so that $P \cdot X = P \cdot C$ and $E(PX') = E(P \cdot C')$ and there is no spill-over of output produced in USA ($\alpha = 0$), then $L = -R \cdot e_s < 0$ implying a net social gain from emigration. Clearly, the case for emigration would be even stronger if the person were un-employed in India so that $P \cdot X = 0$ but $P \cdot C > 0$.

Suppose, we now take a longer-run view. The question, then, is not one of exporting professional manpower (say, engineers)

[10] This 'compensatory' emigration tax is to be distinguished from an 'optimal' emigration tax which wants to maximize the national gain or a 'revenue-maximising' emigration tax which seeks to maximize the tax revenue. The logic as well as the implied tax rates would be different for these three types of emigration tax. See Bhagwati (1976c).

[11] We shall use ~ over a variable to denote its capitalized value.

[12] This possibility remains even if the national cost of education is subtracted from the benefits from emigration as measured by the negative of $\tilde{L}$.

from a given pool but one of producing engineers for export so that the domestic availability of engineers is not affected. Under what conditions can that be a sensible policy? Obviously, the national resource cost of education of an additional engineer will have to be compared with the national gains from exporting an engineer abroad. Let us denote the annual resource cost of education of an extra engineer by T and its capitalized value by $\tilde{T}$. The annual flow of benefit from producing and exporting an extra engineer (relative to status quo) is to be denoted by G_e and its capitalized value by $\tilde{G}_e$. Then, the decision rule should be:

Produce an engineer for export if

$$\tilde{T} < \tilde{G}_e \qquad (2)$$

where

$$G_e = (P - M) . \alpha . X^* + R . e_s + E (P . X') - E (P . C') + P (C_o - X_o).$$

In the above expression (2), C_o and X_o stand for the annual levels of consumption and output, respectively, of the marginal person in India if he had not received an engineering education. $(C_o - X_o)$ is the extra amount available each year to the non-emigrant population due to the marginal man leaving the country, which would not have been possible had he not become an engineer. Hence this is an additional benefit which has to be added on top of the other terms in G_e in this context. Note, G_e in (2) is different from the negative of L in (1) in that $(C - X)$ in the negative of L in (1) is substituted by $(C_o - X_o)$ in (2). This is because in the context of (1) we were considering the losses (or gains) from emigration out of a given pool of already-made engineers while in (2) the issue is one of gains from making and then exporting an engineer. If the difference in the capitalized values of $P (C - X)$ and $P (C_o - X_o)$ is not significant or if the latter is not more than the former,[13] then the gains from producing an engineer for export are not more than that of exporting out of a given pool whereas there is an additional cost of producing an

---

[13] A sufficient (but not necessary) condition.

engineer (which is non-existent for an already-made engineer). Clearly, under these circumstances, even if exporting engineers may be profitable for India in the short-run, it is not a sensible policy in the longer-run perspective.

One may wonder why we cannot apply the conventional international trade theory to judge the desirability of export of engineers, as in the case of merchandise exports. Abstracting from 'distortions' (e.g. externalities, taxes etc.), exporting merchandise is profitable if the export price is greater than its cost of production. In the case of an engineer, the value of his earnings abroad can be treated as the export price (since that is what the rest of the world pays) whereas the cost of education of an engineer can be considered as the cost of production. But, even if the former exceeds the latter, exporting engineers may not be profitable for India primarily because the 'export price' of engineers accrues to the emigrating engineers whose welfare does not constitute part of India's welfare, as we have postulated. Only a part of the export price may accrue to India in the form of remittances etc. In other words, the relevant export price in the present context is $\tilde{G}_e$ (which has little to do with the earnings of the engineer abroad) which has to be weighed against the cost of production or the capitalized cost of education, $\tilde{T}$.

It is often suggested that the national cost of brain drain would be less if the fees for technical education are increased so that the beneficiary of education bears a larger part of the cost of education. Let us have a close look at the problem. If fees for engineering education are increased, the most likely scenario is that either the parents would have to bear the cost or the student would take loans from his parents or banks during the period of education. In the first case, there should not be any effect on T or G_e and hence on the net gain or loss from emigration. In the latter case, T will not be affected. The payment of fees would be a transfer from parents or banks to engineering colleges (all of whom constitute components of the non-emigrant population) in the initial period. To the extend the emigrating engineer repays the loan in subsequent periods to his parents or banks by foreign exchange remittances over and above what he would otherwise have done, G_e increases and the loss from the brain drain becomes correspondingly less.[14]

One may further distinguish between two types of issues for India:

(i) whether to *export* (either out of a given pool or by more production) engineers (for example) or send students for higher studies abroad, for that matter, knowing that most of them (say, three–fourths) would not come back.

(ii) whether to *produce* (not for the purpose of exporting but for domestic use) engineers, knowing that, say, 20 per cent of the additional engineers produced would end up taking up jobs outside India.[15]

So, far, we have focused on the first kind of question. In the computation of L or G_e, the assumed probability of non-return (say, three–fourths) would be reflected in the value of $E(P \cdot X')$ and $E(P \cdot C')$.

For answering the second type of question, however, both the national welfare function and the implied decision rule may have to be modified. In this case, India is contemplating production of engineers primarily for employment at home, with the knowledge that, say, 20 per cent of the additional engineers would eventually emigrate. The welfare of the 80 engineers (out of a marginal group of 100 engineers) who do not migrate should constitute part of India's national welfare, though the welfare of the remaining 20 who settle abroad may be disregarded from India's national welfare point of view. The national gain from an extra engineer is the value of the *additional* output vector (denote it by ΔX) which is attributable to his training as an engineer. Therefore, the social gain from an extra non-migrant engineer is $P \cdot \Delta X$. Note that his

[14] We are abstracting from the complications due to the possibility that higher fees for engineering education may reduce the relative attractiveness and hence the demand for such education.

[15] This is the kind of concern which some people express about engineering education in India.

consumption should not be subtracted since his consumption constitutes part of national consumption yielding national welfare. For the emigrant engineers (who constitute 20 per cent of the group), our measure of G_e as in (2) would still be applicable. Thus, the decision rule should be:

Produce an extra engineer (for domestic use) if

$$\tilde{T} < \tilde{B} \tag{3}$$

where

$$B = (1 - \lambda) P . \Delta X + \lambda . G_e,$$

$\tilde{B}$ = capitalized value of B,

ΔX = additional output (vector) in India of the marginal engineer which is due to engineering education,

λ = probability that a person would emigrate after receiving engineering education in India,

and $G_e = G_e$ as given in (2).

Clearly, if producing engineers for export is not profitable, production for home use may still be, even after taking into account the possibility that some of the trained engineers would land up abroad. Naturally, it would crucially depend upon the probability of migration which has to be based on an empirical knowledge about what fraction of the specified group of professionals is likely to migrate in the given situation. It should be obvious that the opposite possibility also exists. When production of additional engineers for home use is unprofitable, producing them for export may remain a profitable activity, depending upon the parameter values. Also note that our criterion (2) is a special case of the more general criterion (3) when $\lambda = 1$.

4 WHAT IF BRAIN DRAIN IS STOPPED

We may now examine what would happen if we stop the outflow of doctors, engineers, scientists and academics under the present institutional set-up.

Take the case of doctors, for instance. It is well known that there is a surplus of doctors in cities and an acute shortage of doctors in rural areas in India (which is typical of many LDCs). If we put a stop to the emigration of doctors in such a situation, will the doctors move to villages where the social value of their services is enormous or will they simply crowd the cities where they will not provide any significant additional benefits by basically dividing the already cared for patients among a larger number of doctors? If the second outcome is likely, then one is tempted to argue that the net social loss due to the emigration of a doctor is negligible, if not negative, when one takes into account the other gain components, e.g., foregone consumption and remittances. Moreover, one should remember that some of the doctors, after receiving a training abroad, may decide to come back to India. Since there is no sure way of stopping emigration without stopping the flow of medical students for further training abroad (in as much as a student, after the completion of his training, may decide to stay back and there is little that the country of emigration can do about it without help from the country of immigration). One must also consider the potential loss of 'surplus', namely, $E(P.X') - E(P.C')$ in terms of our notations,[16] from the services of foreign-trained doctors who may decide to come back to India. So, all considered, the main problem is one of grossly suboptimal allocation of doctors between rural and urban areas and the issue is whether stopping emigration of doctors would provide the 'right signals' so that the resource allocation would move in the socially desirable directions (i.e. more doctors to villages). One may argue that if doctors are prevented from going abroad, eventually the returns to doctors in cities would be driven to such a point that some of the

[16] It is important to emphasize that it is not the higher productivity (and hence higher earning capacity) of a foreign-trained doctor which is relevant here. It is the gap between the social value of output and consumption which is the consideration. This 'surplus' can be very large if (for instance) patients get a fresh lease of life through complicated surgical operations which could not have been undertaken in the absence of the foreign-trained surgeon.

doctors would be forced to move to rural areas where they would expect to earn more than in cities. In the real world, the doctors are not a homogeneous group — they are differentiated by qualifications, specializations, experience and reputation. Since generally the better qualified specialized doctors emigrate, stopping emigration may not force the same doctor who wanted to migrate to USA to move to a village in India. However, because of a greater availability of specialized and better qualified doctors in the cities (which would certainly lower their *average* earnings in cities, though this may still be substantially greater than the average earnings of doctors in villages) some of the less qualified and less experienced doctors in the hierarchy would be forced ultimately to go to rural areas as the average earnings of this group tends to fall below that of the village doctor. Bhagwati and Rodriguez (1976e) consider this process of internal diffusion of doctors into the hinterland as 'the slow capitalist equivalent of the Maoist policy of "sending" doctors to the countryside' (footnote 8, p. 98, ibid.). The question is: even if slow, can we expect this process to work, at least in the (very?) long run? Let us examine the question carefully.

Suppose, we denote the average earnings of doctors in the 'village', 'city', and 'USA' by W_v, W_c and W_u respectively, assuming, to simplify, that doctors are a homogeneous group. Now, consider a situation of brain drain of doctors with $W_v < W_c < W_u$. Note that $W_v < W_c$ because villagers, being relatively poor, cannot afford to pay the same as city dwellers for the same physical service. Suppose, further, that even if all the available doctors within the country practise in cities, the income differential $W_v < W_c$ would persist.[17] Denote the level of W_v corresponding to

[17] In this sense, W_v may be less than W_c, the expected or average earning in the city, but there would not be any further migration to the city as all doctors have already moved out of the villages. So, a Harris–Todaro (1970) type of equilibrium may not be reached with equality of expected earnings. In a more realistic setting, W_v may be equal to W_c for some low-qualification village doctors but this is irrelevant for our purposes since we are concerned with sending more doctors to the villages as compared to the initial situation.

zero doctor in villages as $\bar{W}_v$.[18] On the other hand, W_u may be many times higher than W_c because of the existence of an (effective) immigration quota imposed by USA which prevents the international equalization of earnings. So long as the international migration of doctors is allowed (though subject to an annual quota) W_c would remain above W_v, provided, of course, the annual flow of doctors from medical colleges is not large enough to augment the total available stock of doctors (after allowing for the annual flow of emigration) so as to take W_c below W_v. Suppose, that is the case.[19] Under such a scenario, if a ban is placed on the emigration of doctors *and* the number of medical graduates each year is not affected by the ban, the total available doctors within the country would increase, ultimately bringing W_c below W_v. At this point, internal migration or diffusion of doctors into villages should begin to take place through the market mechanism. But the market would fail to provide the right signals so long as brain drain continues on a sufficiently large scale.

One of the crucial parameters missing from our story is the expected earnings in an alternative occupation, for example, being a lawyer. Denote this by $\bar{W}_L$. We assume this to be fixed until W_c comes down to it causing more entry into the legal profession, thus bringing down W_L also. If $W_c > \bar{W}_L > \bar{W}_v$ (to start with), the ban on the emigration of doctors, by pushing down W_c towards $\bar{W}_L$, would induce some prospective doctors to become lawyers (over a period of time) and frustrate the 'capitalist' process of diffusion of doctors into the village. How quickly the

[18] In terms of a demand-supply diagram, the intercept of the demand curve for doctors' services in the 'village' is below the intersection point of the demand curve in the 'city' and the total available supply of doctors' services in the country as a whole.

[19] Whether that would, indeed, be the case would obviously depend upon, *ceteris paribus*, how large is the immigration quota relative to the annual flow of doctors from medical colleges. The latter is determined by the attractiveness of medical profession relative to alternative occupations on the demand side and the provision of medical education facilities on the supply side (mostly determined by the government).

process will stop will depend on how close is $\bar{W}_L$ to W_c in the initial situation with brain drain. Thus, merely stopping brain drain of doctors may not achieve the desirable internal diffusion of doctors even in the long run! However, some success may be achieved in reversing brain drain if doctors could be persuaded, either by the compulsory requirement that all doctors, after obtaining their degrees, must serve a few years in the rural areas and that they would not be allowed to go abroad unless they satisfied this requirement or by making practice in rural areas sufficiently attractive by a thorough overhauling of material incentives. With ensuring a sufficiently high rural practicing allowances (the city compensatory allowance system in India is somewhat opposite to the required change in this context) and by improving the state of rural health centres and hospitals, the desirable internal diffusion can be achieved to a large extent, with or without brain drain. So, preventing brain drain *without* the required institutional reforms may not be effective in terms of achieving the objective.

A legitimate question can, however, be raised at this point. In the above example, by stopping brain drain (*without* any other institutional change) India may not be able to send more doctors to the villages but nonetheless may get more skilled personnel in the form of, say, lawyers, engineers and various other intermediate skill categories. Is that not a desirable fallout of stopping the emigration of doctors? Assuming that there are some *net* gains from brain drain (in the form of remittances etc. exceeding the marginal cost of education for an emigrating doctor) the issue is one of comparison of the value of social marginal product in excess of the marginal resource cost of education of an additional lawyer with the foregone net gains from brain drain. In terms of our notation, the issue is whether $(\tilde{B} - \tilde{T})$ for a marginal lawyer is greater than $(\tilde{G} - \tilde{T})$ for a marginal emigrating doctor, provided $(\tilde{G} - \tilde{T}) > 0$. If, on the other hand, there is a net loss from the emigration of doctors so that $(\tilde{G} - \tilde{T}) < 0$ for the marginal doctor, then stopping brain drain of doctors is in national interest if $(\tilde{B} - \tilde{T}) > 0$ for an extra lawyer.

Though quantitatively insignificant, the emigration of scientists and academics attracts widespread attention to brain drain primarily because of the eminence and wide recognition of some of these people. Here the main question is the social value of the potential contribution of these people to the rest of the society in the country of emigration. Many of them are engaged in abstract theoretical research with little immediate applicability for their home countries.[20] The kind of training the researcher receives abroad is often geared to the requirements of developed countries and many of these people, even after their return home, pursue the same type of research with little relation to the pressing problems of their country. I am not trying to belittle the value of the techniques learned abroad by these people which, *if* they are applied to the analysis and possible solutions of the various urgent problems of their home country, can be a source of great gains. My point is simply that it is not done in many cases. This is due to a number of factors — the nature of their training abroad which confers a comparative advantage in pure theoretic research and the high premium placed on such research in the selection of people for employment in universities and research institutes in their home country and abroad. The people engaged in applied work are often summarily considered second-rate people and by this built-in comparative low recognition of such endeavour it is mainly second-rate people (there may, of course, be exceptions) who ultimately go in for this kind of research.[21] The villain is our distorted value system which puts a premium

[20] This is not to imply that their research is useless. Good empirical or applied work must have a sound theoretical basis. For this purpose, one needs theories. But theories can be relevant or irrelevant, though it is not easy to make such a distinction *ex ante*, in some cases. What starts as abstract theorizing may ultimately yield a lot of applications. Nonetheless, it is a fact that the chain connecting abstract theory and its application to practical problems is often long and uncertain.

[21] I should also emphasize that applied work, just like theoretical research, can be good, bad or indifferent. The so-called applied research conducted by mediocre people may as well turn out to be useless repetitions which do not add to knowledge.

on abstract theorizing, even when largely irrelevant, as against the development/application of theories or techniques geared to the pressing problems of the country, either at the micro level or at the macro level.[22] The so-called 'externalities' in the form of the catalytic role of these academicians in building up university departments or research institutes is also of limited value because these institutes in many cases pursue the same type of abstract research in which their mentors excel. Therefore, the emigration of these academics is not that great a loss as is popularly thought. Finally, (and this is perhaps the most important point) whatever value one may ascribe to this type of research output, it would be mostly available through their publications. It is not an accident that some of the best research on Indian economic and social problems have been carried out by people (Indians and foreigners) stationed abroad because of much better research facilities there. Thus, stopping emigration of such people may be counter productive. What is needed is once again a change in our incentive system such that preference is given to people doing work in areas intimately linked to national priorities. Once this can be done, students and teachers may automatically concentrate on such 'useful' research and first-rate people may gradually turn to these areas.

There is, of course, a problem here. Since the premium structure in the international market will not change, the *relative* advantage of staying abroad may increase for people engaged in pure theoretic research. The rate of 'reverse migration' may fall as a result. But, then, at least a larger proportion of those who decide to come back may be tempted to pursue more 'useful' research in terms of national priorities. This way, India may be able to combine the benefits of foreign training to master theories/ techniques and the application of such theories/techniques (suitably modified, where necessary) to real life problems at home.

---

[22] Indian Institutes of Technology (I.I.T.s) are alleged to produce specialist engineers with skills which have far greater use and applicability in the developed Western countries than in the home country.

5 Concluding Remarks

We have approached the problem of brain drain in terms of a social cost-benefit framework. Unlike the general equilibrium models[23] in the brain drain literature, this approach is general and versatile enough to tackle the problem of migration of both skilled and unskilled workers, movement of physical capital along with human capital, to-and-fro and reverse migration and even the case of 'expulsion and appropriation' (e.g. that of Indians from Uganda in the early 1970s),[24] all kinds of distortions (including unemployment, externalities, taxes, wage rigidity, and exchange control), and both short and long run perspectives of the problem. It should, however, be made clear that in our analysis we have generally abstracted from (a) the 'demoralization effect' on those left behind, some of whom may be more talented than those emigrating and could earn many times more abroad, except to the extent that this earning is captured by the change in national output as a result of migration, (b) the income distribution effect within the non-emigrant population though, in principle, it can be captured by attaching suitable welfare weights to income going to different classes in society, and (c) the problem of measuring, in quantitative terms, the values of the variables and parameters involved. The approach also suffers from the limitation (which is a standard problem in cost-benefit analysis) that it ignores the effects of any price changes caused by migration.

The broad conclusion which emerges from the above analysis is that brain drain may not be a serious loss and may even be a source of net gains for a country like India *under the given institutional set up*. More serious is the problem of underutilization and waste in the use of our skilled personnel, with or without brain drain. Unless the system of material incentives for and social recognition of various types of services is altered to reflect national

[23] E.g. Kenen (1971); Johnson (1967) which deal only with *unskilled* labour migration of a *permanent* variety or Bhagwati and Hamada (1976d) and Hamada and Bhagwati (1976) which consider only one distortion at a time.

[24] See Tobin (1974).

objectives and priorities (and in the process increasing the value of the social contribution of our skilled personnel and consequently the value of the potential social loss from emigration), 'locking the doors' would close one of the safety valves of the system inviting more chaos and tension — social, political and economic — without any compensating benefits. Of course, the feasibility of bringing about the required changes may not be independent of the process of brain drain, as we have seen in the context of doctors not moving to villages. To the extent that this is true (but there are limits to which this may be true, as we have also demonstrated in the context of the doctors), there is a stronger case for stopping brain drain. We have also seen that even when exporting technical manpower is a source of national gains in the short-run, it may not be so in the longer run perspective.

References

Adams, W. (1968), *The Brain Drain*, New York: Macmillan.

Berry, R. and R. Soligo (1969), 'Some Welfare Aspects of International Migration', *Journal of Political Economy*, 77.

Bhagwati, J. (ed.) (1976a), *Taxing the Brain Drain: A Proposal*, Amsterdam: North Holland.

— (ed.) (1976b), *The Brain Drain and Taxation: Theory and Empirical Analysis*, Amsterdam: North Holland.

— (1976c), 'The International Brain Drain and Taxation: A Survey of the Issues', in Bhagwati (1976b).

Bhagwati, J. and K. Hamada (1976d), 'The Brain Drain, International Integration of Markets for Professionals and Unemployment', in Bhagwati (1976b).

Bhagwati, J. and C. Rodriguez (1976e), 'Welfare-theoretical Analyses of the Brain Drain', in Bhagwati (1976b).

Dandekar, V.M. (1968), 'India', in Adams (1968).

Dasgupta, P.S., S.A. Marglin and A.K. Sen (1972), *Guidelines for Project Evaluation*, New York: United Nations.

Grubel, H. and A. Scott (1966), 'The International Flow of Human Capital', *American Economic Review*, May.

Hamada, K. and J. Bhagwati (1976), 'Domestic Distortions, Imperfect Information and the Brain Drain', in Bhagwati (1976b).

Harris, J.R. and M.P. Todaro (1970), 'Migration, Unemployment and Development: A Two-sector Analysis', *American Economic Review*, 60, pp. 126–42.

Johnson, H.G. (1967), 'Some Economic Aspects of Brain Drain', *Pakistan Development Review*, 3.

Kenen, P. (1971), 'Migration, the Terms of Trade and Economic Welfare in the Source Country', in J. Bhagwati et al. (eds), *Trade, Balance of Payments and Growth*, Amsterdam: North Holland.

Little, I.M.D. and J.A. Mirrlees (1968), *Manual of Industrial Project Analysis*, vol. II, Paris: OECD Development Centre.

Tobin, J. (1974), 'Notes on the Economic Theory of Expulsion and Expropriation', *Journal of Development Economics*, 1, no. 1.

8

General versus Specialized
Education: An Alternative View*

Amal Sanyal and Anjan Mukherji

1 INTRODUCTION

The dichotomy between general and specialized education has two distinct dimensions. The first relating to their differential rates of net social return is, in principle, quantifiable and figures implicitly or explicitly in most discussions relating to this dichotomy. The second aspect relates to a qualitative difference and does not seem to be as well appreciated as it ought to be, and it is this difference which is of central concern in this paper.

By general education, we will mean the three R's, the basic humanities, and sciences. So defined, it is a sufficient requirement for a large number of general occupations, which students may join at the end of such a course. Alternatively, general education serves as a necessary input into higher education by which we mean the more advanced disciplines and skills. We will begin by noting that the demand for general education is either related to the social productivity of general occupations or is a derived demand related to the productivity of more specialized jobs. The human capital approach based on the analogy between investment and education would then suggest that an optimal allocation

* The authors are grateful to Mukul Majumdar for a suggestion about the modelling of decision-making under complete ignorance and to Binod Khadria and Satish Jain for useful comments on an earlier draft.

of students between general and higher education is one where those dropping out into general occupations will fetch the same social return as those going for higher education and subsequently specialized jobs, net of the extra social cost of higher education. Optimality should also suggest that resource (or time) spent on general education should be just sufficient to teach the minimal set of concepts and facts that would qualify the students to either work in general trades or receive higher education. Any further resource (or time) spent on general education will be socially wasteful. We will argue against these conclusions regarding the optimal amount of general education by showing that a discussion purely based on comparison of social rates of return misses out on an important aspect of the difference between general and higher or specialized education.

The treatment of education as a kind of investment embodied in human agents can be traced at least as far back as Adam Smith, although it was taken up for a more sustained analysis in the 1950's and 1960's by Schultz (1961) and Becker (1964). An alternative view of education is due to Spence (1973) and Arrow (1973), where it is viewed as a signalling device, and we will develop our arguments by comparison with this latter view. A third view due to Bhagwati and Srinivasan (1977) looks at education as an instrument for job competition in a distorted labour market, and will not concern us since we would be discussing a normative rather than a positive theory of education.

Arrow, in his discussion of higher education entirely abstracted from the question of its relative social return as compared to general education. He points out that the 'degree' obtained after the successful completion of higher education has a useful information content, even if higher education does not add to the productivity of the student *per se*. Thus even if higher education adds no additional skill but only tests what is just innate in the students, those who get a 'degree' will have a higher probability of doing better in their trades than those who fail to get a 'degree'. In particular, if there are different skills, corresponding specializations and subsequent occupations, then a 'degree' in a particular specialization indicates a higher probability of doing well in the corresponding occupation. This information content of the 'degree', obtained on successful completion of higher education thus can increase the total product of a given size of labour employed by firms, and thus can be instrumental to a higher social return.

2 GENERAL VS. SPECIALIZED EDUCATION – SOME CRUCIAL DIFFERENCES

It will be useful to develop our argument by relating it to Arrow's. When there are several specializations available, the distribution of success at the end of these courses will depend on how well the individual aptitudes of the student intake were matched with the streams into which they have been enrolled. Assuming that the ten years or so of what we have called general education, simply teaches the basic concepts and facts, but provides little information about aptitudes, at the time of streaming into specialization, there is no pool of information about individual aptitudes to draw upon. If by chance the aptitudes and specializations of the students are appropriately matched, the proportion of success will be very high, while if there is complete mismatch, the proportion will be dismal. The actual outcome of success will lie in between these two limits. The aspect of higher education that Arrow emphasizes is that it generates some information, which when transmitted onward through the 'degree', can increase the productivity of a given size of labour intake. But another aspect, no less important, that should now be clear is that it also generates a large amount of additional, negative information which cannot be used without substantial cost. During specialization, along with the positive information that a number of students have a talent in a given discipline, the negative information about mismatches is also revealed. But the process of specialization is *nearly irreversible*, both because it is expensive and also because it is a process through time, over which the students are getting older. If a student for example displays a lack of innate talent in medicine at the end of a five year medical course, it is costly to redeploy him into say, engineering, where his talents may really lie. The cost not only includes the teaching resources and career time of the student but also the emotional cost incurred by the student, and perhaps the decline in mental agility due to ageing. This student who would either fail to get a 'degree' in Arrow's framework, or will be only modestly productive in his subsequent medicinal career in our model below, could however have contributed a much larger quantum to the social pool of returns if deployed into the proper stream. Regardless of the information that he is wrongly employed in medicine, the outcome has to be simply endured over the career-life of the student.

If the difference between the social returns for the best and worst match situations in a society with different specializations and occupations is large, then clearly the cost to the society of the mismatch of talents can be quite substantial. One way of reducing this potential loss is to retain the flexibility of decision-making until more information is available. This can be achieved by extending the period of general education and utilizing it for deriving information about the aptitudes of the student. Note that general education, coming earlier in the career cycle, retains the flexibility of subsequent branching into any desired discipline, and is thus ideally suited for generating aptitude information that can be utilized without cost. It may appear that it is not necessary to extend the period of general education for this purpose, because it can be so designed as to extract aptitude information during the same span of time that is normally used only to 'educate'. In either case, however, it amounts to spending more resources on general education than is suggested by the pure human capital approach i.e. spending no more resources than are necessary only to 'educate', so as to allow students to either be qualified to receive higher education or drop out into the general jobs' market.

The point that this argument demonstrates is that higher education has a certain irreversibility in comparison with general education. The dichotomy between the two is thus not only in their rates of return, but also in the flexibility of decision-making that one offers and the other does not. To use analogues from the theory of investment, expenditure on general and higher education closely correspond with investment in liquid (convertible) assets and illiquid (non-convertible) assets. Just as liquidity has a premium in an uncertain world, general education has a similar premium in addition to whatever social return it fetches, because of the uncertainty about aptitudes characterizing the relevant 'investment' decision.

Before we proceed to the next section where the argument is formalized within the context of a simple model, we should point out that the inflexibility of decision-making after higher education only makes out a *potential* case for larger resource allocation in general education. Whether actually such an increased allocation is optimal would depend on two distinct factors. One is the extent of potential loss that the aptitude mismatch for a generation entails. It needs to be large enough to justify the additional resource spent on general education, which will delay the ultimate realization of the fruits of higher education. The other factor also related to this delayed fructification of higher education is the rate of time preference of the society. An impatient society, for example, may consider delaying the production of its engineers intolerable, even if that means, engineers of admittedly lower calibre. On the other hand, a society with a lower rate of time discount might feel it is worthwhile to spend large amount of resources to extract aptitude information before final deployment in specialization.

The irreversibility of specialization and some of its implications have been already noted in the literature. For example ILO (1984) both suggests and foresees an increase in the relevance of more flexible general education. On the other hand, early specialization has been advocated by Blaug et. al (1969) to get rid of the 'graduate unemployment', or by Dore (1976) to fight the so-called 'diploma disease'. Khadria (1984) discusses a positive theory of on-the-job skill formation in a situation of imperfect knowledge. Our model below is not a positive theory of choice between general and higher education, but a normative discussion aimed at the location of socially better allocations in a situation of ignorance.

3 A SIMPLE MODEL

Consider a generation of students who have just completed a terminal screening test at the end of a career of general education. Let N be the number of students needed by society for specialization where we assume that the number N has been arrived at by some appropriate decision rule. Suppose also that the terminal test has picked up the top N students who have been correctly identified as the ones most suited for specialization, but no information has been revealed about their aptitudes. We will be concerned with these N students, while the others are presumed to drop out into the market for non-specialized jobs.

The question is whether any of the N students should go through a further period of extended general education which would reveal their natural talents. Such students may then be put into appropriate lines of specialization. Alternatively, students may immediately be assigned to different lines of specialization. The problem in this case may be one of mismatch of aptitude to lines of specialization. These are the two alternatives that we shall focus attention on.

To enable us to set up the model, let T denote the number of periods for which a person works; the number of periods required for specialization in any line is t; let s denote the periods of extended general education at the end of which natural talents stand revealed. To make the problem meaningful, it must be the case that

$$T - t - s > 0 \tag{1}$$

i.e., a student who has spent s periods of extended general education and t periods in specializing has at the end of it some period of his working life left.

In this set up, the planner has to choose how to allocate the N students amongst the two alternatives mentioned above. Let n_1 be the number of students assigned to the periods of extended general education and n_2 the number assigned immediately to specialization, where

$$n_i \geq 0 \; i = 1, 2 \text{ and } n_1 + n_2 = N \qquad (2)$$

To enable the planner to make a decision, we assume that the planner knows the returns that the students provide to the society. It would be convenient to conduct our analysis in terms of the average net return to society per student after completion of t periods of specialization when n students are assigned to be specialized denoted by $r_m(n)$; m denotes the level of mismatch of talents to lines of specialization and may take any value in $(0, 1)$, where $m = 0$ denotes complete mismatch and $m = 1$, full matching. Clearly, we insist that

$$r_m(n) > r_{m'}(n) \leftrightarrow m' > m \qquad (3)$$

As we shall see later, we need to take into account only $r_0(n)$ and $r_1(n)$ i.e., the worst and the best possibilities.

During the s periods of extended general education and during the t periods of specialization, the returns to society are assumed to be zero. This in fact highlights the difference between the two alternatives further; if n students are assigned to specialization, then each would provide after t periods an average return which may be as low as $r_0(n)$; whereas if n students are assigned to an extended period general education and then to appropriate lines of specialization, then each such student provides an average return of $r_1(n)$ after $s + t$ periods. At this point, we would like to state that it is not crucial for our analysis that after s periods of extended general education and t periods of training, a batch of n students provide $r_1(n)$ per student per period; what is crucial is that such a batch provide $r_m(n)$ where $m > 0$. Regarding the functions $r_m(n)$, we require that apart from (3), $r_0(n)$ satisfy the following:

$$r_0(N) \leq r_0(n) \text{ for any } n \text{ satisfying } 0 \leq n \leq N \qquad (4)$$

In other words, in the case of worst possible mismatch, the average return per student per period is at a minimum if all N students have been sent in for specialized training. This may be justified on the basis of infrastructural facilities for training being limited.

The planner, it is further assumed, does not have any *a priori* beliefs about which *m* would occur given a group of students i.e., the planner is completely ignorant about the level of mismatch which may occur. If the planner were to send in *n* students for specialization immediately, then after the completion of *t* periods, either each student would provide a return as low as $r_0(n)$ or it may be as high as $r_1(n)$. Decision-making in such situations has been analysed by Arrow and Hurwich (1972). They show that under an appealing set of axioms, choice would involve a ranking of all possible alternatives based on the best and the worst possible outcomes. A special case of this is the maximin criterion (see Luce and Raiffa (1957)), which is a sensible rule whenever the decision-maker decides to choose cautiously and play safe. We assume that our planner too adopts this rule.

The maximin criterion involves, first, a consideration of the worst possible outcomes of every alternative and then choosing that alternative for which the associated worst outcome is best among the others. With this end in view, we note that a breakup of N into n_1 and n_2 satisfying (2) provides that following net returns in each period j:

$$I_j = 0 \qquad j = 1, 2, \ldots, t-1 \qquad (5)$$

$$\geq n_2\, r_0\,(n_2) \qquad j = t, t+1, \ldots, t+s-1$$

$$\geq n_1\, r_1\,(n_1) + n_2\, r_0\,(n_2) \qquad j = t+s, \ldots, T$$

If *d* is some social rate of discount (the discount factor), then the present value of the stream on the rhs of (5) is

$$n_2\, r_0\,(n_2)\, [1/d^{\,t} + \ldots + 1/d^{\,t+s-1}] + \{n_1\, r_1\,(n_1) + n_2\, r_0\,(n_2)\}$$
$$[1/d^{\,t+s} + \ldots + 1/d^{\,t}]$$

$$= I\,(n_1, n_2), \text{ say.}$$

Now the problem of the planner may be stated:

Max I (n_1, n_2)

$s.t.\ n_1, n_2 \le N$

$\quad n_1, n_2 \ge 0$

That this follows the maximin criterion is obvious when one realizes that $I(n_1, n_2)$ is the worst possible outcome when a choice n_1, n_2 is made. To enable us to analyse the problem, let us rewrite $I(n_1, n_2)$ as follows:

$$I(n_1, n_2) = B \cdot n_2\, r_0\,(n_2) + Cn_1\, r_1\,(n_1)$$

where

$$B = (1/d^t) \frac{d^{T-t+1} - 1}{d - 1} \text{ and } C = (1/d^T) \frac{d^{T-t+1-s} - 1}{d - 1} \tag{6}$$

Further, since n_1, n_2 must satisfy (2), $n_2 = N - n_1$, the expression $I(n_1, n_2)$ may be further simplified to:

$$B(N - n)\, r_0\,(N - n) + Cn\, r_1\,(n) = I(n), \text{ say;}$$

Now the planner's problem is

$$Max\ I(n)$$

$$s.t.\ 0 \le n \le N$$

where $I(0) = BNr_0(N)$ and $I(N) = CNr_1(N)$.

Notice first of all, that the problem is solvable i.e., there is $n^*, O \le n^* \le N$ such that $I(n^*) \ge I(n)$ for all n in (O, N). This follows, because $I(0), I(1), \ldots, I(N)$ are a finite set of N numbers and one among them must be the maximum.

Next, $n^* > 0 \leftrightarrow I(n) > I(0)$ for some $n > 0$ $\tag{7}$

Now $I(n) > I(0) \leftrightarrow B(N - n)\, r_0\,(N - n) + Cnr_1\,(n) > BNr_0(N)$

or $[(N - n)/N]\, r_0\,(N - n) + (C/B) \cdot (n/N)\, r_1\,(n) > r_0(N)$ $\tag{8}$

A sufficient condition for (8) to hold is that

for some $n > 0,\ (C/B) > r_0\,(n)/r_1\,(n)$ $\tag{9}$

for, if (9) holds, then, $(C/B) r_1(n) > r_0(n)$.
Hence,

$$[(N-n)/N] r_0(N-n) + (n/N) . (C/B) . r_1(N)$$
$$> [(N-n)/N] r_0(N-n) + (n/N) r_0(n)$$
$$> Min [r_0(N-n), r_0(n)]$$
$$\geq r_0(N) \text{ by virtue of (4)},$$

which yields (8).

Consequently, how likely is condition (9)? Note that, by virtue of (3),

$$(r_0(n))/(r_1(n)) < 1 \text{ for all } n \text{ in } (0, N)?$$

Moreover, from (6),

$$C/B = (d^{T-t+1-s} - 1)/(d^{T-t+1} - 1) = F(T, t, s, d), \text{ say.}$$

Clearly, for any T, t, s satisfying (1) and any $d > 0$,

$$F(T, t, s, d,) \leq 1.$$

In particular, $F(T, t, 0, d) - 1$ for any T, t, d.

$$F(T, t, s, 0) = 1 \text{ for any } T, t, s.$$

and $\lim_{T \to \infty} F(T, t, s, d) = 1$ for any t, s, and d

Consequently, for d small, s small and T large enough, we may expect C/B to be 'close' to 1 and hence greater than $r_0(n)/r_1(n)$ for some $n > 0$. Thus, we may expect a rather wide class of parameters (T, t, s) satisfying (1), which, also satisfy (9). For each such configuration, the optimum $n^* > 0$.

This demonstrates our basic claim that one may need to spend more time (or resources, as we had indicated in the earlier section) on general education than is warranted by its pure social return consideration. The argument follows from the flexibility lent by general education and its information generating capability together allowing the society to buy time before making an irreversible decision.

4 CONCLUSION

Some of the assumptions made in the last section may be dispensed with without affecting our basic claim and we indicate these now. First of all, note that we have assumed that after s periods of extended general education and t periods of specialized training, a batch of n students provide, on an average, the return $r_1(n)$ per period. This, of course, is not necessary; if instead of complete matching, we had only better matching signified by an average return $r_m(n)$ with $m > 0$, our argument would go through, except instead of (9), a sufficient condition for $n^* > 0$ would now require

$$C/B > r_0(n)/r_m(n) \text{ for some } n > 0$$

and this would be as likely as before.

Secondly, we have assumed that after s periods of extended general education, a student has to go through t periods of specialized education — the same number of periods that students undergo if they were to undertake a specialized line without the period of extended general education. One may clearly make the period of training, after s periods of extended general education, t', to be less than t. This, of course, would make the case for extended general education stronger, and it is because of this that we maintain $t' = t$.

Finally, the nature of the function $r_m(n)$; notice that there are no restrictions on the functions $r_m(n)$, apart from (3) $viz.$, $r_m(n) > r_{m'}(n)$ whenever $m' > m$. But $r_0(n) \geq r_0(N)$ for all n in $(0, N)$. This would be satisfied if, for example, $r_0(n) = a_0 n + b_0$ with $a_0 < 0$. Even if this condition is not met, recall that we need (8) to hold for some $n > 0$. Rewriting (8), we require:

$$(C/B) nr_1(n) > Nr_0(n) - (N-n)r_0(N-n) \text{ for some } n > 0.$$

or $[(C/B)] r_1(n)/r_0(n). > [\{Nr_0(n) - (N-n)r_0(N-n)\}/nr_0(n)] (10)$

for some $n > 0$

This would now be the appropriate condition, instead of (9) which in comparable form is given by $(C/B)\, r_1(n)/r_0(n) > 1$ for some $n > 0$ — clearly (10) is more complicated to interpret but is not, perhaps, analytically stronger.

Note that the parameter d reflects the importance that the planner attaches to the future; for given T, s and t, a higher value of d corresponds to a lower weight being assigned to the future, whereas a lower value of d corresponds to more importance being placed on the future. Consequently, one may note that a planner with a lower d would find (9) more easily satisfied and so assign students to an extended period of general education. Conversely, if the planner has a more short-run view (high d), the less likely would it be to assign students to an extended period of general education. This, perhaps, should not appear to be very surprising, as our earlier discussion indicated.

Some observations about a line of further inquiry may be made at this stage. Within the context of the model suggested above, it should be possible to link up the number of periods of extended general education, s, to m, the degree of matching of aptitudes to lines of specialization. $m(s)$ would then be an increasing function of s. Now in addition to choosing a breakdown of N into n_1 and n_2, the planner has to choose how long must s be. This provides a straight-forward generalization of our model. Our considerations suggest that even within this set-up there would be a wide range of parameters for which s would be chosen to be positive and our basic assertion would remain valid. This would seem to suggest that early specialization suggested by many (Blaug et. al (1969), for example) may not be the correct step to take.

Finally, it should be pointed out that allowing for flexibility in our academic set-up, making higher education not as irreversible as it currently is, even if this means an increased outlay on the flexible higher education, will be beneficial for both the individual and the society. In the above exercise, extended general education allowed the talents of students to be identified and this led to a better match of talents to lines of specializations. Allowing for greater diversity in choice of subjects, lifting of age restrictions for entry into courses and professions and similar relaxations would also allow for a better match. If students are more heterogeneous than what we have assumed them to be, then allowing those whose talents have already been identified, to enter their corresponding lines of specializations, would, by a similar argument, be better than subjecting all to an extended period of general education. Our formal analysis reveals why any flexible alternative may be preferable to a more rigid one, even if it appears to require more resources.

REFERENCES

Arrow, K.J. and L. Hurwich (1972), 'An Optimality Criterion for Decision Making Under Complete Ignorance', in *Uncertainty and Expectations in Economics: Essays in Honour of G.L.S. Shackle*, C.F. Carter and J.L. Ford (eds), Oxford: Basil Blackwell, pp. 1–11.

Arrow, K.J. (1973), 'Higher Education as a Filter', *Journal of Public Economics*, 2, pp. 193–6.

Becker, G.S. (1964), *Human Capital*, New York: Columbia University Press, NBER.

Bhagwati, J. and T.N. Srinivasan (1977), 'Education in a "Job-Ladder" Model and the Fairness in Hiring Role', *Journal of Public Economics*, 7, pp. 1–22.

Blaug, M., R. Layard and M. Woodhall (1969), *The Causes of Graduate Unemployment in India*, London: Allen Lane and Penguin.

Dore, R.P. (1976), *The Diploma Disease*, London: Allen and Unwin.

I.L.O. (1984), *World Labour Report*, vol. I, I.L.O.

Khadria, B. (1984), 'On-the-job Skill Formation Under Imperfect Knowledge', Discussion paper no 196, Sussex: Institute of Development Studies.

Luce, R.D. and H. Raiffa (1957), *Games and Decision*, New York: John Wiley.

Schultz, T.W. (1961), 'Investments in Human Capital', *American Economic Review*, 51, 1.

Spence, M. (1973), 'Job-Market Signalling', *Quarterly Journal of Economics*, 87, pp. 355–74.

Public Goods and Public Policy

Problems relating to the provision of public goods and different public policies have been analysed extensively in economic theory. Such analysis reveals basic departures from standard results associated with perfect markets providing private goods. A recent focus of attention has been on strategic responses of different agents involved in the provision and consumption of public goods, and the incomplete information that agents might have. The chapters by Dipankar Dasgupta and Dilip Mookherjee concentrate on these issues. Ranjan Ray and Ramprasad Sengupta focus on two different types of policies, namely fiscal policy in a federal set-up and energy planning, respectively.

Voluntary Contribution to Public Goods: A Parable of Bad Samaritans

The problem of voluntary contribution to public goods by self-seeking individuals becomes interesting when the number of individuals is small enough for each to matter. Otherwise, an individual's consumption of a public good will become independent of that individual's contribution to providing that public good; hence it would be optimal not to contribute at all. Dasgupta studies the simplest instance in which each agent matters, the case of two agents and one pure public good, using indifference curves and elementary consumer behaviour theory for exposition.

Dasgupta focuses on a central result in this area, which is that voluntary contribution based on self-seeking behaviour leads to *under-provision* of public goods. If I increase my contribution that tends to raise the availability of the public good directly, i.e. *given the contribution of the other person*, it also induces a 'reaction' from the other person and that too affects the availability and, hence, my consumption of the public good. This latter is an external effect, giving rise to the possibility of under-provision and lack of Pareto-optimality. Dasgupta poses the problem in terms of alternative formulations of 'conjectural variations', seen as beliefs about how my 'rival' is expected to react to changes that I may contemplate.

The Economics of Enforcement

Agents in the economic world are incompletely informed about the tastes, the resources and the technologies possessed by other agents. This not only constraints choice of policy but also the *implementation* of a chosen policy. Indeed the major *economic* issue regarding implementation of a desired policy arises from informational *asymmetries* between planners and individual agents regarding tastes, technology, endowments and effort levels of the latter.

However, it is not of course the case that the availability of information is simply given. What makes the problem interesting from an economic view point is that information is costly to acquire and therefore, it would not in general be optimal to select policies that would be chosen under complete information. Mook-herjee provides a perspective on the recent literature concerning costly enforcement of economic policies. The problems discussed include income tax evasion and efficient enforcement of regulations. The main issues concern the design of policies with costly monitoring or investigation, in conjunction with penalties for detected violators.

Optimal Provision and Financing of Public Goods in a Federal State with Illustrative Empirical Evidence

The chapter by Ranjan Ray studies the problem of optimal taxation and public expenditure in a federal nation with many levels of government and different constitutional rights regarding the imposition of tax on the same base. Fiscal federalism has received renewed attention with the reunification of Germany and in some EC countries. He analyses a fully coordinated centralized model, as well as, a decentralized model where different levels of government have different objectives. Contrary to results derived from unitary state models, he shows that individualized lump-sum taxes are fully consistent with *non-zero* commodity taxes, provided that the federal and provincial commodity taxes are proportional across items. He also provides some preliminary results on commodity taxes using the two federal models developed, and Indian budget data.

Energy and Development: Some Macroeconomic Constraints for Energy Planning in India

Energy planning is an important element of any strategy for rapid development and growth. Sengupta studies the nature of the energy market in India, its different segments, and pricing rules. The energy intensity of GDP in India cannot but increase in the future. Even with moderate assumptions about aggregate growth rates, the challenges for ensuring the supply of different forms of commercial fuel can be large and difficult. The state has to play a significant role in the process of ensuring energy security. Price rationalization schemes, conservation, higher efficiency of use, and more effective exploration strategies are discussed. Sengupta also points out that India's oil deficit is bound to increase in the future. Therefore, higher export earnings and a general export promotion policy at the macroeconomic level are essential.

9

Voluntary Contribution to Public Goods: A Parable of Bad Samaritans[*]

Dipankar Dasgupta

1 INTRODUCTION

As an undergraduate student in Presidency College, I studied Price Theory under Professor Bhabatosh Datta. Like all great teachers, he was a bit of a conjurer also. The magic of his lectures held the students in a hypnotic spell, often leading them to misconceptions about their own intellectual capabilities. Such at least was the case with me.

From Professor Tapas Majumdar on the other hand, I had my introduction to Macroeconomics. The first edition of Ackley[1] had just come out at the time and he guided us through the book in all its painstaking details. His lectures were quiet and prosaic and in a way represented the polar opposite of the high drama of Professor Datta's classes. As a result, the priceless service he had rendered us by exposing our minds to the rigour of logical thinking escaped me completely. I was too young then, I am afraid, to have realized that the unmistakable sign of a good theorist lies in the attention paid to finer points of analysis.

---

[*] The ideas expressed in this paper have been strongly influenced by my joint work with Jun-ichi Itaya who is also responsible for my interest in the theory of public goods. I wish to thank (without implicating) him for many hours of useful discussion on the subject.

[1] Ackley, Gardner (1961): *Macroeconomic Theory* (1st ed.), New York: Macmillan.

A few years later, I was selected a Junior Research Fellow in the Centre for Economic Studies at Presidency College. A part of my responsibility, as I found out, was to hold tutorials for Professor Majumdar who was now teaching Microeconomic Theory. My conceit at the time being as boundless as it was baseless, I looked upon my assignment with a feeling akin to contempt. I have no idea, therefore, how many atrocities I had committed before the day of reckoning arrived and he asked me to recount to him what I had been telling his students. His manner, as always, was pleasant but firm, and I knew then and there that at some stage I must have uttered a blasphemy of sorts. As I vaguely remember, it had something to do with the relevance of the Marshallian assumption of a constancy of the marginal utility of money for the law of demand. But I do recall that it was not just a bad slip. It was an error that left me no scope at all to hide my ignorance.

He did not yell at me, nor did he call me a fool. Instead, he merely advised me to look up Hicks' *Value and Capital*. My confidence was rudely shaken by the incident. So I rushed back to read the relevant sections (as well as other parts) of the book. As I see it in retrospect, this was the first piece of economic writing that exposed me to the delights of theory. Since then, I have read and reread the classic many times over and have no doubts at all that the marginal utility of the resulting improvement in my appreciation of our subject matter now far exceeds the marginal disutility of my initial disgrace.

I must confess, on the other hand, that the passage of time has done little to help me forget the incident itself. In fact, I have always felt a little disconcerted in Professor Majumdar's presence since that day. For I am told that it is the first impression that lasts the longest. If so, Professor Majumdar's evaluation of me cannot possibly be one that I should feel flattered about.

When the editors of this volume approached me for a contribution, I decided to choose a subject that has its analytical underpinnings in Consumer Behaviour theory. Needless to say, I have been guided in this by my desire to convey to Professor Majumdar the belated message that his advice was not entirely lost upon me. It is well to admit at the same time, however, that the choice happens to be one of convenience also, for it is partly inspired by a topic of contemporary research. A large body of theoretical as well as empirical literature has recently developed around the subject of public goods. Given a growing awareness of issues relating to global warming, ecological balance, environmental degradation and so on, the resurgence of interest in public goods needs hardly be explained. Policy planners all around the world, and particularly so in developing countries, are in search of incentive compatible mechanisms which might resolve these problems in a satisfactory manner.

On a theoretical plane, it is well-known of course that the contribution by any individual (or a group of individuals) towards a public good (such as the preservation of environment) gives rise to unavoidable externalities and hence an incentive for others to free-ride. As a consequence, the market mechanism fails to achieve a proper allocation of resources.[2]

Recent developments in the noncooperative game theory have, on the other hand, led to the study of *non*market mechanisms for the provision of public goods. This paper is concerned with one of these, viz. a *Nash noncooperative equilibrium*.[3] As an analytical tool, the concept of a *Nash* equilibrium has three advantages. First, it gives rise to easily identifiable equilibria. Second, it brings into sharp focus the factors responsible for a misallocation of resources. And finally, it is based on behavioural assumptions about agents which are not hard to justify in a world where incentives are guided not by philanthropy but by self-interest.

[2] For seminal contributions, see for example, Samuelson, P.A. (1954): 'The Pure Theory of Public Expenditure', *Review of Economics and Statistics*, 36, pp. 387–9 and Samuelson, P.A. (1955): 'A Diagrammatic Exposition of a Pure Theory of Public Expenditure', Review of Economics and Statistics, 37, pp. 350–6.

[3] The original idea in this context is attributable to Chamberlin, J. (1974): *Provision of Public Goods as a Function of Group Size*, American Political Science Review, 68, pp. 707–16. The literature has been extensively reviewed by Cornes, Richard and Todd Sandler (1986): *The Theory of Externalities, Public Goods, and Club Goods*, Cambridge University Press, Cambridge and Sandler, Todd (1992): *Collective Action*, The University of Michigan Press, Ann Arbor.

The results I am about to report are not in the nature of solutions to problems or guidelines for policy makers. Rather, they will attempt to identify the problems themselves in an analytically tractable manner. In particular, I shall attempt to present in terms of an elementary framework, a few of the theoretical implications of the *Nash* theory for an allocation problem involving public goods. Consistent with the *Nash* approach, the society considered below is assumed to be a collection of rational agents, each maximizing his utility subject to a budget constraint and a constraint relating to his perception of the externality he might enjoy on account of contributions by others to the public good. They are bad Samaritans so to speak in so far as each is utterly selfish and consciously attempting to reap a harvest where he never sowed. Further, there being no coercion involved in the mechanisms to be discussed, the contributions to the public good are purely *voluntary*.

2 DEFINITIONS AND INDIVIDUAL EQUILIBRIA

A good is *nonrival* if each unit of it can be consumed simultaneously by more than one individual. An *excludable* good on the other hand is one ' . . . whose benefits can be withheld costlessly by the owner or provider'.[4] Thus, the programmes telecast by state owned TV are nonrival commodities, but cable TV constitutes an excludable (though nonrival) good.[5] A *pure private good* is both *rival* and *excludable*, whereas a *pure public good* is both *nonrival* and *nonexcludable*. In what follows, I shall concentrate on this *pure* variety alone.

To make matters precise and at the same time amenable to diagrammatic analysis, I shall deal with a society composed of

[4] Cornes, Richard and Todd Sandler (1986), ibid., p. 6.

[5] Parking space is an example of the reverse case of an *effectively* nonexcludable though rival good. The example is due to Romer, Paul M. (1990): 'Endogenous Technological Change', *Journal of Political Economy*, 98, p. S74.

two individuals.[6] They consume two goods only, a *pure* private good and a *pure* public good. Individual i's ($i = 1, 2$) demand for the private good is denoted by x_i and his *contribution to the public good by* g_i. By definition, however, each individual consumes the *aggregate contribution G* made by the two agents.[7] Unless otherwise specified, individual i is assumed to be endowed with a *Cobb–Douglas* utility function

$$U^i(x_i, G) = x_i^{\alpha_i} G^{1-\alpha_i}, 0 < \alpha_i < 1, i = 1, 2 \qquad (1)$$

and an exogenously specified level of wealth, say I_i. The wealth represents a resource available to individual i for *allocation* between the private and the public good. For simplicity, and following established practice,[8] the allocative *technology* is also assumed to be linear and written

$$x_i + g_i = I_i, \quad x_i \geq 0, g_i \geq 0, \quad i = 1, 2. \qquad (2)$$

Clearly, (2) may as well be viewed as an agent's budget constraint. Individual i is assumed to maximize (1) subject to (2) and his perception of j's contribution. The latter implies that i is not certain about the amount contributed by j and vice versa. A further uncertainty for i relates to the manner in which j responds to a *change* in i's contribution.

---

[6] Generalizations to the case of an arbitrary collection of individuals may be found in Dasgupta, Dipankar and Jun-ichi Itaya (1992) 'Comparative Statics for the Private Provision of Public Goods in a Conjectural Variations Model with Heterogeneous Agents', *Public Finance*, 47, pp. 17–31 and Itaya, Jun-ichi and Dipankar Dasgupta (1994) 'Dynamics, Consistent Conjectures and Heterogeneous Agents in the Private Provision of Public Goods', Indian Statistical Institute, Delhi Centre, Discussion Paper No. 94–11.

[7] This means, among other things, that the aggregate quantity of the public good is produced by a linear technology involving individual contributions. The simple summation form implies perfect substitutability between the contributions by different individuals. If public goods are *impure* ' . . . individualized weights may have to be applied to the . . . ' contributions. See Sandler, Todd (1992), op. cit., p. 36.

[8] See, for example, Cornes, Richard and Todd Sandler (1986), op. cit., p. 70. Also, Sandler, Todd (1992), ibid., p. 29.

So stated, the problem differs from a typical consumer's maximization problem in that the variables appearing in the objective function are not exactly the same as the ones which define the constraints. This reflects the fact that while (2) represents a private constraint, the utility function must involve the *aggregate* quantity of the public good produced by society. They become comparable, however, by adding g_j^e to both sides of (2) and converting it to

$$x_i + G = I_i + g_j^e, \quad i = 1, 2; \quad i \neq j. \tag{3}$$

where g_j^e represents individual i's expectation about the contribution by individual j. This way of writing the second constraint has a useful role in diagrammatic representations. From i's point of view, the right hand side of (3) stands for his subsidized wealth[9] with the added stipulation that the subsidy itself can be spent on the public good alone. These *modified* budget constraints (mbc's) are depicted in Figure 9.1. The right hand part of the diagram represents 1's mbc. The private good is measured along the horizontal axis and the public good along the vertical. OJ represents the maximum possible consumption of the private good by 1, while OC is the minimum consumption of the public good by society under the assumption that 2 is known to contribute that amount. The maximum possible provision of the public good on the part of 1 is $CT (= OJ)$ and his mbc is therefore represented by the kinked frontier TSJ. Equilibrium choice occurs at E where an indifference curve is tangential to the mbc.[10] Thus, given OC, individual 1 derives maximum satisfaction by consuming OA of the private good and AE of the public good. This implies that his utility maximizing contribution to the public good is EM.[11]

[9] This is often referred to in the literature as *full income*. See Sandler, Todd. (1992), ibid., p. 73.

[10] This is not to suggest that solutions to the choice problem are invariably interior. In fact, much of the literature is concerned with boundary solutions or *(complete)* free riding. The qualification 'complete' has its origin in Cornes, Richard and Todd Sandler (1984) 'Easy Riders, Joint Production, and Public Goods', *Economic Journal*, 94, pp. 580–98.

[11] The mbc's bear more than a superficial resemblance to the intertemporal

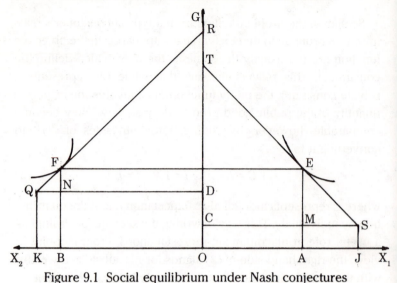

Figure 9.1 Social equilibrium under Nash conjectures

The left hand part of the diagram shows the corresponding situation for individual 2. His *mbc* is given by the frontier *RQK* and desired consumption bundle by the coordinates of the point *F* under the hypothesis that *1* contributes *OD* amount of the public good.

3 SOCIAL EQUILIBRIA

An important point to note here is that any meaningful notion of social equilibrium must involve both individuals consuming the *same* quantity of the public good. As drawn, the diagram obviously satisfies this restriction, since *AE = FB*. A less obvious feature of the figure is that *EM = OD* and *FN = OC*. This means that each individual's expectation about the *level* of contribution by the

budget constraint in Grandmont, Jean–Michel (1983) *Money and Value*, Cambridge University Press, Cambridge. See p. 20, Figure 1.1. The vertical stretch in Grandmont's diagram occurs due to the fact that future *real* resources are ultimately nontransferable to the present. In my case, the vertical portion reflects the fact that the subsidy part of the consumer's budget is tied to the public good. It cannot be *liquidated*, so to speak, to enhance the consumption of the private good.

other is fulfilled in equilibrium. A further subtlety relates to the fact that the slope of TS equals that of RQ and both equal -1.

To appreciate the importance of the last two observations, it is useful to write down the first order conditions (FOC's) for an individual's optimum. This is done[12] by substituting (2) into (1) to get

$$U^i(x_i, G) = (I_i - g_i)^{\alpha_i} (g_i + g_j^e)^{1-\alpha_i}. \tag{4}$$

Differentiating (4) with respect to g_i and equating to zero, the relevant FOC turns out to be

$$-\alpha_i x_i^{\alpha_i-1} G^{1-\alpha_i} + (1-\alpha_i) x^{\alpha_i} G^{-\alpha_i} \left(1 + \frac{dg_j^e}{dg_i}\right) = 0$$

or,

$$\frac{U_1^i(x_i, G)}{U_2^i(x_i, G)} = \frac{\alpha_i G}{(1-\alpha_i) x_i} = \left(1 + \frac{dg_j^e}{dg_i}\right), i = 1, 2; i \neq j. \tag{5}$$

Equations (2) and (5) may be used to solve for the optimal values of x_i and g_i, given i's expectations, i.e. the values of g_j^e and dg_j^e/dg_i. The term $(1 + (dg_j^e/dg_i))$, i.e. the slope of the mbc at E, stands for (the inverse of) i's evaluation of the price (more precisely, the opportunity cost) of a unit of the public good expressed in units of the private good. If i believed j to be totally unresponsive to a change in his own contribution, i.e. $dg_j^e/dg_i = 0$, then the opportunity cost of a unit of the public good to him is a unit of the private good and the slope of the mbc at the equilibrium point is -1 as shown in Figure 9.1. However, if dg_j^e/dg_i is believed to be nonzero, say negative, then the estimated opportunity cost of a unit of the public good is higher for i. This happens because a unit rise in the social supply requires more than a unit rise in i's contribution to compensate for the consequent fall in the contribution by j.[13]

---

[12] See Cornes, Richard and Todd Sandler (1986), op. cit., p. 71 or Dasgupta, Dipankar and Jun-ichi Itaya (1992), op. cit., p. 17 for further details.

[13] Note, however, that $(dg_j^e/dg_i) > -1$ must hold, or else (5) would imply

Generally speaking, i is supposed to be endowed with a function, say $g_j^e = \phi(g_i)$, which summarizes his expectations about j's behaviour. Moreover, $\phi'(g_i)$, i.e. the slope of this function, is usually referred to as his *conjectural variation* with respect to j's contribution. Similarly, j's beliefs are summarized in a corresponding function $g_i^e = \psi(g_j)$. A large part of the literature under survey is based on the assumption that each individual holds a zero conjectural variation about the other, i.e. $\phi'(g_i) = \psi'(g_j) = 0.$[14] Such conjectures are usually known as *Nash* conjectures. Therefore, the significance of the fact that the slope of the *mbc* is -1 at E is that individual *1* holds *Nash* conjectures about his opponent's behaviour. Moreover, $EM = OD$ and $FN = OC$ at equilibrium imply, as already noted, that each agent's expectation about the level of the other's contribution is self-fulfilling. In other words, Figure 9.1 represents a social equilibrium with the following properties:

(*i*)   each individual maximizes utility subject to his *mbc;*
(*ii*)   each individual's expectation about the level of the other's contribution is fulfilled; and
(*iii*) each individual entertains *Nash* conjectures regarding the other, i.e. the slopes of *TS* and *RQ* are both equal to -1.

These properties of the social equilibrium qualify it as a *Nash* noncooperative equilibrium under *Nash* conjectures, or simply as a *Nash* equilibrium (*NE*).

An alternative[15] representation of the above equilibrium calls forth the notion of *reaction curves* or *functions*. A reaction curve represents an individual's optimal responses to alternative

---

$G = 0$, which is suboptimal under the *Cobb–Douglas* utility specification. The point was noted by Cornes, Richard and Todd Sandler (1985) 'On the Consistency of Conjectures with Public Goods', *Journal of Public Economics*, 27, pp. 125–9.

[14] Cornes, Richard and Todd Sandler (1986), op. cit., Chapter 5. Warr, P. (1982) 'Pareto optimal Redistribution and Private Charity', *Journal of Public Economics*, 19, pp. 131–8; Warr, P. (1983) 'The Private Provision of a Public Good is Independent of the Distribution of Income', *Economics Letters*, 13, pp. 207–11.

[15] The representation that follows is taken, *mutadis mutandis*, from Cornes, Richard and Todd Sandler (1986), op. cit., p. 77.

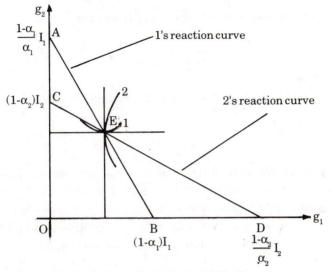

Figure 9.2 Social equilibrium under Nash conjectures
in terms of reaction curves

choices by the other. Substituting $G = g_1 + g_2$ and (2) into (5) and using the notion of *Nash* conjectures, we obtain the reaction curves of *1* and *2* as

$$g_1 = -\alpha_1 g_2 + (1 - \alpha_1) I_1 \qquad (6)$$

and

$$g_2 = -\alpha_2 g_1 + (1 - \alpha_2) I_2. \qquad (7)$$

respectively. These are shown in Figure 9.2 as *AB* and *CD* whose intersection point *E* represents the *Nash* equilibrium under discussion.[16]

---

[16] Strictly speaking, the reaction curve of *1* is the union of *AB* and the vertical stretch above *A*, while the reaction curve of *2* is the union of *CD* and the horizontal stretch beyond *B*. Thus, it is possible to have a *Nash* equilibrium where one of the individuals contributes a zero amount to the public good. In what follows, however, we assume away such possibilities and concentrate only on equilibria with positive contributions by both individuals. As can be easily verified from Fig. 2, a sufficient condition for this to happen is that

Inverting the reaction function in (6) we obtain

$$g_2 = -\frac{1}{\alpha_1} g_1 + \frac{1-\alpha_1}{\alpha_1} I_1 \qquad (6')$$

In the diagram, AB is shown to be steeper than CD which happens if

$$1 > \alpha_1 \alpha_2.^{17} \qquad (8)$$

When this is the case, E constitutes a *stable* equilibrium. That is to say, a logical process which, in a small neighbourhood of E, views each individual to be revising his contribution as a function of the discrepancy between his proposed contribution and the one ordained by his reaction function, must converge to E.[18]

4   Consistency and Inconsistency

The stability of the path of contributions, however, is hardly a cause for satisfaction. For, despite the fact that g_i keeps changing in response to changes in g_j, individual j is all along assumed to hold *Nash* conjectures and *vice versa*. In other words, an individual's optimal reactions to *changes* in the other's contribution are based on the assumption that they are change*less*.

The *NE* described above involves agents making conjectures

$$(1 - \alpha_1) I_1 > \alpha_1(1 - \alpha_2) I_2 \text{ and } (1 - \alpha_2) I_2 > \alpha_2 (1 - \alpha_1) I_1$$

or,

$$\frac{1 - \alpha_2}{\alpha_2(1 - \alpha_1)} > \frac{I_1}{I_2} > \frac{\alpha_1(1 - \alpha_2)}{1 - \alpha_1}.$$

This condition is more likely to be satisfied the closer are the values of α_i to zero, i.e. the weaker are individual preferences for the private good as compared to that for the public good. The reaction curve of I is invertible in a neighbourhood of the equilibrium point whenever the above condition is satisfied.

[17] Notice that this is automatically satisfied under the sufficient condition stated in fn 16.

[18] See Cornes, Richard and Todd Sandler (1986), op. cit., p. 92.

about each other that are inconsistent with their actual behaviour (symbolically, $(dg_j^e/dg_i) \neq (dg_j/dg_i)$). As a result, they equate their marginal rates of substitution to distorted price ratios computed on the basis of falsely perceived opportunity costs of the public good. This gives rise to a loss in each individual's welfare. The resulting equilibrium is therefore expected to be *Pareto* suboptimal. That this is indeed so is seen by comparing the slopes of the indifference curves at the equilibrium point in the $g_1 - g_2$ plane. For $i = 1$, for example, we have along any indifference curve,

$$dU^1(I - g_1, g_1 + g_2) = 0 = -U_1^1 \, dg_1 + U_2^1 \, (dg_1 + dg_2)$$

i.e. $$\frac{dg_2}{dg_1} = \frac{U_1^1}{U_2^1} - 1.$$

Using (5) and *Nash* conjectures, the last expression reduces to

$$\frac{dg_2}{dg_1} = 0 \tag{9}$$

at the individual's equilibrium point. In Figure 2, this is apparent from the tangency of a horizontal line with 1's indifference curve at E. By a similar exercise, we may show that

$$\frac{dg_1}{dg_2} = \frac{U_1^2}{U_2^2} - 1 = 0 \tag{10}$$

so that 2's indifference curve is tangential to a vertical line at E. Thus, the indifference curves of the two individuals have unequal slopes at the equilibrium point implying thereby that E is not a *Pareto* optimal allocation.

It is clear that agents would soon discover through a process of trial and error that the *Nash* conjectures are *inconsistent*, and consequently that they yield (individually) suboptimal choices. They would naturally be led therefore to revise their beliefs. On the other hand, the manner in which 1 revises his conjectures regarding 2 depends on the way 2 actually responds and the latter in turn is guided by *2*'s beliefs about the way *1* reacts to a change in *2*'s contribution and so on *ad infinitum*. These are serious dynamic issues and must be resolved in terms of a properly formulated dynamic model. Any such attempt would take us far beyond the scope of the present exercise. Instead, I will attempt a shortcut that purists in Game theory shrink away from. Following Bresnahan, Perry and Cornes and Sandler,[19] I will ask if the model under consideration is capable of producing a *consistent conjectures equilibrium (CCE)*.[20] Such an equilibrium lies at the opposite extreme from the *NE* discussed so far. More precisely, one asks in this case if it might be possible to have a *consistent* conjectural variation for an agent in a local sense, i.e., can the conjecture about an agent be identical to his optimal response at the equilibrium which itself is based upon that conjecture? This means that a *CCE* involves changing (*iii*) in the definition of *NE* by

(*iii'*) each individual entertains *consistent* conjectures regarding the other (or, symbolically, $(dg_j^e/dg_i) = (dg_j/dg_i)$, $i, j = 1, 2; i \neq j$).

A *CCE* is displayed diagrammatically in Figure 9.3. If agent *2* is not endowed with *Nash* conjectures, he would expect changes in his contribution to bring forth perceptible responses from *1*. In a local neighbourhood of a given point such as *A* in the $g_1 - g_2$ plane, agent *2*'s beliefs about *1*'s behaviour could then be summarized by the slope of a line like *CD*. The fact that *2*'s conjectures are non-*Nash* is captured by the fact that *CD* is not a vertical line.[21] If

[19] Bresnahan, T.F. (1981): Duopoly Models with Consistent Conjectures, *American Economic Review*, 71, pp. 934–45; Perry, M. (1985) 'Oligopoly and Consistent Conjectural Variations', *Bell Journal of Economics*, 13, pp. 197–205, Cornes, Richard and Todd Sandler (1986), op. cit., p. 154.

[20] It should be noted that a *CCE* is no longer popular amongst Game theorists. A criticism that may be levelled against the concept is that it represents a questionable attempt to reduce an essentially dynamic problem to a static one.

[21] *CD* is supposed to have a negative slope in the figure. One could as well assume that the slope is positive. However, as Sugden (1985, op. cit.) argued, this will not be the case under normal circumstances. The matter is discussed below in greater detail.

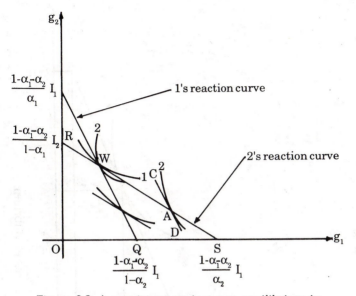

Figure 9.3 A consistent conjectures equilibrium in terms of reaction curves

now agent 2's conjectural variations were to be the same as the slope of the line CD everywhere in the $g_1 - g_2$ plane, then his reaction function would be the locus of points at which his indifference curves have this slope also. The curve RS in Figure 9.3 depicts such a reaction function for agent 2.

A *CCE* is characterized by the fact that 2's conjectural variations regarding A are identically the same as 1's true behaviour in a neighbourhood of the equilibrium and vice versa. This entails 1's reaction curve having the same slope as CD around the equilibrium allocation. Similarly, 2's reaction function must have the reciprocal property. The point W in Figure 9.3 satisfies this property and qualifies as a *CCE*.

Figure 9.4 is an alternative representation of a *CCE* and corresponds to Figure 9.1 of the *Nash* conjectures case. The major change in Figure 9.4 is that the slopes of the top parts of the two *mbc*'s (viz. *TS and RQ*) cease to be -1. This follows because the opportunity cost of a unit of the public good is no longer a unit

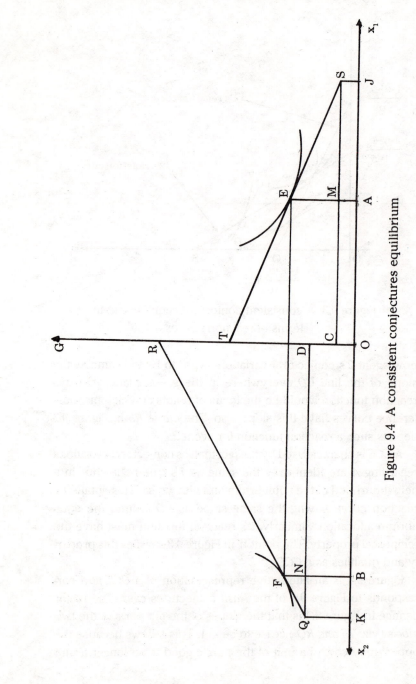

Figure 9.4 A consistent conjectures equilibrium

of the private good now (unless of course the *Nash* conjectures are themselves consistent, but more about that later on). Criterion (*ii*) of the social equilibrium however remains unchanged, so that we have $EM = OD$ and $FN = OC$. Of course, we do not know as yet whether the slopes of TS and RQ increase or decrease. But this is found out easily.

Suppose b_1 and b_2 are the conjectural variations of *1* and *2* respectively (viz. the slopes of $\phi(.)$ and $\psi(.)$) at the equilibrium. Once again, substituting $G = g_1 + g_2$ and (2) into (5), but instead of *Nash* conjectures, using this time the fact that

$$\frac{dg_2}{dg_1} = b_1 \text{ and } \frac{dg_1}{dg_2} = b_2$$

the two reaction curves now become

$$g_1 = -\frac{\alpha_1}{\alpha_1 + (1 - \alpha_1)(1 + b_1)} g_2 + \frac{(1 + b_1)(1 - \alpha_1) I_1}{\alpha_1 + (1 - \alpha_1)(1 + b_1)} \quad (11)$$

and

$$g_2 = -\frac{\alpha_2}{\alpha_2 + (1 - \alpha_2)(1 + b_2)} g_1 + \frac{(1 + b_2)(1 - \alpha_2) I_2}{\alpha_2 + (1 - \alpha_2)(1 + b_2)}. \quad (12)$$

For a *CCE*, the slopes of (11) and (12) must equal b_2 and b_1 respectively. This yields a pair of quadratic equations,[22] viz.

$$b_2 = -\frac{\alpha_1}{\alpha_1 + (1 - \alpha_1)(1 + b_1)}$$

and

$$b_1 = -\frac{\alpha_2}{\alpha_2 + (1 - \alpha_2)(1 + b_2)}$$

whose solutions are given by

[22] The exercise is taken from Itaya, Jun-ichi and Dipankar Dasgupta (1994), op. cit.

$$(b_1^*, b_2^*) = (-1, -1) \text{ or, } \left(-\frac{\alpha_2}{1-\alpha_1}, -\frac{\alpha_1}{1-\alpha_2} \right) \tag{13}$$

However, the first of the solutions is easily discarded since for these values of b_i, equation (5) would imply that the optimum values of G and x_i must satisfy

$$\frac{G}{x_i} = 0.$$

This means, as in footnote 13, that $G = 0$, a suboptimal choice given *Cobb–Douglas* utility functions.

The negativity of b_i^* implies that the slopes of the *CCE* reaction curves are negative too. Further, (5) shows that the *TS* and *RQ* stretches in the respective *mbc*'s become flatter with a rise in the opportunity cost of the public good. Substituting for b_1^* and b_2^* in (11) and (12) we obtain

$$g_1 = -\frac{\alpha_1}{(1-\alpha_2)} g_2 + \frac{(1-\alpha_1-\alpha_2) I_1}{(1-\alpha_2)} \tag{14}$$

and

$$g_2 = -\frac{\alpha_2}{(1-\alpha_1)} g_1 + \frac{(1-\alpha_1-\alpha_2) I_2}{(1-\alpha_1)} . ^{23} \tag{15}$$

In Figure 9.3, the two reaction curves PQ and RS are drawn to satisfy (14) and (15). Further, since

$$\frac{1-\alpha_1}{\alpha_1} > \frac{1-\alpha_1-\alpha_2}{\alpha_1},$$

it is easily seen that OA of Figure 9.2 is strictly larger than $O'P$ of Figure 9.3. Similarly, OB of Figure 9.2 is larger than $O'Q$ of Figure 9.3, since

$$\frac{(1-\alpha_1-\alpha_2) I_1}{(1-\alpha_2)} = 1 - \frac{\alpha_1}{1-\alpha_2} < 1 - \alpha_1.$$

[23] A necessary condition for the existence of an interior social equilibrium for this case is given by $\alpha_1 + \alpha_2 < 1$ and a sufficient one by $(1 - \alpha_2/\alpha_2) > (I_1/I_2) > (\alpha_1/1 - \alpha_1)$.

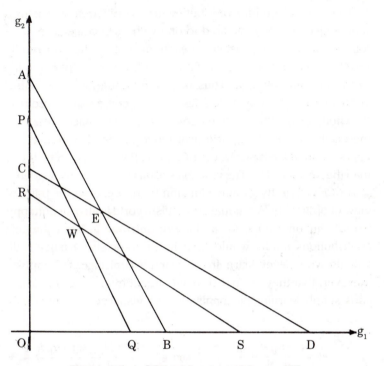

Figure 9.5 A CCE is dominated by an NE

Therefore, superimposing Figure 9.2 on Figure 9.3, we obtain in Figure 9.5 the result that PQ (of Figure 9.3) lies wholly inside AB (of Figure 9.2). Similarly, RS lies wholly inside CD. Hence, the point W (Figure 9.3) is dominated by the point E (Figure 9.2). In other words, a CCE involves contributions that are even *lower* than those under *Nash* conjectures. And it continues to be Pareto suboptimal of course.[24]

---

[24] More rigorously, the solution of (14) and (15) gives the CCE equilibrium contributions to be

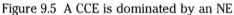

$$g_1^c = (1 - \alpha_1)\, I_1 - \alpha_1\, I_2 \text{ and } g_2^c = (1 - \alpha_2)\, I_2 - \alpha_2\, I_1.$$

The corresponding *Nash* equilibrium values are obtained by solving (6) and (7). These are

The reason for undercontribution in an equilibrium with consistent conjectures as compared to one with *Nash* conjectures is as follows. Since b_1^* is negative, at each level of g_2, the opportunity cost to *1* of a unit of the public good is *higher* as compared to the *Nash* conjecture situation. Thus, he will contribute less to the public good for each value of g_2 and his reaction curve will accordingly lie wholly below the reaction curve under *Nash* conjectures. Symmetrically, *2*'s reaction curve will move inside also. Hence, the intersection of the two, viz. the *CCE* allocation is likely to be lower than the *NE* allocation. The essentials of this was noted by Sugden.[25]

A *CCE* is a pretty gloomy situation therefore, from the point of view of optimality. A rational and selfish world is also an unhappy world! Our only hope for a cheerful outcome in the voluntary contributions model would then lie in a society of naive individuals who never learn from their past mistakes.[26] Suppose, however, that they are not so naive, that they do in fact learn. A fairly simple learning mechanism would visualize the individuals

---

$$g_1^n = \frac{(1 - \alpha_1) I_1 - \alpha_1(1 - \alpha_2) I_2}{1 - \alpha_1 \alpha_2} \text{ and } g_2^n = \frac{(1 - \alpha_2) I_2 - \alpha_2(1 - \alpha_1) I_1}{1 - \alpha_1 \alpha_2}$$

It is easy to verify that the latter solution dominates the former vectorwise. The fact that an *NE* allocation is hard to improve upon has been observed in other contexts also. For example, a classic *neutrality* result due to Warr (1982, 1983), op. cit. says that an *NE* allocation stays undisturbed in the face of a wealth redistribution. In other words, both predictions of the Fundamental Theorem of Welfare Economics are invalid for an *NE* with public goods. The equilibrium is not Pareto optimal and no Pareto optimal allocation can be sustained as an *NE* through income redistribution. The result was proved in greater generality in Bergstrom, Theodore, Lawrence Blume and Hal Varian (1986) 'On the Private Provision of Public Goods', *Journal of Public Economics*, 29, pp. 25–49. For a recent in depth study, see Saijo, Tatsuyoshi and Yoshikatsu Tatamitani (1995) 'Characterizing Neutrality in the Voluntary Contribution Mechanism', *Economic Design*, 1, pp. 119–40.

[25] Sugden, Robert (1985), op. cit., p. 121.

[26] The situation is comparable to the much discussed rational expectations equilibrium of macroeconomic theory. Government policy is likely to be successful only if individual agents are incorrectly informed!

to be revising their conjectural variations on the basis of the discrepancy between the actual behaviour of the rest of society and their initial beliefs. Where would this lead? As shown in Itaya and Dasgupta,[27] the path of revised conjectures so generated must lead to consistent conjectures in the limit. The result therefore merely adds to the depression.

This brings back to mind the following insightful comment by Sugden:[28]

We have, it seems, reached an impasse. It would hardly be satisfactory to claim to explain voluntary contributions to public goods by assuming that individuals hold systematically false beliefs about one another's behaviour. After all, if someone really wants to know whether other people would match an increase in his own contribution, it is easy enough to put the matter to the test. Why should people continue to believe in a myth of matching behaviour, in the absence of any evidence to support it? But if we require conjectures to be consistent or self-fulfilling we are led, seemingly inescapably, to the conclusion that no public good would ever be supplied in significant amounts by voluntary contributions.

5 REFINEMENTS

The negativity of the slopes of the reaction functions raises a further question. Can they ever be non-negative? I take up the question in two parts. First, I ask if the slope of a reaction function can be positive, irrespective of the consistency or inconsistency of conjectures. Secondly, I shall analyse the possibility of reaction curves with zero slopes and ask if *Nash* conjectures may be consistent.

5.1 Positively Sloped Reaction Functions

I have shown that the *CCE* examined in the previous section involves negatively sloped reaction curves. That reaction curves

---

[27] Itaya, Jun-ichi and Dasgupta, Dipankar (1994), op. cit.

[28] Sugden, Robert (1985), op. cit., p. 123. As opposed to Itaya and Dasgupta (1994), however, Sugden did not consider any explicit dynamics in his model.

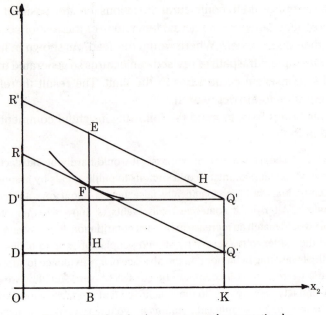

Figure 9.6 Sugden's argument for negatively
sloped reaction curves

would generally satisfy this property was noted by Sugden.[29] His
argument is easily understood with reference to Figure 9.6. We
assume that in the initial equilibrium, *2* consumes *OB* of the private
good and *BF* of the public good. His contribution to the public good
is *FN* while *1's* contribution to it is *OD*. His *mbc* is *RQK* and we make
no particular assumptions about the slope of *RQ*. (Notice that this
introduces a third possibility, a *Nash* equilibrium with *non-Nash*,
though possibly inconsistent, conjectures.)[30]

Suppose now that for one reason or the other, *1's* contribution
rises from *OD* to *OD'*. This shifts *2's mbc* to *R'Q'K*. How would
it affect his contribution to the public good? If both goods are
normal, then the new equilibrium point will lie in the region *EH*.

[29] See Sugden Robert (1985), op. cit., pp. 119–21.

[30] See Cornes, Richard and Todd Sandler (1986), op. cit., Ch. 9 and Dasgupta,
Dipankar and Jun-ichi Itaya (1992), op. cit., p. 20.

This in turn would imply that his consumption of the public good would increase by less than the rise in *1*'s contribution. Hence, his contribution must *fall!*

Alternatively, if the public good is inferior,[31] then the new equilibrium for *2* will lie in the zone *HQ'*, so that *2*'s consumption of the public good along with his contribution falls. The only case left out then is the *unlikely* one where the *private* good is inferior. Here the new equilibrium would lie in the region *ER'* with the result that *2*'s contribution would *rise* with that of *1*. In other words, *2*'s reaction function is rather unlikely to be positively sloped and hence it is not sensible to consider the case of an equilibrium in which individuals hold positive conjectural variations about one another.

Sugden used his argument to criticize a suggestion by Cornes and Sandler that individuals might believe that other people's contributions are positively related to their own.[32] If this were so, then the opportunity cost of the public good would fall (in

---

[31] I have already indicated in the title for this section that we are now moving onto theoretical niceties. Nevertheless, the case of an inferior public good may not be entirely imaginary. If both *G* and *x* are to be looked upon as macro aggregates of heterogeneous collections of public and private goods, it might be natural to conclude that each is *non-inferior*. A less aggregative approach would suggest a different viewpoint however, especially where side by side with a public good, a more expensive and superior variety of the commodity is available in a private form and the agent is concerned with an optimal allocation of his budget between the two. The obvious examples are public and private schools, public and private health care, communally hired security services and private security, etc.

The following excerpt from the editorial (dated 28 September 1994) of The Times of India confirms the point:

Over the last decade and a half, the private health care sector has grown rapidly while the public, nonprofit sector has languished due to paucity of funds. In normal times and for nonemergency cases, private hospitals are being increasingly preferred because patients believe they can secure better care. . . .

[32] Cornes, Richard and Todd Sandler (1984): The Theory of Public Goods: Non-Nash Behaviour, Journal of Public Economics, 23, pp. 367–79. Sugden, Robert (1985), op. cit., p. 118.

comparison with the *Nash* conjectures case) and contributions rise. Clearly, Sugden's critique implies that such beliefs are unwarranted.

Dasgupta and Itaya,[33] however, demonstrated rigorously that positively sloped reaction functions could in fact turn out to be the case if the public good was inferior and conjectures were not required to be consistent. This conclusion did not of course contradict Sugden's claim, since the latter was based on the assumption of a society of homogeneous individuals, whereas our work explicitly introduced heterogeneity into the model. And it was *heterogeneity* alone that was offered as the cause of a reversal of results. The diagrammatic argument of Figure 9.6 on the other hand is perfectly valid whether the individuals are homogeneous or not! Where then is the catch?

To see this, let us extend the model slightly to include *three* instead of *two* agents. Let us suppose moreover (as in Sugden's case) that the individuals are homogeneous in all respects and that the public good is inferior. (Needless to say, we are well out of the *Cobb–Douglas* world here.) Suppose now, that beginning from an initial equilibrium situation, the total contribution by *2* and *3* rises as a result of a rise in the contribution by *1*. Therefore, they consume *more* of the public good. Since *2* and *3* are identical in all respects, it is clear that the contribution by *each* must rise, and rise by the same amount. This means, in particular, that the subsidized wealth (or full income) of *2* (resp. *3*) for example must definitely rise (on account of the rise in contributions by *1* and *3* (resp. *2*)). But the public good is inferior. Consequently, *2*'s consumption of it must *fall*. A contradiction! Hence, his contribution has to fall.

Consider next a nonhomogeneous world in which the public good is inferior for *2* and *3*, and possibly, though not necessarily, for *1* also. Suppose further that in the initial equilibrium, *2* is at *F* in Figure 9.7. Consequent upon a rise in *1*'s contribution by the amount *DD'*, holding *3*'s contribution fixed, *2*'s equilibrium shifts

---

[33] Dasgupta, Dipankar and Jun-ichi Itaya (1992), op. cit., p. 25.

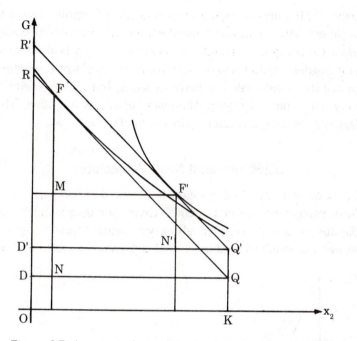

Figure 9.7 Argument for positively sloped reaction curves

drastically down to the point F'. From the point of view of 3 now, this amounts to a *change* in his wealth subsidy by $DD' - (FN - F'N') = DD' - FM$. Given his taste pattern on the other hand, this must lead to a rise in his consumption of the public good as well as his contribution when $DD' - FM < 0$. Further, if the latter rise more than compensates for the initial fall in 2's contribution, then the net effect will be a rise in the joint contribution by 2 and 3 in response to a rise in 1's contribution.

Needless to say, I am not looking here into the indirect chain that would be generated as second, third and n^{th} round effects, which amounts to an assumption that the first round effect dominates. This does not worry me too much, however, since the result that the slopes of reaction curves may turn out to be positive when the public good is inferior was demonstrated quite generally (by solving the relevant simultaneous equation system) in our paper.[34] My purpose here is merely to add a footnote of sorts to point out what I had not realized earlier, viz. that heterogeneity *alone* cannot give the result. The size of the society is also important. Sugden continues to be right in a two person world, whether or not the individuals are heterogeneous. But heterogeneity is only one aspect of reality. Minimality of size is the other. The Dasgupta and Itaya result requires both of these.

5.2 Consistent Nash Conjectures

I now come to the final question to be asked in this paper. Can *Nash* conjectures be consistent?[35] Given our diagrammatic apparatus, the question is relatively easy to handle. Figure 9.8, which shows the equilibrium of individual *2*, is clearly a case in point.

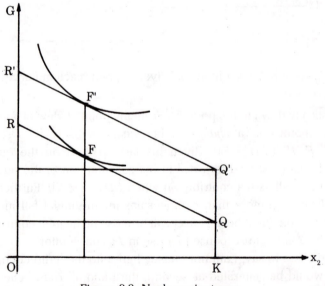

Figure 9.8 Nash conjectures

[34] Ibid., p. 25.

[35] This question was also raised in Cornes, Richard and Todd Sandler (1984), op. cit., p. 372. They noted that only a limited class of utility functions would satisfy this property. I am merely suggesting here what might be a member of that class.

The distinguishing feature of the diagram is that F' lies vertically above F. In other words, a rise in 1's contribution by the amount QQ' leads to an identical rise in the social consumption of the public good, thereby leaving both the private good consumption by 2 as well as his contribution to the public good completely unchanged. So it is consistent for 1 to have *Nash* conjectures regarding 2.

This is reminiscent of what Professor Majumdar taught me about Hicks' analysis of the Marshallian demand curve. Hicks told us that the demand function for a nonmoney good remains unaffected in the face of a rise in money income if the utility function is separable and the marginal utility of money is a constant. Now, as I have already argued, for the model under consideration, an increase in individual 1's contribution to the public good does act like a wealth subsidy for individual 2, providing a parallel for the exogenous increase in money income in Marshall's model. Hence, the situation of Figure 9.8 would indeed occur if the marginal utility of the public good is a constant and the utility functions are separable. An example of such a utility function would be

$$U^i(x_i, G) = u^i(x_i) + \lambda_i\, G, \qquad (16)$$

where $u^i(x_i)$ is the utility of the private good and λ_i (a positive constant) the marginal utility of the public good for each i.[36]

Can these *Nash* conjectures sustain a *CCE* however? To answer this question we should recall that a necessary condition for this is to require that the slopes of the mbc's be -1 at equilibrium. Figure 9.8 is deliberately drawn to violate the condition. But can it be satisfied at all? The slope of an indifference curve for the utility function in (16) is

$$\frac{dG}{dx_i} = -\frac{\dfrac{\partial u^i}{\partial x_i}}{\lambda_i}$$

[36] Dasgupta, Dipankar and Jun-ichi Itaya (1992), op. cit., p. 25 argued for an alternative explanation of *Nash* conjectures in terms of inferiority of the public good for one class of agents and its normalcy for another with the opposite effects cancelling out.

where λ_i is a constant. What is a sufficient condition that guarantees that this ratio assumes a specific value? Surely the other Marshallian assumption, viz. diminishing marginal utility of x_i, would do the trick.[37] While we are at it, let us therefore be Marshallian all the way and make that assumption also.[38]

Finally, there is of course condition (*ii*) of a social equilibrium to verify. This again is a simple matter. It would definitely be satisfied if, for example, the individuals shared perfectly homogeneous characteristics, i.e. a common utility function and common levels of wealth ($u^i = u$, $\lambda_i = \lambda$ and $I_i = I$ irrespective of i).[39] Under *Nash* conjectures, the *FOC* will be

$$\frac{\partial u^i}{\partial x_i} = \lambda \text{ for } i = 1, 2 \qquad (17)$$

By virtue of the law of diminishing marginal utility and the constancy of λ, the optimal value of x_i is determined uniquely (as x^*, say). We may assume moreover that $I - x^* > 0$, so that the solution is interior. Each individual's contribution will then be $g_i = g^* = I - x^*$ and the total consumption of the public good equals $G^* = 2g^*$. Obviously, both G^* *and* g^* are determined residually by the size of I alone, given that x^* is determined independently of

[37] Actually, even Marshall needed a little more in the form of regularity conditions. These were

$$\lim_{x_i \to 0} \frac{\partial u^i}{\partial x_i} = \infty \text{ and } \lim_{x_i \to \infty} \frac{\partial u^i}{\partial x_i} = 0.$$

[38] See Varian, Hal (1994): Sequential Contributions to Public Goods, Journal of Public Economics, 53, pp. 165–86, for what may be considered the polar opposite of this utility function. Varian's utility function (ibid., p. 167) has the form $u_i(G) + x_i$, where u_i satisfies the law of diminishing marginal utility. In this case, we would obtain offsetting contribution by each individual to a rise in his wealth subsidy. See also Cornes, Richard and Todd Sandler (1986), op. cit., p. 83–4.

[39] Homogeneity is not as bizarre an assumption as might appear at first sight as a large part of the literature on voluntary contribution to public goods makes it. See, for example, Sugden (1985), op. cit. Dasgupta, Dipankar and Jun-ichi Itaya (1992), op. cit., was one of the first papers in the area which gave serious thought to the case of heterogeneity.

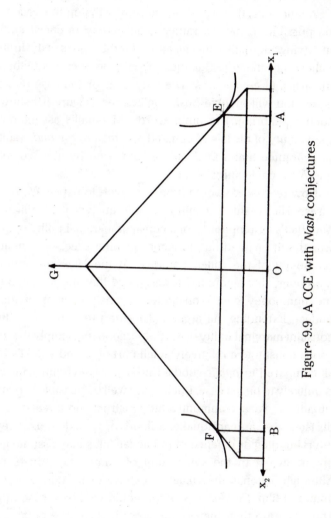

Figure 9.9 A CCE with *Nash* conjectures

it (subject of course to the interior restriction). Under the assumed circumstances, $g_1 = g^*$ is the best response to $g_2 = g^*$ (and vice versa), and it would continue to be so even if g_2 were to change. But that is what the consistency of *Nash* conjectures is all about.[40]

A little reflection will show moreover that in this case it might be possible to have a rather wide variety of social equilibria, involving alternative specifications for the values of the individual beliefs, i.e. the b_i's. But these would be social equilibria with inconsistent conjectures. The only *CCE* for the case under consideration will involve *Nash* conjectures. (Figure 9.9 shows one such equilibrium.) In other words, Marshall's assumptions for the validity of his law of demand are, *mutatis mutandis*, sufficient to guarantee that a *CCE* will be supported by *Nash* conjectures and *Nash* conjectures alone!

How *reasonable* would it be, however, to expect *Nash* conjectures? Hicks' interpretation of the analytical significance of Marshall's assumption[41] (of a constant marginal utility of money) was that it enabled him to ignore income effects and hence the possibility of the Giffen paradox. In the Hicksian framework, moreover, this amounted to assuming that the expenditure on the nonmoney good constituted a small fraction of the total budget. Extending the argument to the present context then, a constant marginal utility of the public good must imply that *private* goods constitute a relatively small part of an individual's budget as compared to *public* goods. Under *normal* circumstances, this is unlikely to be the case. But it could well be possible in *ab*normal situations. To a community either struck or threatened by a disaster, e.g., an earthquake, a flood, or an external aggression, the rebuilding or defence of public facilities may assume greater importance than the satisfaction of immediate private needs. Although fictional, the villagers' behaviour in Akira Kurosawa's immortal film *The Seven Samurai* could well be a case in point. They gave up their meagre ration of food (a pure private good)

---

[40] It is to be noted in passing that the arguments apply with equal force to the *n* person case.

[41] Hicks, J.R. (1946) *Value and Capital*, Oxford, UK: Clarendon Press, p. 32.

in order to purchase the services of the Samurai warriors (a pure public good) employed to guard their village against a marauder![42]

CONCLUSION

This completes my tale of the Bad Samaritans. As might be expected, there are parallel tales of the Good ones, as well as the ones who lie in between. I was concerned above with the Bads alone, because the analytical structure of their story provided a short cut to my heady days at Presidency College. But the Good and the Not So Good are as important as the Bad. Indeed, they might even be the *only* ones who matter for the perpetuation of human society.[43]

[42] Some might argue of course that this is really a case of intertemporal substitution, the villagers substituting present consumption to buy inputs (defence in this case) necessary to extend the boundary of their future production possibility frontier.

[43] See Sugden, Robert (1982) 'On the Economics of Philanthropy', *Economic Journal*, 92, pp. 341–50 and Sugden, Robert (1984) 'Reciprocity: The Supply of Public Goods through Voluntary Contributions', *Economic Journal*, 93, pp. 772–87 for the first category. Examples of the second type, the *pompous* contributors, is to be found in Andreoni, James (1989) 'Giving with Impure Altruism: Applications to Charity and Ricardian Equivalence', *Journal of Political Economy*, 97, pp. 1447–58 and Andreoni, James (1990) 'Impure Altruism and Donations to Public Goods: A Theory of Warm Glow Giving', *Economic Journal*, 100, pp. 464–77.

10

The Economics of Enforcement

*Dilip Mookherjee**

1 INTRODUCTION

Welfare economics is concerned primarily with economic policy, particularly its normative connotations. Following important contributions of Bentham. Mill and other utilitarians in the 19th century, and later of Pigou and Marshall, this field became especially active since the 1930s following the work of Robbins, Bergson, Samuelson, Hicks, Kaldor, Scitovsky and Arrow. Professor Tapas Majumdar was an important figure in that early stage of development, whose work helped to clarify notions of social choice and preference. Later developments in the subject bear a large debt to this early literature, which succeeded in clarifying these notions sufficiently to allow issues of concern to shift considerably in recent years. In particular, attention has moved from questions of *aggregation* of individual preferences towards *implementation* of socially desired choices.

The literature on implementation, following closely on the pioneering work of Hurwicz (1972), Gibbard (1973) and Groves (1973), usually postulates the existence of informational asymmetries between economic planners and economic agents. Agents are presumed to be better informed than planners about important

* My interest and understanding of the topic of this paper owes much to numerous conversations and joint research with Ivan Png. I thank Nahum Melumad, Mitch Polinsky and Ivan Png for detailed comments on an earlier draft, and Yoji Yasukawa for able research assistance.

parameters concerning tastes, technology and endowments. This is usually referred to as the problem of adverse selection or hidden information. In addition, certain aspects of the behaviour of agents may be difficult to observe by the planner, such as effort levels or conformity with prescribed laws; this is usually referred to as the problem of moral hazard or hidden action.

These informational asymmetries generate important constraints on the formulation of economic policies. To give an example, if abilities and efforts of individual agents could be perfectly and costlessly observed by a planner, completely progressive income taxes could simultaneously achieve the twin objectives of efficiency and equality.[1] The presence of perfect information at the disposal of the planner would enable such 'first-best' outcomes to be achieved via 'command and control'. Specifically, given knowledge of an individual's ability, a planner can compute the efficient effort level to be assigned to this individual; the absence of moral hazard subsequently ensures that compliance with decreed effort levels can be costlessly monitored. In the absence of such perfect information conditions, feasible policies must respect 'incentive compatibility' constraints that prevent attainment of first-best outcomes. Attempts to elicit information about abilities would be self-defeating as individuals would seek to hide their true abilities. Moreover, taxes that are excessively progressive would cause individuals to withdraw efforts. These information constraints thus lie at the heart of efficiency-equality tradeoffs underlying choice of tax policies.[2] In general, policy choices are required to incorporate implementation constraints.

Most of the literature on implementation, however, specifies an exogenously given structure of imperfect information within which policy choices are to be conducted: the government either knows or does not know something. In other words, the information available to planners are not conscious objects of choice. This is a convenient simplifying assumption, no doubt. But one can hardly dispute that in reality information is costly to acquire, and

---

[1] See Mirrlees (1971, 1974) for elaboration.

[2] For further discussion, see Mirrlees (1971) and Hammond (1979, 1987).

that an important part of policy-implementation concerns strategic acquisition of information on which policies may be based. It is this aspect of implementation that is the main concern of this paper, and referred to as *enforcement*.

For example, an important consideration in income tax policy is that individuals have better information about their incomes than the government. Such policies are enforced via a procedure whereby individuals are asked to report their own incomes: the government selectively audits the returns of some individuals, and levies penalties on those detected to have underreported. The design of enforcement policies has to incorporate the way that taxpayers are likely to respond strategically to these policies. The information available to the government regarding the income of any given individual thus has to be *endogenously* determined. In particular, one needs both normative and descriptive theories of optimal enforcement policies, comprising audit probabilities and penalties for detected evaders. In addition, enforcement costs should figure as a prominent consideration in the determination of optimal tax rates, if the latter are to be enforced successfully.

In a similar vein, consider the enforcement of regulations concerning externality causing activities. Examples include laws concerning traffic movements, emissions of pollutants, installation of anti-pollutant devices, safety and quality standards, collusive behaviour, payment of minimum wages, hoarding, gambling, black market activity, fraud or theft. Strategic enforcement of these regulations requires the government to decide the quantity of resources to be allocated in monitoring the behaviour of potential offenders, in the prosecution of guilty parties, and what kinds of penalties ought to be inflicted upon them. Again, the chief issue of interest concerns costly acquisition of information by law enforcers, and the manner in which such information is utilized. The difference from the income tax evasion context arises only in so far as the information acquired by enforcement agencies concerns the *behaviour* of individuals (i.e. whether or not they committed an offense), rather than some *attribute* such as wealth or income concerning which they have private information.

The purpose of this paper is to provide some perspective on recent developments in the literature on enforcement. No attempt is made to provide an exhaustive survey; many important contributions will probably receive insufficient attention. This paper may be viewed rather as a sample of issues that have received recent attention and selected by the author on a subjective basis. Moreover, there is no emphasis on technicalities or generalized results; on the contrary, the simplest conceivable examples are employed to illustrate the main ideas.

One overall caveat: there is no consideration of the likelihood of collusion between potential offenders and enforcement authorities. Models of strategic interaction between them are typically of the one-shot non-cooperative variety. An important research need for the future is to analyse possibilities for corruption in the process of enforcement, and policy alternatives for dealing with such problems.[3]

Section 2 of the paper deals with the enforcement of income taxes, comprising both normative and descriptive issues. Drawing upon developments in the literature on the game theory and principal agent models, this literature focusses on the strategic interaction between taxpayers and revenue authorities. The models allow one to derive the implications of alternative assumptions regarding the objectives of the government or the enforcement agency, and the ability of the latter to commit to enforcement policies. We devote specific attention to the implications of these models for the effectiveness of alternative policies to control tax evasion.

Two different classes of tax evasion models are described. The first comprises normative models (in the principal-agent tradition) deriving optimal enforcement policies for a social welfare or revenue maximizing government that can commit to its audit policies. The assumption about commitment ability amounts to

---

[3] Following the early work of Becker and Stigler (1974), and Rose Ackerman (1978), a number of recent papers have appeared on this topic, such as Besley and Mclaren (1989), Chander and Wilde (1991), Chu (1987), Goswami, Gang and Sanyal (1991), Gangopadhyay, Goswami and Sanyal (1991), Lui (1986), Mookherjee and Png (1991), and Virmani (1987). These papers are not reviewed here.

assuming that the government is a Stackelberg leader, i.e., it announces an enforcement policy, to which taxpayers respond strategically. Policies are thus designed to deter tax evasion efficiently. These models permit assessment of efficient audit policies, as well as the enforcement costs associated with alternative income tax policies. By abstracting from a number of possible institutional constraints on policy design, it is argued that this approach provides a useful normative benchmark for appraising alternative institutional frameworks for the design of enforcement policies.

The other class of models are more descriptive in spirit: they usually postulate a given institutional setting for the formulation and implementation of enforcement policies. For instance, enforcement may be delegated to revenue authorities whose objectives may be narrower than the government's own objective (e.g., maximization of net revenue rather than social welfare). Further, the authorities may be unable to commit to their enforcement policies, i.e., audit policies may be chosen simultaneously with (or subsequent to) the filing of income reports by tax payers. Using a simple example, we contrast the outcomes of these two alternative formulations of optimal enforcement policy, and discuss the implications of alternative policies (such as altering tax rates, penalties or the structure of incentives of enforcement authorities) on the extent of tax evasion. In particular, the analysis throws light on the revenue and welfare implications of alternative institutional frameworks for policy design, varying for instance in terms of the degree of delegation of authority over policies to bureaucrats, and associated budgetary and incentive schemes. The section concludes with a discussion of factors apart from reported incomes that may affect audit decisions, and some recent empirical analyses of tax evasion.

The tax evasion models described in Section 2 do not satisfactorily discuss the design of penalties for convicted offenders. In particular, they yield the result that increased penalties unambiguously enhance revenues and welfare. This implies that optimal penalties should be maximal, no matter how mild the offence. Such drastic penalties run counter to common intuition, as well as the ethical precept of letting 'the punishment fit the crime'.

Section 3 discusses this matter in more detail. The optimality of maximal evasion penalties happens to be a special version of a more general result originally discussed by Becker (1968), and referred to as the 'Becker conundrum'. Section 3 discusses alternative resolutions of this conundrum, some of which have appeared in the law and economics literature dealing with the design of legal rules. The role of factors such as risk aversion of offenders, Type I and II errors in detection of offenders, multiple offense levels and heterogeneity of the population of potential offenders, on the level of optimal penalties are discussed here.

2 INCOME TAX EVASION

Following Gary Becker's pioneering application of economic analysis to crime and punishment, Allingham and Sandmo (1972) modelled the tax evasion decision for an individual as a problem of portfolio choice under uncertainty. This permitted an assessment of the 'partial equilibrium' effect of altering the probability of auditing, or fines for evasion. The Allingham–Sandmo paper formed the basis of a large body of empirical analysis and policy discussions of tax evasion in the 70's and early 80's. The more recent literature is distinguished by a study of the strategic interaction between revenue collection authorities and individual taxpayers. Instead of viewing enforcement policies as exogenous parameters, this literature studies the endogenous choice of these policies by government officials.

This recent literature, however, falls into either of two broad categories. The first utilizes a principal agent framework, where the government moves first in announcing an enforcement policy, and taxpayers condition their reporting decisions on the announced policy. By assuming that the enforcers have relatively few constraints on their ability to coordinate different aspects of enforcement policy, and also commit to these in the long term, possible institutional constraints on enforcement policy are ignored. The results of these models are thus appropriately viewed as a normative benchmark, isolating the implications of the presence of enforcement costs and associated incentive compatibility constraints (from additional institutional constraints on policy making). Papers in this tradition include Townsend (1979, 1988), Reingamum–Wilde (1985), Border–Sobel (1987), Roemer and Ortuno–Ortin (1988) and Mookherjee–Png (1989a, 1990).

The other class of papers attempts a more descriptive analysis by incorporating institutional details such as the fact that income tax audit policy is usually delegated to a revenue authority (hereafter referred to as the Internal Revenue Service (IRS)), while tax policies or penalties for offenders are chosen by other branches of the government. Not only is there a possible lack of coordination in the design of these different aspects of enforcement policy, there is also a divergence of objectives between the different government branches. For instance, the formulation and implementation of audit policies are usually delegated to bureaucrats in charge of tax enforcement, whose objective is to maximize revenues collected (either gross or net of audit costs). On the other hand, tax policy is formulated by legislatures more concerned with broader notions of social welfare, which include the efficiency effects and incidence of tax policies. Another important distinction from the first category of models is that revenue enforcement officials are presumed unable to commit to their audit policies, i.e., instead of acting as a Stackelberg leader, the government chooses its audit rule simultaneously or subsequent to the filing of reports by taxpayers.

The two classes of models, however, share a number of common features. Both consider large populations of taxpayers distinguished by a unidimensional income measure. The distribution of income is publicly known and exogenously given. Enforcement authorities, however, do not know who has what income, while individual taxpayers know their own incomes. It is costless for taxpayers to send a report to the authorities concerning their incomes, but it is costly for the authorities to audit a given report.

An audit reveals an individual's true income without error. Those detected misreporting are automatically convicted and assessed a pecuniary penalty (limited by their true incomes) according to a preassigned rule. The interaction between taxpayers and the authorities is of a one-shot nature, not repeated over time. These assumptions are unrealistic, but they do help focus attention on some key strategic issues. Later in this section, we will discuss some literature dealing with the implications of modifying these assumptions.

Within this setting, different models can be distinguished according to the following broad features:

(a) *The degree of coordination between tax policy, audit policy and legal penalties for evasion*: The 'normative' models tend to assume that a welfare maximizing government simultaneously chooses all three policies freely.[4] The 'descriptive' models assume that the IRS chooses an audit policy in a setting where they take as given both tax policy and penalties for convicted tax offenders.

(b) *The identity and objectives of enforcement authorities*: Some of the normative models assume that the enforcement authority is a unitary government seeking to maximize a measure of social welfare that incorporates efficiency and equity objectives.[5] The descriptive models typically assume that the IRS is delegated authority over income tax audits, and is concerned to maximize total revenues collected, net of audit costs.[6] This presumes a given relationship between the legislative or executive body (that formulates tax policy) and its enforcement agency, i.e. a specific pattern of delegation, combined with an incentive scheme for IRS managers that induces net revenue maximization.

[4] However, some versions do incorporate some constraints on coordination, by assuming a given structure of penalties, or 'fairness-like' constraints.

[5] In contrast, Reingamum–Wilde (1985) and Border–Sobel (1987) are examples of principal-agent models where the objective of the principal is assumed to be maximization of net revenues collected.

[6] Reingamum–Wilde (1984) examine a variant of this where the IRS is restricted by a given budget. This is discussed in more detail later in this section.

(c) *The degree of commitment to audit policies*: Principal-agent formulations of the tax audit process are distinguished by the assumption that the principal can commit to audit policies. The descriptive models, however, employ an 'equilibrium' approach, i.e., embodying the assumption that the IRS cannot commit to a stated audit policy.[7] This feature has an important influence on the outcome of strategic interaction between auditors and taxpayers. For instance, in a full commitment setting, the purpose of auditing is to deter all forms of tax evasion. A policy that does succeed in deterring evasion is *ex post* wasteful — i.e. if it is common knowledge that all taxpayers report truthfully, then audits do not reveal any useful information, and at the same time involve deadweight costs. So an authority lacking the ability to commit will be tempted to deviate from the stated audit policy, in the interests of reducing its *ex post* audit costs. Anticipating such deviations, taxpayers will significantly evade. Equilibria in 'no-commitment' contexts will consequently be characterized by mixed strategies, both on the part of taxpayers and the revenue authorities — i.e. a fraction of taxpayers will evade, and the IRS will audit a certain fraction of all reports. In contrast, most principal-agent models are characterized by an audit policy that completely deters all forms of evasion. This represents a rather fundamental feature of a wide range of enforcement problems: if monitoring and apprehension intensities are sufficiently severe to deter most crime, no criminals are actually apprehended and there is an *ex post* temptation to reduce the enforcement budget by scaling back these activities.

These are three important features of models of the enforcement process. Mixing and matching alternative specifications of these yield qualitatively distinct conclusions, as we shall attempt to describe below. Indeed, perhaps the most important contribution of

---

[7] Melumad and Mookherjee (1989) study intermediate degrees of commitment, e.g. where the enforcement authority can commit only to aggregate dimensions of audit policy, and a hierarchical model in which the government can commit to an incentive scheme for IRS managers, who in turn, cannot commit to their audit policies with respect to the taxpayer population.

the recent literature on enforcement of tax compliance is to high-
light the importance of the institutional setting of the enforcement
processes, as embodied by these three features.

2.1 A Normative, Principal-Agent Formulation

We start by illustrating a model of a welfare maximizing government designing a coordinated tax-cum-enforcement policy in the
absence of any constraints on its commitment abilities. We follow
the analysis of Mookherjee–Png (1989a, 1990) and Melumad–
Mookherjee (1989); towards the end of this subsection we shall
explain the relation to other principal-agent formulations.

There are a finite number of possible levels of income
$Y_1, \ldots Y_n$, with $0 < Y_i < Y_{i+1}$ for all i. The distribution of income
is exogenously given : $\lambda_i > 0$ is the proportion of the population
with true income Y_i, where $\Sigma_i \lambda_i = 1$. Each individual is small with
respect to the population in the sense that his exclusion does
not affect the proportions λ_i. This model can be extended to
include incentive effects on labour supply and thereby on income
distribution (e.g. see Mookherjee–Png (1989a)).

Every taxpayer shares a common von Neumann–Morgenstern
utility function $u(C)$ defined over his consumption, C, equal to
income less taxes and penalties paid. This function is strictly
increasing, and concave; it is defined over the range $(\underline{C}, \infty)$ where
$\underline{C}$ is a minimum subsistence level of consumption. We assume
that $u(\underline{C})$ is finite, and correspondingly normalize $u(\underline{C})$ to 0.[8] In
addition to the consumption of the private good, individuals obtain
benefits from a public good provided by the government. The
amount of public good generated is a function of net revenues
collected, R. Preferences over the private and the public good are
assumed to be additively separable of the form $u(C) + V(R)$, where
V is a strictly increasing function.

---

[8] If $u(\underline{C})$ approaches $-\infty$, then the enforcement problem tends to disappear:
the threat of auditing with arbitrarily low probability, and punishing evaders by
pushing them to subsistence consumption, is sufficient to deter all evasion.
Consequently, any tax policy can be enforced at infinitesimally small costs.

The distribution of income $\lambda_1, \ldots, \lambda_n$ is known to the government, but not the true income of any specific taxpayer. However, the government can decide to audit the taxpayer's income; this costs the government an amount $A_i > 0$ (which may thereby depend on the true income Y_i of the audited individual).[9] An audit identifies the individual's true income without error, not only from the point of view of the auditor, but also for third parties such as courts that administer penalties for evaders. Correspondingly, an evader is automatically convicted following an audit.[10]

It is costless for taxpayers to report their incomes to the government: consequently it makes sense for the government to condition their audit decisions on reported incomes. Let the tax policy be denoted by T_i, where an individual of income Y_i owes tax T_i. The enforcement policy tools are audit probabilities (p_i for an individual reporting income Y_i) and penalties following audits (F_{ij} for an individual reported Y_j and detected to have true income Y_i). The government seeks to maximize a utilitarian social welfare function; the concavity of u implies that it is sensitive to the distribution of consumption, as well as the average level of consumption.[11] The government also seeks to balance the provision of public goods vis-à-vis private goods in conformity with taxpayer preferences. Finally, the government may be be bound by some ethical constraints such as horizontal equity (equal treatment of individuals with identical true incomes) or letting the 'punishment fit the crime' (where penalties for evasion depend on the extent of taxes evaded). In what follows, we shall ignore these constraints.[12]

[9] For simplicity, we assume that audits impose no costs on the individual. See Mookherjee–Png (1989a) for the case where the taxpayer also incurs costs in the process of being audited.

[10] Prosecution costs are therefore assumed to be absent.

[11] The extension to the case where the government exhibits greater inequality aversion is also straightforward, irrespective of whether the aversion is to inequality in *ex ante* or ex post welfare levels.

[12] The interested reader may consult Roemer and Ortuno–Ortin (1988) and Mookherjee–Png (1990) for analyses of optimal policies under these constraints.

A key analytical step in principal-agent models of this kind is the Revelation Principle, which states that there is no loss of generality in confining attention to policies that induce truthful reporting by every taxpayer. The argument is, however, somewhat more complicated than usual, and runs as follows. Corresponding to any policy which induces untruthful reports from some taxpayers, the risk aversion of taxpayers implies the existence of a Pareto dominating policy which induces truthful reporting from all taxpayers. The new policy is constructed in the following manner. Note that untruthful reports cause a divergence between 'nominal' tax liabilities and their 'effective' levels, i.e., the amounts owed and actually paid respectively. In addition, they cause these individuals to bear risk, according to whether or not they will be audited and subsequently be penalized. It is then possible to reform tax policy, by altering the nominal tax levels to a level equal to the *average* amount actually paid under the previous policy, where the average is taken over taxpayers of the given class that are respectively audited and not audited. Nominal tax liabilities increase, relative to previous nominal liabilities; but they are equal to the effective level paid previously (on average, i.e. including penalties paid by the fraction audited). With corresponding adjustments in audit probabilities and penalties from their 'nominal' to their 'effective' levels, individuals are induced to report truthfully, and in this new equilibrium they avoid the risk associated with the audit process.[13] Finally, the construction ensures that exactly the same net revenues are collected by the government.

Given the Revelation Principle, the principal-agent problem reduces to the following nonlinear optimization exercise:

$$maximize_{p_i, T_i, F_{ij}} \sum_i \lambda_i \{p_i u(Y_i - T_i - F_{ii})$$
$$+ (1 - p_i) u (Y_i - T_i)\} + V(R) \tag{1}$$

[13] Roemer and Ortuno–Ortin (1988) show that with more than a single consumption good, this argument requires additional, restrictive assumptions on preferences. Also, if taxpayers incur costs while being audited, they continue to bear risk associated with the government's audit decision. But this risk is substantially lessened with the new policy.

subject to: $p_i u(Y_i - T_i - F_{ij}) + (1 - p_i) u (Y_i - T_i)$

$$\geq p_j u(Y_i - T_j - F_{ij}) + (1 - p_j) u (Y_i - T_j)$$

for all $j \neq i$ such that

$$Y_i - T_j - F_{ij} \geq \underline{C}, \; Y_i - T_j \geq \underline{C} \tag{2}$$

$$R = \sum_i \lambda_i [T_i - p_i (A_i - F_{ii})] \tag{3}$$

and

$$Y_i - T_i - F_{ij} \geq \underline{C}, \; Y_i - T_i \geq \underline{C}, \; 1 \geq p_i \geq 0, \tag{4}$$

in addition to constraints on T_i, F_{ij} imposed by notions of fairness. Constraint (2) is the incentive compatibility constraint, requiring that truth-telling be an optimal response of every taxpayer to the enforcement policy of the government.

The first set of questions in this context relates to the character of optimal audit strategies for the government. Should auditing be random, i.e., p_i lie between 0 and 1? How should they vary with reported income? Reinganum–Wilde (1985) criticized Sandmo (1981) for confining attention to audit strategies that were independent of reported income, i.e. $p_i = p$ for all i. They demonstrated that 'lower-tail' policies, those involving $p_i = 1$ for all Y_i less than some cut-off level Y^* and $p_i = 0$ above Y^*, may dominate a constant audit probability strategy in some settings. Townsend (1979) in the meantime had shown that lower-tail policies were optimal within the class of all nonrandomized audit strategies (where $p_i = 0$ or 1 for all i).[14]

The optimal audit strategy can be characterized rather sharply, in terms of the optimal tax and penalty policy. For the sake of illustration, consider the case where $F_{ii} = 0$, i.e. a taxpayer verified to have reported truthfully in an audit is not required to pay or receive any additional amount over and above taxes already

---

[14] However in the context of an example, he demonstrated that a randomized audit policy may dominate such lower-tail policies.

paid: this may be imposed as a fairness (horizontal equity) constraint.[15] Given the optimal tax-penalty policy $\{T_i, F_{ij}\}$, the optimal audit policy must maximize $[\sum_i \lambda_i u \, (Y_i - T_i) + V(R)]$, i.e., minimize aggregate audit costs $\sum_i \lambda_i \, p_i \, A_i$, subject to feasibility constraints (4), in addition to the incentive constraint (2), which takes the form $u(Y_i - T_i) \geq p_j u \, (Y_i - T_j - F_{ij}) + (1 - p_j) \, u \, (Y_i - T_j)$. From this it follows that the optimal audit probabilities are given by

$$p_j = Max_{\substack{i \neq j \\ F_{ij} \neq 0}} \left\{ \frac{u \, (Y_i - T_j) - u \, (Y_i - T_i)}{u \, (Y_i - T_j) - u \, (Y_i - T_j - F_{ij})}, \, 0 \right\} \tag{5}$$

Since all taxpayers report truthfully, and auditors do not commit errors, the penalties F_{ij} (for $i \neq j$) are never actually applied (the government only threatens to apply them). Since an increase in these penalties enhances the incentive of taxpayers to report truthfully, it enables a reduction in audit frequencies without violating the incentive constraints. So it is optimal to set penalties at their maximal levels: $F_{ij} = Y_i - T_j - \underline{C}$ for $i \neq j$. Ethical notions of 'letting the punishment fit the crime' may, however, prevent the establishment of such draconian penalties for those who evade by small amounts. Nevertheless, most ethical norms would be consistent with the application of *some* penalty for evasion, i.e., $Y_i - T_j - F_{ij} < Y_i - T_i$. As long as penalties satisfy this minimal condition, inspection of equation (5) leads to the conclusion that *optimal audit policies must be random, i.e. $p_i < 1$ for all i*. This implies in particular that lower-tail policies are never optimal.

Condition (5) also yields other qualitative properties of optimal audit policies. If income Y_j is associated with the highest tax ($T_j = \max_i T_i$), then $p_j = 0$. On the other hand, if Y_k is not associated with the highest tax ($T_k < \max_i T_i$), then $1 > p_k > 0$. So constant audit probability strategies are also never optimal.

How do the random audit probabilities vary with reported income? If there are no constraints on penalties, so $Y_i - T_j - F_{ij} = \underline{C}$ for $i \neq j$; then it is clear that *audit probabilities are decreasing in reported income, as long as taxes are increasing in income*. Higher

---

[15] The optimality of $F_{ii} = 0$ is discussed below.

income taxpayers should thus be audited less frequently. This may appear counterintuitive; however, our result applies to taxpayers who are otherwise indistinguishable by occupation, source of income, domicile, etc. The normal idea of auditing high income taxpayers more intensively usually refers to the relative treatment of two distinguishable populations of taxpayers. A more intuitive way of describing this result is that individuals within a certain category of taxpayers (identified by given observable attributes) should be audited more intensively if they opt for more deductions when filing taxes.

It may be noted that this result need not hold with limited penalties for tax evasion. Suppose that penalties are assessed as a fixed fraction of the tax evaded, as is the practice in many countries. Then taxpayers may be more tempted to evade taxes by an intermediate amount, than to evade by large amounts, since the penalty subsequent to detection is lower in the former case. In such instances the government should audit intermediate incomes more intensively than low income reports.[16]

Border and Sobel (1987) formulate a principal agent analysis of optimal auditing which differs from the preceding model in two respects: the objective of the government is to maximize net revenues collected, subject to constraints (2) and (4); and taxpayers are risk neutral. In this context, they are able to obtain a sharp characterization of optimal enforcement policies. In particular, (while optimal evasion penalties are maximal), optimal audit probabilities are always monotone decreasing in reported income levels, and optimal taxes are correspondingly monotone increasing.

Returning to the context of a welfare maximizing government, we now turn to other questions that can be answered within the principal agent framework. In the preceding discussion, we assumed that $F_{ii} = 0$, i.e. no additional transfers follow verification of truthful reporting in an audit. In Mookherjee–Png (1989a) it is

---

[16] Examples of this emerge in the numerical computations of optimal enforcement policies for parameter values representative of the U.S. economy: see Mookherjee and Png (1990).

shown that this is *never* optimal: it is always desirable to set $F_{ii} < 0$, i.e., reward taxpayers when they are verified by an audit to have reported truthfully. This implies that taxpayers reporting truthfully should strictly prefer to be audited! The result holds irrespective of the degree of risk-aversion, or other parameters.[17] It is based on a Standard Envelope Theorem argument: starting from $F_{ii} = 0$, a small reduction in F_{ii} coupled with an increase in T_i has a second-order effect on risk and utility (from consuming the private good) of those with income Y_i. But it allows a first-order reduction in p_i, and thereby of audit costs, allowing more public goods to be provided. This is a rather striking and counterintuitive recommendation, one which has probably never been followed in practice.

Finally, what can be said about the optimal tax levels T_i, when enforcement costs are incorporated? In the absence of enforcement costs ($A_i = 0$) a utilitarian government would impose completely progressive taxes, with 100 per cent marginal rates (since the current model abstracts from labour supply considerations). It is possible to show that with costly auditing such policies are always dominated by schemes that are less than fully progressive. Lowered progressivity has second-order effects on consumption inequality and thereby on welfare valuation of private consumption; but allows first-order reduction in enforcement costs. Apart from this, little more can be said. In fact, not much is known about conditions under which the optimal taxes are increasing in reported income.[18] However, the model permits numerical computations of optimal progressivity of income taxes in the presence of enforcement costs: Mookherjee–Png (1990) carry out

---

[17] It also holds if the taxpayer bears some of the costs of audits: in that case he should be reimbursed a sum (following truthful verification) which over-compensates him for costs incurred.

[18] Mookherjee–Png (1990) show that optimal taxes are increasing in income if there is a horizontal equity constraint requiring $F_{ii} = 0$, and the distribution of income is uniform. However, see Dye (1986) and Wagenhofer (1987) for models involving investigation of endogenous effort levels where optimal payments are monotone increasing.

such calculations for parameter values representative of the U.S. economy in 1986.

A notable shortcoming of the entire class of principal-agent models is that they impose very little institutional structure on the tax enforcement process, while postulating unrealistically high degrees of coordination between the formulation of tax policy and its implementation. In practice, enforcement is delegated to a revenue authority whose objectives may not be to maximize social welfare, and who may be unable to publicly commit to detailed aspects of its audit policies.[19] Besides, they are of limited use in answering policy questions like 'how do we efficiently reduce the presently high levels of tax evasion?' As we have seen, there is no evasion in the principal-agent solution, by virtue of the Revelation Principle; the model is thus not very useful in comparing regimes associated with differing amounts of evasion. Its usefulness lies rather in defining the highest welfare achievable in the presence of institutional constraints on the formulation and implementation of policies. As the following discussion illustrates, this benchmark is useful in comparing the outcomes of different specific institutional frameworks.

2.2 A 'Realistic' Equilibrium Formulation of Auditing

The discussion of this section draws heavily upon the work of Graetz, Reinganum and Wilde (1984, 1986). The model postulates that audit policy is delegated to the IRS, which chooses its policy to maximize net revenue collected. The IRS takes the existing tax policy, as well as the structure of legal penalties for tax evasion, as given. Further, it lacks the ability to commit to a stated audit policy. The IRS chooses the proportion of taxpayer reports in any given category (classified by reported income level) to audit: its objective is to maximize revenues (net of audit costs) in the short run. The outcome of strategic interaction between taxpayers and

---

[19] However, Melumad and Mookherjee (1989) argue that the principal-agent solution can be implemented with a simple, aggregative incentive scheme for the revenue authority; this is discussed further below.

the IRS is modelled as the noncooperative equilibrium of the simultaneous move (one-shot) game played between them. Nevertheless, the model is useful for generating predictions about the revenue and welfare effects of varying tax rates and evasion penalties. In many respects, the 'endogenization' of the behaviour of the IRS turns out to result in comparative static effects considerably distinct from those of the Allingham–Sandmo (1972) model.

The simplest exposition of this model supposes that there are two income levels in the population, denoted Y_L and Y_H, where $Y_H > Y_L > 0$. An exogenous proportion of taxpayers have the high income Y_H. Further, a certain fraction $(1 - \rho)$ of the high income group are either 'pathologically' honest, or lack the ability to lie about their true incomes (e.g., because of the nature of their occupation).[20] The remaining fraction ρ can potentially underreport their incomes: they will behave strategically in order to maximize their expected utility levels.

The nominal tax liabilities associated with the two income levels are given: T_L and T_H, where $T_H > T_L$, and $T_i < Y_i$ for both i. There is a given fine $F > 0$ imposed on any high income taxpayer discovered to have reported income Y_L. The minimum consumption level is normalized to 0, and F satisfies $T_L + F \le Y_L$, $T_H + F \le Y_H$. It costs the IRS an amount $A > 0$ to audit any given taxpayer, and it is assumed that the net revenue gain to the IRS of auditing a high income taxpayer who is underreporting, is positive:

$$T_H + F - T_L > A. \tag{6}$$

It is clear that the IRS has no incentive to audit any individual who declares a high income. Conversely, since no penalties can be imposed on an individual whose true income is low, such an individual will always report truthfully. What remains to be determined is α, the fraction of 'strategic' high income taxpayers that

---

[20] The theory could be further simplified by assuming that $\rho = 1$. However, the purpose of complicating the model in this manner is to show that it does not matter (in terms of affecting the qualitative results). In other words, the validity of the analysis is not vitiated by the presence of a fraction of taxpayers who never conceal their incomes, no matter how large the temptation.

report a low income, and p, the fraction of low income reports audited by the IRS.

The expected utility of a high income taxpayer who reports Y_L with probability α, is

$$(1 - \alpha)\, u\,(Y_H - T_H) + \alpha\,[pu\,(Y_H - T_H - F) + (1 - p)\,(Y_H - T_L)]\quad (7)$$

whereas the IRS net revenue conditional on receiving a low income report is

$$\mu(\alpha)\,[p(T_H + F - A) + (1 - p)\,T_L] + [1 - \mu(\alpha)]\,[p(T_L - A) \\ + (1 - p)\,T_L]\qquad (8)$$

where $\mu(\alpha) \equiv \rho q \alpha / (\rho q \alpha + 1 - q)$ denotes the probability assessed by the IRS that a taxpayer is of high income, following receipt of a low-income report. The outcome of the game is defined by a *Nash* equilibrium $\{\alpha^*, p^*\}$ where α^* maximizes (7) given p^*, and conversely p^* maximizes (8) given α^*.

This model has the virtue that it generates a simple measure of the extent of tax evasion, namely $q\rho\alpha^*$, the proportion of the population evading taxes, or $q\rho\alpha^*\,(T_H - T_L)$, the amount of taxes evaded. Moreover, it is characterized by a unique *Nash* equilibrium, as described by the following result.

Proposition 1: There is a unique *Nash* equilibrium in the game between taxpayers and the IRS:

(i)   If $\mu(1)\,(T_H + F - T_L) \leq A$, the equilibrium is $\alpha^* = 1, p^* = 0$.

(ii)   If

$$\mu(1)\,(T_H + F - T_L) > A,\qquad (9)$$

the equilibrium is

$$\alpha^* = \frac{A(1 - q)}{\rho q\,(T_H + F - T_L - A)},\; p^* = \frac{u\,(Y_H - T_L) - u\,(Y_H - T_H)}{u\,(Y_H - T_L) - u\,(Y_H - T_H - F)}\quad (10)$$

Note that there can never be a truthful equilibrium — unlike the outcome of the principal agent setting. If all strategic high income taxpayers report truthfully ($\alpha = 0$), then it does not pay the IRS to audit at all, i.e. $p = 0$. But if there is no auditing, strategic high income individuals will underreport. Consequently, the equilibrium must involve some lying. If equation (9) is not satisfied, it does not pay the IRS to audit, even if all (strategic) high income individuals lie; hence the resulting equilibrium is $\alpha^* = 1, p^* = 0$. However, if (9) is satisfied, then this cannot be an equilibrium. The only equilibrium then involves randomized strategies for both the IRS and the high income taxpayers. The equilibrium (10) is computed by applying the requirement that both parties must be indifferent between their respective pure strategies (i.e. lying and not lying for the taxpayers; audit and not audit for the IRS).

The level of social welfare at this equilibrium may now be compared with the welfare level at the principal-agent solution, i.e., where audits are decided by a welfare-maximizing government with the ability to commit to its audit policy. Note first that the equilibrium audit policy, p^*, is precisely equal to the commitment solution (5).[21] Furthermore, the *ex ante* utilities from consumption of the private good are also equal: low income taxpayers get $u(Y_L - T_L)$, while high income taxpayers are indifferent between lying and not lying, and therefore get $u(Y_H - T_H)$. However, there is greater ex post inequality in the no-commitment solution: some of the strategic high income taxpayers that lie are audited and subsequently fined, while others escape with a low tax payment. Moreover, the two outcomes differ in the level of net revenues realized.

Proposition 2: The net revenue collected and therefore the welfare level in the principal-agent solution is higher than in the no-commitment solution.

---

[21] This is because both outcomes involve indifference between underreporting and truthful reporting for high income taxpayers. In the principal agent model, this arises because the principal seeks to minimize the audit cost of enforcing truthful reporting by high income taxpayers, while the other model is characterized by mixed strategy equilibria which must involve such indifference. The reader should note that the result does not generalize when there are more than two possible income levels.

Proof: In the principal-agent solution, the net revenues are $qT_H + (1-q)(T_L - p^*A)$. In the no-commitment solution, they are $q[(1-\rho)T_H + \rho\{(1-\alpha^*)T_H + \alpha^*[p^*(T_H + F - A) + (1-p^*)T_L]\}] + (1-q)(T_L - p^*A)$. It therefore suffices to compare the net revenues collected from the strategic high income individuals: T_H with $p^*(T_H + F - A) + (1-p^*)T_L$. But these individuals are indifferent between lying and not lying, i.e. $u(Y_H - T_H)$ equals $p^*u(Y_H - T_H - F) + (1-p^*)u(Y_H - T_L)$. The concavity of u implies that $T_H \geq p^*(T_H + F) + (1-p^*)T_L$, and the result follows from the fact that $A > 0$.

Q.E.D.

Somewhat paradoxically, therefore, *the IRS's pursuit of a short-term revenue objective leads to a loss in revenues collected!* It is perhaps worthwhile to find out whether this stems from the inability of the IRS to commit to its audit policy, or from the nature of its objective. This question requires us to consider the outcome of net revenue maximization by an IRS that can commit to its audit policy. This is given by the solution to the following problem.

$$\max_{0 \leq p \leq 1} q[(1-\rho)T_H + \rho\{(1-\alpha(p))T_H + \alpha(p)\{p(T_H + F - A) + (1-p)T_L\}\}] + (1-q)(T_L - pA) \tag{11}$$

where $\alpha(p)$ is the optimal response of the (strategic) high-income taxpayers to the audit rule p, given by $\alpha(p) = 1$ for $p \leq p^*$, and 0 otherwise.[22] Clearly, it can never pay the IRS to set p above p^*, as p can be lowered without affecting taxpayers' behaviour, thereby increasing net revenues. Hence, the outcome either coincides with the principal-agent solution: $p = p^*$, $\alpha = 0$, or it involves lying by all (strategic) high-income individuals: $\alpha = 1$ and $p < p^*$. Straightforward computation yields the following result.

---

[22] Strictly speaking, if $p = p^*$, then $\alpha(p)$ is the entire interval $[0, 1]$. In this case it makes sense to set $\alpha(p^*) = 1$ because this gives rise to higher net revenues for the government without affecting high income individuals' expected utility from the private good. It may also be true that individuals prefer to be truthful when there is no strategic advantage from lying.

Proposition 3: If the IRS can commit to its audit policy, and maximizes net revenues, then the outcome coincides with the principal-agent solution if and only if

$$A \leq \max \left[\frac{q\rho(T_H + F - T_L)}{q\rho + (1-q)}, \frac{q\rho(T_H - T_L)}{(1-q)p^*} \right] \qquad (12)$$

If (12) is violated, the outcome is $\alpha = 1, p = 0$.

Although the IRS is postulated to maximize net revenues, this result states that if the IRS can commit to its audit policy, then under a broad range of circumstances it will choose the same audit policy as a planner aiming to maximize social welfare. The result suggests that it is the lack of commitment ability that leads to revenue losses in the Graetz–Reinganum–Wilde model. However, for some range of audit costs, i.e. those violating (12), the consequence of the IRS's revenue objective (in combination with its commitment ability) leads to higher net revenues and greater tax evasion, and thereby a lower level of welfare.

It should be mentioned that the implementability of the second best welfare outcome via delegation of audit policy to a revenue maximizing IRS (with commitment ability), does not extend to the case where there are more than two income levels. Sanchez (1987) and Scotchmer (1987) have shown that if taxpayers are risk-neutral, income levels form a continuum, and tax and penalty rules are linear, then the optimal audit policy of a revenue-maximizing IRS with commitment ability is a cut-off rule of the form: $p = \bar{p}$ if reported income falls below some cut-off level Y^*, and $p = 0$ otherwise. The revenue objective of the IRS causes them to create a 'regressive bias' in auditing, whereby low income individuals are over-audited, while high income individuals are under-audited.

Returning to the no-commitment model of Graetz, Reinganum and Wilde, comparative static effects of varying tax rates, fines or audit costs can be worked out. Such analyses permit assessment of the effectiveness of alternative policies in reducing tax evasion. Consider first the effect on α^*, the equilibrium proportion of (strategic) high-income taxpayers that underreport, as given by (10). The most interesting result concerns increasing the marginal tax rate, as measured by $T_H - T_L$. Clearly, this lowers the amount of tax evasion! This runs contrary to conventional intuition, as well as to the results of the Allingham–Sandmo analysis. The reasoning is as follows. An increase in $T_H - T_L$ does increase the temptation for high income taxpayers to underreport, provided the audit policy is fixed. But with an endogenous behaviour rule for the IRS, the change in the tax rule will lead to a change in the audit policy. An increase in $T_H - T_L$ also increases the additional revenue gain from auditing a high income individual who under-reports — causing the IRS to audit low income reports more intensively. This effect outweighs the former (Allingham–Sandmo partial equilibrium) effect.

The effects of varying the penalty F, or audit costs A, are more conventional. Increasing F lowers α^*, as the IRS is motivated to audit more intensively, while high income taxpayers are less tempted to underreport, given the audit intensity. The two effects work in the same direction: the 'partial equilibrium' effect is intensified in this case. Increasing A increases α^*, as the IRS is less inclined to audit if audit costs increase.

The Graetz–Reinganum–Wilde model can also be used to discuss the impact of alternative policies on a utilitarian measure of welfare. In particular, the model is useful for organizing possible responses to the policy question 'what can be done about the tax evasion problem?', by suggesting welfare improving reforms. We consider a number of possible policy alternatives below.

Redesign the Incentive Structure of Managers of the IRS: Taking as given the inability of the IRS to commit to its audit policy, it may be worthwhile to redesign incentive schemes for IRS managers in an effort to modify their objective of maximizing net revenues. In particular, the models suggest that the performance of the IRS should be evaluated in terms of some measure different from net collections. Realistic performance evaluations will perhaps involve variables that are measured relatively easily, such as aggregate measures of audit performance. The same concern perhaps rules out attempting to measure their performance directly in terms of social welfare or utility levels achieved by taxpayers. Melumad and Mookherjee (1989) have argued that there do exist such 'simple' incentive schemes that implement the principal-agent solution. Specifically, let the government fix a target B^* for aggregate audit costs, equal to the aggregate audit cost in the principal-agent solution. The IRS could be evaluated in terms of (and thereby induced to maximize) gross collections (GC) including taxes and fines, with a small quadratic penalty for deviations of the actual budget from the target B^*. That is, the performance measure would be $GC - \gamma (B - B^*)^2$, where γ is a small positive number. This can be shown to induce a simultaneous move game between the IRS and taxpayers, with an equilibrium achieving the second best welfare level (irrespective of the value of γ). Moreover, any other equilibrium will lie arbitrarily close to the principal-agent solution (for values of γ sufficiently close to 0).

The reasoning is as follows. If taxpayers report truthfully, the IRS cannot increase gross collections by increasing audit frequencies (since fines or tax arrears cannot be collected from taxpayers reporting truthfully). Consequently, the IRS will seek to minimize deviations from the target budget, which is achieved by auditing according to (5). Conversely, given the IRS auditing rule (5), no individual will find it advantageous to lie: this is ensured by the very nature of the principal-agent solution. Hence the principal-agent solution can be achieved as an equilibrium. Moreover for γ sufficiently small, every equilibrium will involve an arbitrarily small number of individuals lying, and the IRS auditing rule varying only slightly from (5). For if this were not true, a significant fraction of taxpayers would lie, and the IRS would be tempted to increase gross collections by increasing its audit frequencies. If γ is sufficiently small, it will increase the intensity of auditing so severely as to make it unworthwhile for any taxpayer to underreport.[23]

---

[23] The argument also indicates that the truthful equilibrium is the unique equilibrium satisfying the behavioural postulate that taxpayers indifferent

Altering Other Aspects of IRS Management: One approach may be to allow administrative changes that enhance the ability of the IRS to commit to its audit policy. This may include autonomy for the IRS, combined with restrictions on turnover of IRS managers. Such changes may restrict the extent to which politicians with short-term revenue interests (or reacting to special interest groups) can manipulate audit policies, as well as enhance long term goals for IRS managers. This would amount to giving the revenue service a status similar to that accorded to bodies responsible for short-term monetary management, such as the Federal Reserve Board in the United States. However, the results of Scotchmer (1987) and Sanchez (1987) referred to earlier, suggest that enhancing commitment abilities alone will not serve to improve welfare levels; some corresponding adjustment in the goals of the IRS are also required, as the IRS may have a tendency to over-audit low-income individuals. To counteract this, budgetary restrictions on the IRS may be worthwhile.[24]

It is important to note, however, that the impact of budgetary restrictions may depend importantly on what the commitment abilities of the IRS are. Graetz, Reinganum and Wilde (1984) consider the impact of budget restrictions in their simple two-income model where the IRS cannot commit. If the budget restriction binds, the impact is to increase noncompliance: the only equilibrium involves all (strategic) high–income taxpayers under-reporting.[25]

---

between lying and not lying will report truthfully. The reason is that γ being small implies that the only untruthful equilibria involve mixed strategies where taxpayers lie despite being indifferent between lying and not lying.

[24] Isabel Sanchez and Joel Sobel have recently reported work in progress on this question.

[25] Let $\bar{B}$ be the budget restriction, less than $p^* A$, the (unconstrained) budget in the equilibrium depicted earlier. Then the only equilibrium involves $\alpha = 1$, and the IRS choosing the maximal audit frequency $p = (\bar{B}/A + q - 1)(q\rho)^{-1}$. Since $p < p^*$, it is straightforward to verify that this is an equilibrium. To show that there is no other equilibrium, i.e. with $\alpha < 1$, consider first the case where $\alpha < \alpha^*$. Then the optimal response of the IRS is to not audit: $p = 0$, to which the optimal response

The welfare implications of this are, however, unclear. Consider the effect of increasing the budget limit $\bar{B}$, starting from a point where it does bind. The effect this has on the resulting equilibrium is to increase the audit frequency p, while high income taxpayers continue to lie. Net revenues increase, but the effect on welfare from consumption of the private good is unclear, as high income taxpayers are worse off. This has to be traded off against the benefit of increased revenues as well as a more equitable post-tax income distribution. If one is inclined to disregard the utility loss of tax evaders on moral grounds, then the strategy of allowing the IRS larger budgets can be defended.[26] Descriptively, the comparative static effect of varying budget size may explain persistent political pressure for limiting IRS budgets.

Increase Penalties for Evasion: The effect of increasing the penalty F is unambiguous on all fronts. It reduces tax evasion, as well as audit frequencies, while *ex ante* utilities of taxpayers from the private good are unaffected. Net revenues increase for three reasons: the direct effect of higher fines, lower evasion and lower audit costs. The optimal penalty is therefore maximal, and ought to be set in order to reduce the consumption of detected evaders to the minimum subsistence level. It is important to note that these arguments rely on the assumption of absence of errors in auditing: those honest taxpayers convicted by mistake would be subject to large penalties. As the discussion in the following section illustrates, the presence of Type 1 errors in auditing does not necessarily imply that an increase in the penalty rate (combined with a reduction in the audit rate) is welfare reducing.[27] It is therefore

---

of taxpayers is $\alpha = 1$. So suppose $\alpha \geq \alpha^*$. The IRS budget constraint implies that the maximal audit probability is no higher than $(\bar{B}/A + q - 1)(q\rho\alpha^*)^{-1}$, and therefore definitely less than p^*. The optimal response of taxpayers is to set $\alpha = 1$, contradicting the original hypothesis.

[26] This should be qualified in the presence of (intentional or otherwise) errors in the auditing process. Proposals to increase IRS budgets in the United States in recent years have been criticized by the public for allowing increases in taxpayers 'abuse' by the IRS.

[27] The basic reason is that such a variation also reduces the fraction of the

possible that optimal penalties are still maximal in the presence of audit errors.

Alter Tax Rates: We have seen that increasing the tax rate lowers evasion, thereby suggesting the possibility of increasing tax rates as a policy option. However, the welfare effects are complicated. Increasing the tax T_H on high income individuals will lower their utility, but increase net revenues; the welfare effect will therefore depend on the relative valuation of private and public goods. Consider instead a mean preserving increase in tax progressivity, where T_L is lowered and T_H is increased so that $qT_H + (1 - q)T_L$ is left unaffected. There is a direct distributive advantage from a less unequal distribution of post-tax income. The effect on revenues is in general ambiguous, but some algebra reveals that if taxpayers are risk-neutral then net revenues actually decrease. If u is linear, the government is also insensitive to distribution; increased tax progressivity then reduces welfare. The same is true if u is only 'slightly' concave. For moderate or high levels of risk-aversion and inequality aversion, it is difficult to calculate the welfare effects of increased progressivity.

2.3 Other Determinants of Audit Policies

In practice, audit decisions can be conditioned on a number of information sources apart from reported income. For example, they may depend on source of income, occupation, age, domicile, nature of deductions opted for, past history of tax payments and income reports, and whether or not a tax practitioner was hired by the taxpayers to file a tax return. For characteristics that are easily observed, like age or marital status, one may extend our earlier discussion to apply to separate categories of the population defined by given age and marital status. In so far as these characteristics are correlated with true income, one would expect

---

population that is mistakenly convicted, since the audit rate declines. There are thus two effects in opposing directions, and the net balance depend on audit costs, among other parameters.

optimal audit policies to be conditioned on their realization. Scotchmer (1987) discusses the equity implications of such a practice. In so far as individuals with identical true incomes are audited differently based on factors like age and marital status, a violation of horizontal equity is created. On the other hand, Scotchmer demonstrates that conditioning on such information may improve vertical equity.

Additional analytical considerations arise when audits are conditioned on variables under the control of taxpayers, such as occupation, source of income, past tax record, and the decision to use tax practitioners. Such conditioning creates additional contexts of strategic interaction. Recently, Scotchmer (1989) and Reinganum–Wilde (1989) have explored models where taxpayers strategically decide whether to seek professional advice or help in preparing returns; the Reinganum–Wilde paper also deals with the strategic decision of the IRS to condition audits on whether or not the return was filed by a practitioner. These models throw light on the preferences of taxpayers and the IRS with respect to the use of tax practitioners, and their effects on evasion, revenues and welfare.

Meilijson–Landsberger (1982) and Greenberg (1984) make a strong case for conditioning audit decisions on the past record of a taxpayer. In an infinite horizon framework where individuals do not discount the future, they explore the implications of 'simple' Markovian audit policies where taxpayers are classified at any date into two or three categories, according to their status and outcome of audit (if any) in the previous period. The tax and penalty functions are exogenously given, and are allowed to take a very general form. Further, the IRS may be subject to a constraint on its audit budget every period. Meilijson–Landsberger show that if taxpayers are risk-neutral, such Markovian audit policies can yield considerable increases in net revenues. Greenberg shows that with general monotonic von–Neumann–Morgenstern utility functions for taxpayers, it is possible to devise a Markovian policy where 'almost' everyone reports truthfully.

2.4 Errors in Audits and Ambiguities in the Tax Code

An important topic receiving attention of late, is the role and implication of ambiguity concerning the 'true' tax code, as well as of errors in the audit process. These concerns are an important element of policy discussions concerning tax enforcement. Scotchmer–Slemrod (1987), Reinganum–Wilde (1988) and Scotchmer (1989) have shown how uncertainty regarding 'true' tax liabilities can enhance the net revenues collected by the IRS. These supplement the earlier work of Weiss (1976) and Stiglitz (1982) demonstrating the possible desirability of randomized mechanisms owing to their favourable effects on incentives (concerning, for instance, labour supply). However, such uncertainties generally reduce the welfare of risk-averse taxpayers, *ceteris paribus*. Scotchmer and Slemrod show that if the increased net revenues are rebated to taxpayers, it will always be optimal to 'obfuscate' the tax code to a certain extent. Reinganum and Wilde obtain related results: they show that there is an 'optimum' amount of uncertainty, from the point of view of IRS revenues and equilibrium compliance levels.

Lee (1989) focuses on the programme of IRS 'tax rulings', where taxpayers may seek information from the IRS regarding the tax status of certain business activities, before deciding whether to carry them out. The IRS is bound subsequently by the content of its ruling. He explores equilibrium and welfare implications of rulings programmes, explaining in particular the frequent reluctance of the IRS to issue rulings in certain areas. As in the analyses of Scotchmer–Slemrod and Reinganum–Wilde, it is not optimal from the IRS's point of view to minimize uncertainty, owing to the unfavourable incentive effects of reduced uncertainty.

A relatively neglected area is the implication of errors in the audit process, whereby auditors assess an individual's income with error. Some of the models concerning tax ambiguity may be interpreted, however, as models of 'noisy' auditing. From this standpoint, errors in audits may have a functional role in reducing tax evasion. Shibano (1989) studies a model of equilibrium interaction between a single auditee and single auditor, in the presence of stochastic audit errors. The auditor has to choose among a variety of audit rules with varying degrees of conservativeness (i.e., ratios of Type I and II error probabilities), while auditees decide whether or not to underreport. His focus, however, is on private accounting firms whose role is to certify the financial health of companies for the benefit of private investors, and accordingly discusses the effects of alternative regulations of accounting practices. It would be worthwhile to extend his approach to the tax evasion context.

2.5 Empirical Research on Tax Evasion

We discuss a few notable advances in empirical modelling that have occurred recently; one expects more research to be forthcoming in this area. In the United States, empirical research has been stimulated by a large dataset prepared by the IRS, called the Taxpayer Compliance Measurement Program (TCMP), which contains approximately 50,000 individual tax returns each of which was thoroughly audited by an IRS examiner. The dataset provides detailed information on the filer (taxes paid, income, occupation, etc. in addition to socio-economic and demographic characteristics) as well as on the IRS side (audit rates, prosecution rates, seriousness of penalties for tax fraud, and the identity and characteristics of assigned auditors).

Earlier work with the TCMP dataset by Clotfelter (1983) and Witte and Woodbury (1985) was based on the Allingham–Sandmo model of the optimal income reporting decision for a risk averse taxpayer confronted with an exogenous audit probability, tax and penalty rates. This generates a tobit model of the form

$$Y^{\cdot} = X \beta + \varepsilon_1.$$

$$Y_1 = \begin{cases} Y^{\cdot} & \text{if} \quad Y^{\cdot} \geq 0 \\ 0 & \text{otherwise} \end{cases} \tag{13}$$

where Y_1 denotes extent of evasion and X includes audit probability, tax and penalty rates, in addition to socio-economic characteristics affecting the taxpayer's risk attitudes. Witte and Woodbury used aggregated TCMP data to estimate (13) separately for seven different audit classes using Zellner's method of seemingly unrelated regressions. They found significant effects of audit rates, of the prevalence of tax withholding as well as of educational efforts made by the IRS. Somewhat surprisingly, the level of penalties for the fraud had an insignificant effect. Witte and Woodbury did not, however, include the tax rate in their analysis. Gorilla Alexander and Feinstein (1987) introduce a number of novel features in their econometric approach to tax evasion, relative to the standard tobit analysis. Unlike Witte and Woodbury they study individual (rather than aggregate) versions of the TCMP data. They first separate the decision of a taxpayer to evade, from the decision of how much to evade (conditional on an evasion decision). They use (13) to model the first decision, and conditional on $Y_1 > 0$, the extent of evasion is given by

$$Y_2 = X_2 \beta_2 + \varepsilon_2, \tag{14}$$

where Y_2 is constrained to be positive. Secondly, and more importantly, they allow for the fact that all evaders may not have been detected, by modelling the detection process. Conditional on a filer having evaded (i.e. $Y_1 > 0$), detection occurs if the variable W^* is positive, where

$$W^* = Z \pi + \mu + \varepsilon_3, \tag{15}$$

Z being a set of variables which determines the intensity of detection, such as the experience of the auditor, while μ represents a fixed effect differentiating one auditor from another. An instance of evasion is observed to occur if Y_1, Y_2 and W^* are all positive. Cases where Y_1, Y_2 are positive and W^* negative are ones where a tax evader escaped detection; such cases are unobservable. Modelling the detection process corrects the bias resulting from observing only the cases which are detected.

The third novelty in the Alexander–Feinstein approach is their attempt to correct for involuntary filing errors by taxpayers. Looking at instances where incomes were overreported, and assuming a symmetric distribution for involuntary errors around 0, enables them to separate out strategic evaders from those making errors.

Alexander and Feinstein use this approach to estimate the effects of income level, source of income, occupation, age and tax rate on tax evasion and detection in the TCMP dataset. Those more likely to evade are those with self-employment, or with farm income or capital gains; those with lower incomes; those facing higher tax rates; those who are younger and those who are married. They also find significant heterogeneity amongst different auditors in terms of their success in detection.

The most interesting aspect of their model is that it permits one to estimate the total amount of tax evasion in the system, including the extent of evasion that was undetected. Based on the TCMP data, approximately 15 per cent of all filers were estimated to have evaded taxes as well as detection.

An important shortcoming of the Alexander–Feinstein approach is that it ignores strategic interdependencies between taxpayer's decisions to evade, and the auditor's decisions, e.g. as in the Graetz–Reinganum–Wilde model. To accommodate this, Feinstein (1988) proposes a modification of (15) where the IRS has access to information about taxpayer characteristics determining evasion decisions:

$$W^* = Z\pi + \mu + \delta\Phi(X_1\beta_1) + \varepsilon_3 \qquad (16)$$

but even this falls short of an explicit model of interdependence between taxpayers and the IRS.[28]

We conclude this section by mentioning the work of Dubin, Graetz and Wilde (1987), which emphasizes the endogeneity of

[28] Notice, for instance, that Alexander and Feinstein do not include the audit probability as one of the variables determining the taxpayer's decision. It could be argued that this is already incorporated within the detection equation. But then why should taxpayer decisions be formulated independently of their assessments of the detection process?

audit rates, in contrast to all other empirical studies. An additional point of contrast is that they find that increased tax rates decrease tax evasion, as predicted by the Graetz–Reinganum–Wilde model. They also use a different dataset: a pooled cross section-cum-time series set for variables aggregated at the state level in the United States. Having rejected the hypothesis of exogeneity of the audit rate, they estimate the coefficients of evasion with respect to audit rates, state income tax rates, education, age, unemployment, income, proportion of work force in manufacturing, inflation and a time trend. Apart from the negative affect of tax rates on evasion, they find that increases in audit rates have a considerable deterrent effect.

3 OPTIMAL FINES: FURTHER DISCUSSION

In the previous section we have seen that optimal evasion penalties were maximal, in both the principal-agent formulation, as well as the equilibrium formulation. The logic of this is similar to the conundrum discussed by Gary Becker in his classic piece on the economic analysis of crime and punishment. Offenders are deterred by a combination of the likelihood of detection, and the penalties that follow such detection. It is thus possible to preserve a given level of deterrence (of a given offence) by lowering the probability of detection and simultaneously increasing the penalty. Since the former results in a lowering of enforcement costs, while the latter (fines representing transfers from some citizens to others) involve zero deadweight loss, such a variation is welfare improving. So Becker concluded that optimal deterrence requires fines to be increased as far as possible, for any kind of offense, no matter how mild. This echoes an earlier argument of Jeremy Bentham:

Pecuniary punishments are highly economical, since all the evil felt by him who pays turns into an advantage for him who receives.

Theory of Legislation, ch. vi.

We now present Becker's formal argument, which is set in the context of an offense which generates negative externalities. This framework is slightly different from the tax evasion context, and we shall employ it for the remainder of this section. It is therefore appropriate to describe some of its salient features.

First, the government has imperfect information regarding the *behaviour* rather than *attributes* (such as income levels) of private citizens. In other words, the fundamental problem is one of moral hazard rather than adverse selection. It therefore appears plausible that there is no point in eliciting reports from citizens, on which audit or investigations of the government can be based: no citizen would have an incentive in reporting that they had committed an offense.[29] Hence the government must choose a single probability of apprehension rather than conditioning it on information generated by private citizens.[30] Second, the tradition in the literature is to weigh the utilities of offenders and victims equally in calculating social welfare, the typical utilitarian approach to externality problems. So the analysis may not apply to 'felonies' involving murder or rape where society may not wish to weigh the utilities of criminals.[31] Finally, issues concerning incentives of enforcement authorities are ignored. Except for Grieson and Singh (1988), all models utilize a principal-agent framework, where no distinction is made between 'society',

[29] This point has not, however, been formally verified in the literature, to the best of my knowledge.

[30] It is possible, of course, that victims of the externality may report its occurrence, and the government may condition its investigation intensity on this information. By ignoring this possibility, we are in effect focussing attention on 'victimless' crimes (such as black marketeering, gambling, prostitution or 'invisible' environmental damage) where the external costs are widely diffused, or not evident to victims, to ensure that they are unlikely to be reported. Mookherjee–Png (1989b) refer to such forms of enforcement as 'monitoring' rather than 'investigation'.

[31] However, we shall argue below that some of the results follow from arguments concerning 'efficient' enforcement of given behaviour patterns, and therefore do not rely upon weighing the utilities of 'externality creators' equally with those of victims. Hence, the scope of the analysis may include felonies as well.

'government' or 'enforcement authority'. Possible commitment problems are also ignored.

We shall concentrate on the determinants of optimal fines, in particular on the consequences of errors in apprehension or conviction, and of agent heterogeneity — variables that have received relatively less attention in the income tax evasion literature. We shall, however, ignore issues pertaining to nonmonetary sanctions, for a discussion of which the interested reader is referred to Becker (1968), Polinsky–Shavell (1984) and Shavell (1987).

Becker's analysis runs as follows. Let O denote the level or number of offenses committed within a given population, $H(O)$ the harm inflicted on victims and $G(O)$ the gain obtained by offenders from committing offense O, where both H and G are expressed in pecuniary equivalents, and are increasing functions (with H convex and G concave). Let p denote the probability that a given offender will be apprehended, and $C(p, O)$ denote the social cost incurred in apprehension, where C is increasing in both arguments. If f denotes the penalty imposed on a convicted offender (per unit offense), and if bf is the associated social cost of this penalty, then the total social cost of punishments is $bpfO$.[32] Becker postulates that $b = 0$ for punishment by fines, but $b > 1$ for punishment by imprisonment or other means, on the ground that the former involve net transfers which carry no deadweight loss, unlike the case of imprisonment.

Finally, Becker postulates that the 'supply' of offenses depends upon the probability of apprehension p and the penalty rate f: $O = O(p, f)$ which is decreasing in both arguments. The aggregate social loss associated with the enforcement policy (p, f) is then given by

$$L = H(O) - G(O) + c(p, O) + bfpO \qquad (17)$$

which should be minimized via choice of p and f, subject to the supply constraint $O = O(p, f)$. This is the basic Becker framework,

---

[32] We are assuming that the penalty rates and social costs are linear, but this does not affect the conclusions.

which most subsequent literature has attempted to extend in various directions.

Becker's argument for the optimality of maximal penalties is as follows. If offenders are risk-neutral, the supply of offences is a function of the product of p and f. Social loss is then reduced by increasing f and reducing p in such a way as to leave pf unaffected. The supply of offences remains unchanged, but society has to devote less resources to apprehending criminals.

It is worth noting that Becker's result is actually more general than the form in which it was originally expressed. For instance, it doesn't really hinge on the use of an utilitarian framework, or one that assigns any weight to an offender's utility. Given whatever level of offenses society agrees to tolerate, then (provided offenders are risk neutral) the process of increasing penalties allows a reduction in costs of enforcing the given level of offenses. So the argument should apply to felonies as well (though the contrast with moral intuition is perhaps less striking in such cases).

Moreover, for the case of pecuniary penalties where $b = 0$, the argument does not depend on risk-neutrality of offenders at all. As long as the supply of offenses is decreasing in both p and f, an increase in f combined with a reduction in p that leaves the supply of offenses unchanged, must result in a social improvement.[33]

Stigler (1970) discussed two possible factors ignored by Becker's analysis that may help explain why extreme penalties may not always be optimal. First, errors in apprehension would cause innocent people to be convicted; consideration of the welfares of such people may argue against extreme penalties. The argument is not altogether clear, because the variation proposed by Becker would lower p and therefore convict fewer innocent

---

[33] Other interesting implications of the Becker framework are as follows. Fines dominate imprisonment: so convicted offenders should be imprisoned only in so far as pecuniary penalties do not suffice to provide sufficient disincentives. Mild offenses ought therefore to be fined, while more serious offenses may require imprisonment. Further, richer people should be punished by fines, poorer people more by imprisonment, assuming that the disutility from going to prison is independent of income.

people (while those convicted mistakenly would pay larger penalties). The second factor suggested by Stigler is the notion of marginal deterrence: offenses vary in severity and extreme penalties for all offenses would provide no marginal disincentive for an offender not to commit a more serious crime. This argument, too, is somewhat unclear: marginal deterrence could be achieved by varying probability of apprehension according to the severity of crime, rather than by varying the penalties.

Subsequent literature has more carefully explored a variety of alternative resolutions of the 'Becker conundrum':

(i)   Risk-aversion of offenders (Polinsky–Shavell (1979)).
(ii)   The likelihood of convicting innocent people by error (Bolton (1986)).
(iii) Marginal deterrence, i.e. variations in severity of offenses (Shavell (1989), Mookherjee–Png (1989b)).
(iv)   Heterogeneous levels of wealth of offenders (Polinsky–Shavell (1989)).

In what follows, we shall illustrate how the above features modify the nature of optimal penalties, using a simple set of examples. It will be argued that factors (i) and (ii) are analytically similar, and generate the result that maximal penalties are optimal if the costs of apprehension are large, but not when they are small. In addition, optimal penalties may be non-maximal in some contexts involving (iii) and (iv). Hence, these factors provide possible explanations for the desirability of non-maximal penalties.

Start by considering the benchmark 'Becker' case where offenders are homogeneous, and may be apprehended at a certain cost. Furthermore, enforcement officials do not apprehend a non-offender by mistake, and an individual either commits the offense or not; offenses do not vary in severity. Let $\tilde{a}$ denote the act chosen by a potential offender, which may take two possible values: $\tilde{a} = 1$ denotes an offense, and $\tilde{a} = 0$ denotes no offense. The von Neumann–Morgenstern utility function of a potential offender is given by $u(C) + G\tilde{a}$, where C denotes nonnegative consumption level of a private good, and G the private gain to the individual from committing the offence. All potential offenders share a common wealth level w; the consumption of any one of them is given by $w - f$, were f is the level of fine to be paid to the government in the event of being apprehended. The function u is assumed to be increasing, differentiable and concave.

Apprehending an offender costs the government c units of money; so the expected cost of resources devoted to apprehension is equal to cp, where p denotes the probability of apprehension. The expected loss of public revenues (expressed per potential offender) is then

$$cp - \tilde{a}pf = \begin{cases} cp & \text{if } \tilde{a} = 0 \\ cp - pf & \text{if } \tilde{a} = 1 \end{cases} \qquad (18)$$

Suppose that the social harm caused by the offense is sufficiently large that it is socially optimal to ensure that no offense is actually committed.[34] Then the optimal enforcement policy $\{p, f\}$ must be chosen to minimize the enforcement cost (18), subject to the constraint of deterring the offense:

$$\min_{p, f} cp \qquad (19)$$

$$\text{subject to } p[u(w) - u(w - f)] \geq G \qquad (20)$$

$$w - f \geq 0 \text{ and } 1 \geq p \geq 0. \qquad (21)$$

If $u(0) = -\infty$, then no optimum exists; given any feasible policy (p, f), the cost of enforcement can be lowered by raising f and lowering p further. On the other hand, if $u(0)$ is finite, the optimal solution is to set the penalty f at its maximal level $f = w$, and $p = (G/u(w) - u(0))$. This is the 'Becker conundrum'.

It is apparent from the preceding argument that the conundrum does not rely upon risk neutrality of potential offenders. In order to explain the results of Polinsky–Shavell (1979), we introduce

----

[34] If, on the other hand, enforcement costs are sufficiently high (relative to social harm from the offence) that the socially optimal policy involves $\tilde{a} = 1$, there is no need for regulation at all: the activity can be legalized and enforcement costs will drop to zero.

heterogeneity amongst potential offenders.[35] Specifically, suppose there are two types ($i = 1, 2$) of offenders, differing in their private benefits from committing the offense. Type i has the utility function $u(C) + G_i\tilde{a}$, where $G_2 > G_1 > 0$. Let λ_i denote the proportion of the population that is of Type i. Suppose that the social harm committed by these offenses are such that it is optimal to deter Type 1 from committing the offense, but not Type 2.[36] Unlike the previous case, Type 2 offenders will commit the offense at the optimum; those apprehended will have to pay the penalty. *Ex ante*, Type 2 offenders will thus bear the risk associated with whether or not they will be apprehended. A utilitarian planner sensitive to the welfare of all individuals (including offenders) would then include the cost of this risk as a social cost. The utilitarian optimal enforcement policy would solve the following problem:

$$\text{maximize}_{p,\,f}\ \lambda_2[pu(w - f) + (1 - p)\, u\,(w)] + \lambda_2 pf - cp \qquad (22)$$

$$\text{subject to } G_2 \geq p[u(w) - u(w - f)] \geq G_1, \qquad (23)$$

and constraint (21).

Before describing the solution to this problem, we show that it is analytically equivalent to the problem studied by Bolton (1986). Bolton considers a homogeneous population of potential offenders (with utility $u(C) + G_2\tilde{a}$). His model differs from Becker's only in so far as an innocent person can be convicted by mistake. Let p denote the probability of monitoring, an activity which (with a given degree of stochastic error) observes whether or not a given individual commits the offense. If $\tilde{a} \in \{0, 1\}$ denotes the act actually chosen by an individual who is monitored, let $\hat{a} \in \{0, 1\}$ be the information received by the government regarding this act. That is, the

---

[35] The importance of heterogeneity may not be obvious from a quick reading of the Polinsky–Shavell paper. The population may be *ex ante* homogeneous in their model. But ex post they must face heterogeneous circumstances: the *ex ante* distribution over these circumstances can be homogeneous.

[36] This is indeed optimal if the harm is sufficiently large, while $G_1 < u(w) - u(0) < G_2$. Then it is impossible to deter Type 2, but it is possible to deter Type 1.

government believes the offense was committed if it observes $\hat{a} = 1$. In the case where monitoring is error-free, $\tilde{a} = \hat{a}$. In general, let β_1 denote $Prob[\hat{a} = 0 \mid \tilde{a} = 1]$ and $\beta_0 = Prob[\hat{a} = 0 \mid \tilde{a} = 0]$, the respective probabilities of acquittal when the individual is and is not guilty. We assume that the government's evidence is informative on average, so $\beta_1 > \beta_0$.

Suppose that the harm committed by an offense is sufficiently large to make it socially worthwhile to deter them entirely. The incentive constraint then reads:

$$(1-p)\, u\, (w) + p\{\beta_1 u(w) + (1 - \beta_1)\, u\, (w - f)\} + G_2 \geq (1 - p)\, u\, (w)$$
$$+ p\{\beta_0 u(w) + (1 - \beta_0)\, u\, (w - f)\},$$

which reduces to

$$p(\beta_0 - \beta_1)\, \{u(w) - u\, (w - f)\} \geq G_2. \tag{24}$$

Since the public revenue loss equals

$$cp - p(1 - \beta_0)f \tag{25}$$

the utilitarian optimal enforcement policy would solve:

Maximize $_{p,\, f} p(1 - \beta_0)f - cp + [(1 - p)\, u\, (w) + p\{\beta_0 u(w)$
$$+ (1 - \beta_0)\, u\, (w - f)\}] \tag{26}$$

subject to (24) and (21).

Note that upon setting λ_2 equal to $(1 - \beta_0)$, maximizing (26) is exactly equivalent to maximizing (22), the objective function in the Polinsky–Shavell model. Further, the incentive constraint (24) has a structure similar to the right-hand inequality in (23). As it turns out, the two problems have similar solutions.

Proposition 4: Consider either the Polinsky–Shavell problem of maximizing (22) subject to (21) and (23), or the Bolton problem of maximizing (26) subject to (21) and (24).

(i)   If potential offenders are risk-neutral, it is optimal to set $f = w$ and $p = G_2/f$.

(ii)   If potential offenders are strictly risk averse (i.e., u is strictly concave), and

  (a) c is close to 0, the optimal p is close to 1, and the optimal value of f is less than w.

  (b) c exceeds $\lambda_2 w$ or $(1 - \beta_0)w$, and $u(0)$ is finite, the optimal value of $f = w$ and $p = G_2/[u(w) - u(0)]$. If on the other hand $u(0) = -\infty$, then an optimum does not exist: any feasible policy $\{p, f\}$ is dominated by another with a higher fine and lower probability of apprehension.

Proof: (i) With risk-neutrality, the problem reduces to minimizing cp subject to constraints on pf. Any increase in f accompanied by an equiproportionate decrease in p is then a welfare improving policy.

  (ii) (a) If c equals 0, we first show that the optimal value of p equals 1. Suppose otherwise, that there exists an optimal p less than 1. The incentive constraints require that $f > 0$. We can lower f and increase p so that $p[u (w) - u (w - f)]$ is unaffected, i.e.:

$$\frac{dp}{df} = -p \, \frac{u'(w - f)}{u(w) - u(w - f)} \qquad (27)$$

with $df < 0$. By construction, this variation is feasible. The effect on the objective function equals

$$\lambda_2 \left[f\frac{dp}{df} + p \right] df = \lambda_2 p \, \frac{[u(w) - u (w - f) - fu'(w - f)]}{u(w) - u(w - f)} \, df$$

which is positive by virtue of the strict concavity of u. This contradicts the premise that we started with an optimal value of $p < 1$.

  Given that the optimal value of p equals 1 with $c = 0$, the corresponding optimal value of f maximizes $\{f - [u(w) - u(w - f)]\}$ subject to a constraint of the form $u(w) - u(w - f) \geq k_2$, for some constant k_2. It is readily checked that the solution is $f = w - min \, \{\hat{w}, w^*\} < w$, where $u'(\hat{w}) = 1$ and $u(w) - u(w^*) = k_2$.

  The result now follows from the Theorem of the Maximum, and the fact that $p = 1$, $f = w - Min \, \{\hat{w}, w^*\}$ is the unique optimum when $c = 0$.

(b) Consider a variation with $df > 0$ and dp/df as given by (27). The effect on the objective function is $(\lambda_2 f - c)dp + \lambda_2 pdf > 0$, since $c > \lambda_2 w \geq \lambda_2 f$. So in this case, it is always better to lower p and increase f, from which the result follows.

Q.E.D.

The element similar to both models is that the probability of monitoring (p) and fine (f) affect the risk borne by some individuals that count in social welfare. The intuitive argument can be phrased thus: a decrease in the penalty accompanied by an increase in the probability of apprehension that preserves incentives also leaves unaffected the *level* of *ex ante* expected utility of offenders. Consequently, the welfare effects of such variations depend entirely on their effect on enforcement costs (less collections from fines). Now, risk-aversion implies that the expected fine increases (and so do collections from fines on an average, if the population is large). Hence, if enforcement costs are small, such a variation is desirable, and the 'Becker conundrum' reappears! On the other hand, if enforcement is costly enough, the increase in enforcement cost outweighs the increase in collected fines, and optimal penalties are non-maximal.

We now turn to the notion of marginal deterrence, where offenders are to be induced to select appropriately among different levels of seriousness of the offense. Suppose there are three possible acts for a potential offender: do not commit an offense $(\tilde{a} = 0)$, commit a mild offense $(\tilde{a} = 1)$, or commit a serious offense $(\tilde{a} = b)$, where $b > 1$. Furthermore, as in the Polinsky–Shavell model, assume there are two types of offenders: type i has utility $u(C) + G_i \tilde{a}$, where $G_2 > G_1 > 0$. Enforcement officials and courts cannot distinguish between the two types of offenders. Moreover, enforcement authorities cannot condition the intensity of monitoring on the seriousness of the offense. As discussed earlier, this is natural for 'victimless' offenses which are not likely to be reported by victims.[37]

---

[37] For an alternative interpretation in terms of specific versus general enforcement, see Shavell (1989).

Suppose that Type 2 offenders cannot be prevented from committing the serious offense, (i.e., $u(0) + G_2 b > u(w) + G_2$). Moreover, $G_1 > u(w) - u(0) > G_1(b - 1)$, so Type 1 individuals can be deterred from undertaking the serious offense, but not from undertaking the mild offense. Suppose also that the incremental social harm caused by escalation of the offense is so large that it is optimal to deter Type 1 individuals from committing the serious offense. It then follows that the penalty f_s, following the serious offense must exceed f_m, the penalty following the mild offense. This is because both offenses are, by assumption, monitored with the same probability: if the penalties were also similar, then Type 1 individuals would prefer to commit the more serious offense. Hence the mild offense must be associated with a non-maximal penalty, and penalties are graduated according to seriousness of the crime. This conclusion would not follow if the enforcement authorities could condition the probability of monitoring on to the seriousness of the offense (as in the case where investigation starts after offenses are reported by victims): in such situations the optimal policy would be to set penalties at maximal levels, and achieve marginal deterrence by suitably varying the probability of monitoring.

We conclude this section with a brief discussion of the case where potential offenders have heterogeneous wealth, and the wealth of a potential offender can be observed costlessly subsequent (but not prior) to apprehension. Consequently, probabilities of apprehension cannot be based on observed wealth levels, while fines can. Let there be two types 1 and 2 with λ_i being the proportion of type i, characterized by income w_i, where $w_2 > w_1 > 0$. Each type i can either commit an offense ($\tilde{a}_i = 1$) or not ($\tilde{a}_i = 0$), and has the same utility function $u(C) + G\tilde{a}_i$. Assume that $u(0)$ is finite, $u'(w_1) < 1$ and that the harm caused by an offense is large enough to make it socially optimal to minimize the number of offenses. It may be verified that the nature of the optimal enforcement policy is as follows (where f_i denotes the fine imposed on an offender with wealth w_i):

(i) If $G < u(w_1) - u(0)$, so that the optimum involves complete deterrence ($\tilde{a}_1 = \tilde{a}_2 = 0$), the associated enforcement policy is

$f_1 = w_1$, and f_2 set at any value between f_2^* and w_2, where $u(w_2 - f_2^*) = u(w_2) - u(w_1) + u(0)$, and $p = G/(u(w_1) - u(0))$.

(ii) If $u(w_1) - u(0) < G < u(w_2) - u(0)$, so that the optimum involves deterrence for wealthy individuals only ($\tilde{a}_1 = 0, \tilde{a}_2 = a$), the associated enforcement policy involves $f_1 = x^* < w_1$, where $u'(w_1 - x^*) = 1$. Further, if $\lambda_1[x^* + u(w_1 - x^*) - u(w_1)] > c$, the optimal value of p equals 1 and f_2 lies anywhere between f_2^{**} and w_2, where $u(f_2^{**}) + G = u(w_2)$. But if $\lambda_1[x^* + u(w_1 - x^*) - u(w_1)] < c$, it is optimal to set $f_2 = w_2$ and $p = G/(u(w_2) - u(0))$.

The prior unobservability of wealth makes it impossible for authorities to condition the probability of monitoring on wealth levels. Consequently, the optimal (uniform) probability of monitoring is set according to the requirement of marginally deterring potential offenders of a particular wealth level. Fines for offenders at other wealth levels can then be varied without correspondingly varying the probability of monitoring, and without altering incentives. They may be set according to distributive as well as revenue considerations, and may therefore be non-maximal.

REFERENCES

Alexander, C. and J. Feinstein (1987), 'A Microeconometric Analysis of Income Tax Evasion', mimeo, MIT Dept. of Economics.

Allingham, M. and A. Sandmo (1972), 'Income Tax Evasion: A Theoretical Analysis', *Journal of Public Economics*, 1, pp. 323–38, November.

Basu, K., S. Bhattacharya and A. Mishra (1990), 'A Note On Bribery and Control of Corruption', mimeo, Delhi School of Economics.

Becker, G. (1968), 'Crime and Punishment: An Economic Approach', *Journal of Political Economy*, 76, pp. 169–217.

Becker, G. and G. Stigler (1974), 'Law Enforcement, Malfeasance and Compensation of Enforcers', *Journal of Legal Studies*, 3, pp. 1–18.

Bentham, J., *Theory of Legislation*, C.K. Ogden (ed.), New York, NY: Harcourt, Brace Co., 1931.

Besley, T. and J. McLaren (1990), 'Tax Compliance and Corruption Deterrence: The Role of Wage Incentives', mimeo, Woodrow Wilson School, Princeton University.

Bolton, P. (1986), 'The Principle of Maximum Deterrence Revisited', mimeo, Dept. of Economics, Harvard University.

Border, K. and J. Sobel (1987), 'Samurai Accountant: A Theory of Auditing and Plunder', *Review of Economic Studies*, 54, pp. 525–40.

Chander, P. and L. Wilde (1991), 'Corruption and Tax Compliance', mimeo, New Delhi: Indian Statistical Institute.

Clotfelter, C. (1983), 'Tax Evasion and Tax Rates: An Analysis of Individual Returns', *Review of Economics and Statistics*, 65, pp. 363–73.

Cyrus Chu, C.Y. (1987), 'Income Tax Evasion with Venal Tax Officials: The Case of Developing Countries', Discussion Paper 8704, The Institute of Economics, Academia Sinica, Taiwan.

Dubin, J., M. Graetz and L. Wilde (1987), 'The Effect of Tax and Audit Rates on Compliance with the Federal Income Tax', Social Science Working Paper No. 638, California Institute of Technology.

Dye, R. (1986), 'Optimal Monitoring Policies in Agencies', *Rand Journal of Economics*, Autumn, pp. 339–50.

Feinstein, J. (1988), 'Detection Controlled Estimation', mimeo, Graduate School of Business, Stanford University.

Gangopadhyay, S., O. Goswami and A. Sanyal (1991), 'To Catch a Thief: Corrupt Auditors, Tax Enforcement and an Optimal Monitoring Hierarchy', mimeo, New Delhi: Indian Statistical Institute.

Gibbard, A. (1973), 'Manipulation of Voting Schemes: A General Result', *Econometrica*, 41, pp. 587–601.

Goswami, O., I. Gang and A. Sanyal (1991), 'Bureaucratic Corruption, Income Tax Enforcement and Collection', mimeo, New Delhi: Indian Statistical Institute.

Graetz, M., J. Reinganum and L. Wilde (1984), 'A Model of Tax Compliance with Budget Constrained Auditors', Social Science Working Paper 520, California Institute of Technology.

—— (1986), 'The Tax Compliance Game: Toward an Interactive Theory of Law Enforcement', *Journal of Law, Economics and Organization*, 2, pp. 1–32.

Greenberg, J. (1984), 'Avoiding Tax Avoidance: A (Repeated) Game Theoretic Approach', *Journal of Economic Theory*, 32, pp. 1–13.

Grieson, R. and N. Singh (1988), 'Regulating Externalities Through Testing', mimeo, Santa Cruz: Dept. of Economics, University of California.

Groves, T. (1973), 'Incentives in Teams', *Econometrica*.

Hammond, P. (1979), 'Straightforward Individual Incentive Compatibility in Large Economies', *Review of Economic Studies*, 46, pp. 263–82.

—— (1985), 'Welfare Economics', in G.R. Feiwel (ed.), *Issues in Contemporary Microeconomics and Welfare*, London: Macmillan, pp. 405–34.

Hurwicz, L. (1972), 'On Informationally Decentralized Systems', in C. McGuire and R. Radner (eds), *Decisions and Organization*, Amsterdam: North Holland.

Lee, E.S. (1989), 'Tax Treatment Uncertainty and the IRS Individual Rulings Program', Ph.D. dissertation, Graduate School of Business, Stanford University.

Lui, F.T. (1986), 'A Dynamic Model of Corruption Deterrence', *Journal of Public Economics*, 31, pp. 215–36.

Meilijson, I. and M. Landsberger (1982), 'Incentive Generating State Dependent Penalty System', *Journal of Public Economics*, 19, pp. 333–52.

Melumad, N. and D. Mookherjee (1989), 'Delegation as Commitment: The Case of Income Tax Audits', *Rand Journal of Economics*, Summer, 20 (2), pp. 139–63.

Mirrlees, J. (1971), 'An Exploration in the Theory of Optimal Income Taxation', *Review of Economic Studies*, 38 (2), pp. 175–208.

—— (1974), 'Notes on Welfare Economics, Information and Uncertainty', in M. Balch, D. McFadden and S. Wu (eds), *Essays in Economic Behaviour Under Uncertainty*, Amsterdam: North Holland, pp. 243–58.

Mookherjee, D. and I. Png (1989a), 'Optimal Auditing, Insurance and Redistribution', *Quarterly Journal of Economics*, 104 (2), pp. 399–415.

—— (1989b), 'Monitoring Versus Investigation in Law Enforcement and Regulation', mimeo, Graduate School of Management, UCLA.

—— (1990), 'Enforcement Costs and the Optimal Progressivity of Income Taxes', *Journal of Law, Economics and Organization*, Fall issue.

—— (1991), 'Corruption, Welfare and Compensation of Law Enforcers', mimeo, Graduate School of Management, UCLA.

Polinsky, M. and S. Shavell (1979), 'The Optimal Trade-off between the Probability and Magnitude of Fines', *American Economic Review*, 69 (5), pp. 880–91.

—— (1984), 'The Optimal Use of Fines and Imprisonment', *Journal of Public Economics*, 24, pp. 89–99.

—— (1989), 'A Note on Optimal Fines when Wealth Varies Among Individuals', Working Paper No. 58, Olin Program in Law and Economics, Stanford Law School.

Reinganum, J. and L. Wilde (1984), 'An Equilibrium Model of Tax Compliance with a Bayesian Auditor and Some "Honest" Taxpayers', Social Science Working Paper, California Institute of Technology.

— (1985), 'Income Tax Compliance in a Principal Agent Framework', *Journal of Public Economics*, 26, pp. 1–18.

— (1988), 'A Note on Enforcement Uncertainty and Taxpayer Compliance', *Quarterly Journal of Economics*, 103, pp. 793–8.

— (1989), 'Equilibrium Enforcement and Compliance in the Presence of Tax Practitioners', Working Paper, Dept. of Economics, University of Iowa.

Roemer, J. and I. Ortuno–Ortin (1988), 'Implementation with Inspection', Working Paper, Dept. of Economics, University of California, Daws.

Rose Ackerman, S. (1978), *Corruption: A Study in Political Economy*, New York: Academic Press.

Sanchez, I. (1987), 'Principal Agent Models of Income Tax Compliance', Working Paper, University of Rochester.

Sandmo, A. (1981), 'Income Tax Evasion, Labour Supply and the Equity-Efficiency Trade-off', *Journal of Public Economics*, 16 (3), pp. 265–88.

Scotchmer, S. (1987), 'Audit Classes and Tax Enforcement Policy', *American Economic Review*, 77 (2), pp. 229–33.

— (1989), 'Who Profits from Taxpayer Confusion?', *Economics Letters*, 29, pp. 49–55.

Scotchmer, S. and J. Slemrod (1987), 'Optimal Obfuscation in Tax Enforcement', Working Paper, Graduate School of Public Policy, Berkeley: University of California.

Shavell, S. (1987), 'The Optimal Use of Nonmetary Sanctions as a Deterrent', *American Economic Review*, 77 (4), pp. 584–92.

— (1989), 'Specific Versus General Enforcement of Law in a Model of Optimal Deterrence', mimeo, Harvard Law School.

Shibano, T. (1989), *Equilibrium Models of Attestation*, Ph.D. dissertation, Graduate School of Business, Stanford University.

Stigler, G. (1970), 'The Optimum Enforcement of Laws', *Journal of Political Economy*, 78, pp. 526–36.

Stiglitz, J. (1982), 'Utilitarianism and Horizontal Equity: The Case for Random Taxation', *Journal of Public Economics*, 18 (1), pp. 1–33.

Townsend, R. (1979), 'Optimal Contracts and Competitive Markets with Costly State Verification', *Journal of Economic Theory*, 21, pp. 265–93.

Townsend, R. (1989), 'Information Constrained Insurance', *Journal of Monetary Economics*, 21, pp. 411–50.

Virmani, A. (1987), 'Tax Evasion, Corruption and Administration: Monitoring the People's Agents under Symmetric Dishonesty', Development Research Division Discussion Paper No. 271, the World Bank, Washington DC.

Wagenhofer, A. (1987), 'Investigation Strategies with Costly Perfect Information', in *Agency Theory, Information and Incentives*, edited by G. Bamberg and K. Spremann, Springer–Verlag, Berlin–Heidelberg.

Weiss, L. (1976), 'The Desirability of Cheating Incentives and Randomness in the Optimal Income Tax', *Journal of Political Economy*, 84, pp. 1343–52.

Witte, A. and D. Woodbury (1985), 'The Effect of Tax Laws and Tax Administration on Tax Compliance: The Case of the US Individual Income Tax', *National Tax Journal*, 38, pp. 1–14.

11

Optimal Provision and Financing of Public Goods in a Federal State with Illustrative Empirical Evidence

Ranjan Ray

1 INTRODUCTION

Samuelson's (1954, 1955) celebrated condition for optimal provision of public goods in the first best case has, recently, generated
considerable interest in public goods provision in the presence
of distortionary taxes. Pigou's (1947) observation that distortionary taxes increase the marginal cost of public goods because of
the indirect damage caused by additional taxation has received
formal attention in several recent papers [Stiglitz and Dasgupta
(1971); Atkinson and Stern (1974); Wildasin (1984); King (1986);
Wilson (1991)]. As these papers have shown, Pigou's suggestion
that the social marginal cost of a public good exceeds the production cost in the presence of distortionary taxes does not hold in
general. Atkinson and Stern (1974); King (1986) give examples
where the exact reverse of Pigou's assertion is implied.

The conditions for the optimal provision of public goods have
been derived and analysed within the framework of a unitary
State which is the sole supplier of the public good with an
exclusive right to design and levy taxes to finance its production.
The recent interest in 'fiscal federalism'[1] largely stems from the

---

[1] See, for example, Arnott and Grieson (1981); Gordon (1983); Mintz and

limited applicability of results in public economics in the case of federal countries such as Australia, Canada, Germany, USA and India. Discussions on the supply and financing of public goods in the federal case have taken on a new significance with the recent re-unification of Germany and the proposed economic integration of the member countries of the European Economic Community.

This paper attempts an integrated treatment of optimal taxation and public expenditure within a framework that incorporates some of the key characteristics of a federal nation. These include (i) many levels of government[2] each with a constitutional right to levy taxes, partly on the same base, (ii) statutory definition in several federal countries (e.g. India) of some commodity taxes as federal instruments while others belong to the provinces, and (iii) distinction between a 'national public good' (e.g. defence) which is provided by the national government, financed by its federal tax and consumed uniformly by all nationals, and a 'local public good' (e.g. roadways) which is supplied and financed by the province out of provincial tax revenue and consumed exclusively by residents of that particular province. Following Gordon (1983), we distinguish between 'fully co-ordinated' (i.e. 'centralised') and 'decentralised decision making' in the federal setup. In the former, the Central and provinces' tax and spending behaviour are fully co-ordinated i.e. the Centre simultaneously designs federal and provincial taxes taking into account regional (i.e. inter-province) as well as intra province income distributional weights, its own revenue constraint and those of the provinces. This procedure captures the external effects of changes in federal, provincial taxes on the revenue of the other. By contrast, in the decentralized

---

Tulkens (1986); Murty and Nayak (1989); Murty and Ray (1990). See, also, Oates (1990) for a recent survey of research in 'Fiscal Federalism', and the volume edited by Rosen (1988) for a selection of quantitative studies on state and local government finance in the USA.

[2] These will be referred to as the 'federal' and 'provincial' authorities. Note, also, that the terms 'federal', 'national' and 'Central' are used synonymously in this paper.

procedure, each provincial government acts independently, in the light of provincial objectives, taking as given the fiscal decisions made by the Centre and other provincial governments. In this latter procedure, therefore, the constituent units of the federal union do not take into account the external effects of changes in their respective tax instruments on the others' revenue and regional income distributional preferences of the Centre.

The methodology of this paper follows King (1986, p. 274)[3] in exploiting 'the dual relationship that exists between the prices of private goods and the quantities of public goods on the one hand, and willingness to pay for public goods on the other'. We extend the King methodology to establish conditions for the optimal financing and provision of public goods in the federal context. The plan of this paper is as follows. Section 2 presents the basic duality results for local and national public goods. The various optimality conditions in the 'centralised' federal context are derived and analysed in Section 3. This section also derives an interesting relation between federal and provincial resource constraint parameters that must hold at the optimum. Section 4 presents the 'decentralised' version of the federal model and re-examines the optimality conditions in this context. Section 5 shows how the framework and concepts presented in this paper can be made operational and presents illustrative numerical evidence for India confirming the principal analytical result derived earlier. The paper ends on the concluding note of Section 6.

2 REVIEW OF DUALITY CONCEPTS AND RESULTS

The federal system consists of a Centre and S provinces. The former supplies a national public good (Z) consumed uniformly by all citizens, while each province, s, supplies a local public good (g^s) whose consumption is restricted to residents of that province.

---

[3] We have retained King's symbols, as far as possible, for ready comparability with his results.

We ignore inter province migration[4] of goods and individuals. There are J private goods which are traded at consumer price p. Leisure, which is a private good, is not taxed. Assuming full shifting of taxes, the consumer price of item i in province s has three elements

$$p_i^s = \bar{p}_i + \theta_i + t_i^s \tag{1}$$

$$s = 1, \ldots, S; i = 1, \ldots, J$$

where θ_i is the federal tax set by the Centre, t_i^s is the province-specific commodity tax, and producer price $\bar{p}_i$ is assumed to be constant across provinces. The preferences of a resident of province s are represented by the indirect utility function.

$$v^s = v^s(p^s, g^s, Z, y^s) \tag{2}$$

$$s = 1, \ldots, S$$

where p^s is a $J \times 1$ vector of consumer prices, g^s, Z are quantities of local, national public goods, and y^s is the resident's exogenous full income i.e. the value of all endowments including time. Inverting (2), assuming invertibility, we obtain the corresponding expenditure function.

$$e^s = e^s(p^s, g^s, Z, v^s) \tag{3}$$

$$s = 1, \ldots, S$$

Note that (3) extends the traditional concept of a cost function defined in a strictly private goods economy [see, e.g. Varian (1978)] to incorporate public goods (g^s, Z). The resident's money metric utility or 'equivalent income', y_E^s is defined as the level of income in province s which, at some reference vector of consumer prices and public goods provision ($p^{R.s}, g^{R.s}, Z^s$), yields the same utility as under the actual budget situation (p^s, g^s, Z, y^s)

i.e. y_E^s is the result of (2) and (3)

$$y_E^s = e^s(p^{R.s}, g^{R.s}, Z^R, v^s) \tag{4a}$$

---

[4] See Arnott and Grieson (1981); Mintz and Tulkens (1986) for analysis of the implications of migration of goods and individuals for the optimal tax results.

$$= f^s (p^{R.s}, g^{R.s}, Z^R, p^s, g^s, Z^s, y^s) \qquad (4b)$$

where the superscript 'R' denotes reference values.

Assuming v, e, and, hence, f to be continuous, the 'marginal willingness to pay' for the local, national public goods are given, respectively, by

$$w^s (p^s, g^s, Z, y^s) = - \left. \frac{\partial y^s}{\partial g^s} \right|_{v = \bar{v}} \qquad (5a)$$

$$\tilde{w}^s (p^s, g^s, Z, y^s) = - \left. \frac{\partial y^s}{\partial Z} \right|_{v = \bar{v}} \qquad (5b)$$

Differentiating (2) with respect to g^s, Z holding the utility level constant, we obtain

$$\frac{\partial v^s}{\partial g^s} + \frac{\partial v^s}{\partial y^s} \cdot \frac{\partial y^s}{\partial g^s} = 0 \qquad (6a)$$

$$\frac{\partial v^s}{\partial Z} + \frac{\partial v^s}{\partial y^s} \cdot \frac{\partial y^s}{\partial Z} = 0 \qquad (6b)$$

Combining (5a), (6a) and (5b), (6b), respectively, we obtain the following analogue of Roy's Identity for local, national public goods

$$w^s = - \frac{\dfrac{\partial v^s}{\partial g^s}}{\dfrac{\partial v^s}{\partial y^s}} \qquad (7a)$$

$$\tilde{w}^s = - \frac{\dfrac{\partial v^s}{\partial Z}}{\dfrac{\partial v^s}{\partial y^s}} \qquad (7b)$$

Again, combining (3), (5a) and (3), (5b), respectively, we obtain the following analogue to Shephard's Lemma.

$$w^s = - \frac{\partial e^s}{\partial g^s} \qquad (8a)$$

$$\tilde{w}^s = -\frac{\partial e^s}{\partial Z} \tag{8b}$$

Note, incidentally, that though the national public good, Z, is consumed uniformly by all nationals, the 'marginal willingness to pay' for it will vary across and within provinces.

The compensated and uncompensated demands for private goods in province s are given, respectively, by

$$x_i^s = \frac{\partial e^s}{\partial p_i^s} = x_i^{c.s}(p^s, g^s, Z, v^s) \tag{9}$$

$$x_i^s = -\frac{\dfrac{\partial v^s}{\partial p_i^s}}{\dfrac{\partial v^s}{\partial y^s}} = x_i^s(p^s, g^s, Z, y^s) \tag{10}$$

The compensated effect of change in local, national public goods on the demand for the ith private good in province s, denoted by S_{ik}^s, S_{iZ}^s, respectively, are given as follows.

$$S_{ig}^s = \frac{\partial x_i^{c.s}}{\partial g^s} = \frac{\partial x_i^s}{\partial g^s} + \left[\frac{\partial x_i^s}{\partial y^s}\right]\left[\frac{\partial e^s}{\partial g^s}\right] \tag{11a}$$

$$S_{iZ}^s = \frac{\partial x_i^{c.s}}{\partial Z} = \frac{\partial x_i^s}{\partial Z} + \left[\frac{\partial x_i^s}{\partial y^s}\right]\left[\frac{\partial e^s}{\partial Z}\right] \tag{11b}$$

Combining (8a), (11a) and (8b), (11b), respectively, we obtain the Slutsky equation for local, national public goods.

$$\frac{\partial x_i^s}{\partial g^s} = S_{ig}^s + w^s \frac{\partial x_i^s}{\partial y^s} \tag{12a}$$

$$i = 1, \ldots, J$$
$$s = 1, \ldots, S$$

$$\frac{\partial x_i^s}{\partial Z} = S_{iZ}^s + \tilde{w}^s \frac{\partial x_i^s}{\partial y^s}$$

(12b)

$$i = 1, \ldots, J$$
$$s = 1, \ldots, S$$

The equations relating changes in the quantities of public goods to changes in the willingness to pay for them in province s are given as follows.

$$\frac{\partial w^s}{\partial g^s} = S_{gg}^s + w^s \frac{\partial w^s}{\partial y^s}$$

(13a)

$$\frac{\partial w^s}{\partial Z} = S_{gZ}^s + \tilde{w}^s \frac{\partial w^s}{\partial y^s}$$

(13b)

$$\frac{\partial \tilde{w}^s}{\partial g^s} = S_{Zg}^s + w^s \frac{\partial \tilde{w}^s}{\partial y^s}$$

(13c)

$$\frac{\partial \tilde{w}^s}{\partial Z} = S_{ZZ}^s + \tilde{w}^s \frac{\partial \tilde{w}^s}{\partial y^s}$$

(13d)

$S_{gg}^s, S_{gZ}^s, S_{Zg}^s, S_{ZZ}^s$ denote, respectively, the effect of compensated change in the quantities of local, national public goods on the willingness to pay for them in province s. Note that, by the usual symmetry argument, $S_{gZ}^s = S_{Zg}^s$.

In the above discussion, willingness to pay for public goods plays a role that is analogous to that of commodity demands in a strictly private goods economy. The equilibrium values of these variables can be obtained by differentiating (4a)–(4b) with respect to actual prices and quantities and using Roy's identity. These are given by

$$x_i^s = \frac{\partial f^s}{\partial p_i^{R.s}} \Bigg|_{\substack{p^{R.s} = p^s \\ g^{R.s} = g^s}} = -\frac{\dfrac{\partial f^s}{\partial p_i^s}}{\dfrac{\partial f^s}{\partial y^s}}$$

(14)

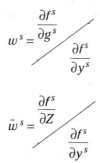

$$w^s = \dfrac{\dfrac{\partial f^s}{\partial g^s}}{\dfrac{\partial f^s}{\partial y^s}} \qquad (15a)$$

$$\tilde{w}^s = \dfrac{\dfrac{\partial f^s}{\partial Z}}{\dfrac{\partial f^s}{\partial y^s}} \qquad (15b)$$

3 Optimal Financing and Provision of Public Goods in a Centralized Federal State

In the federal economy, while there is a finite number (S) of provinces, each province consists of a continuum of individuals who differ in respect of some attribute ϕ (scalar), with its distribution function denoted by $F^s(\phi)$. Assuming what Gordon (1983, p. 573) calls 'fully coordinated decision making behaviour' and following King (1986) in defining the social welfare function (SWF) over individual levels of equivalent income, the optimization involves maximizing the nation's SWF given by

$$SW = \sum_{s=1}^{S} \int_{\phi} W^s\!\left(y_E^s(\phi) \right) d F^s(\phi) \qquad (16)$$

subject to the provincial and federal budget constraints. In the following analysis of the centralized federal specification, we initially admit a provincial poll tax, denoted by l^s that is uniform within a province but varies between provinces. We, subsequently, allow the national government to levy a lump sum tax, $\tilde{l}$, that is invariant between and within provinces. If $\bar{x}_i^s$ denotes mean demand for private good i in province s, then the provincial and federal budget constraints are, initially, given by

$$l^s + \sum_{i=1}^{J} t_i^s \bar{x}_i^s \geq c^s g^s \tag{17}$$

$$s = 1, \ldots, S$$

$$\sum_{s=1}^{S} \sum_{i=1}^{J} \theta_i \bar{x}_i^s \geq \tilde{c} Z \tag{18}$$

where c^s is the per capita marginal cost of the local public good, and $\tilde{c}$ the per capita marginal cost of the national public good.

The constrained maximization of the nation's *SWF* [(given in eqn. 16)] is carried out with respect to three sets of policy instruments at the disposal of the provincial and Central authorities. These are (i) commodity tax rates (t^s, θ), (ii) quantities of public goods (g^s, Z) and (iii) the $(S \times 1)$ vector of poll taxes, l, whose typical element is l^s.

The exercise implies the following Lagrangean

$$L = \sum_{s=1}^{S} \int_{\phi} W^s \left(y_E^s(\phi) \right) d F^s(\phi) + \sum_{s=1}^{S} \lambda^s \left\{ l^s + \sum_{i=1}^{J} t_i^s \bar{x}_i^s - c^s g^s \right\}$$

$$+ \mu \left\{ \sum_{s=1}^{S} \sum_{i=1}^{J} \theta_i \bar{x}_i^s - \tilde{c} Z \right\} \tag{19}$$

where $\lambda^s \ (s = 1, \ldots, S)$, μ denote the budget constraint multipliers and can be interpreted as, respectively, the shadow price of the revenue of the provincial and federal authorities or, in other words, the social marginal utility of federal and provincial government revenue.

Using the facts that $\partial f^s/\partial l^s = -\partial f^s/\partial y^s$, and $\partial f^s/\partial t_j^s = \partial f^s/\partial \theta = \partial f^s/\partial p_j^s$ and denoting $W'^s = \partial W^s/\partial y_E^s$, $\hat{t}_i^s = t_i^s + (\mu/\lambda^s) \theta_i$, the five first order conditions for the optimum levels of the policy instruments, mentioned above, are as follows.

$$\int_\phi W'^s \frac{\partial f^s}{\partial p_j^s} dF^s(\phi) + \lambda^s \left\{ \bar{x}_j^s + \sum_{i=1}^{J} \bar{t}_i^s \int_\phi \frac{\partial x_i^s}{\partial p_j^s} dF^s(\phi) \right\} = 0 \tag{20a}$$

$$j = 1, \dots, J$$
$$s = 1, \dots, S$$

$$\sum_s \int_\phi W'^s \frac{\partial f^s}{\partial p_j^s} dF^s(\phi) + \sum_{s=1}^{S} \lambda^s \sum_{i=1}^{J} \bar{t}_i^s \int_\phi \frac{\partial x_i^s}{\partial p_j^s} dF^s(\phi) + \mu \sum_{s=1}^{S} \bar{x}_j^s = 0 \tag{20b}$$

$$j = 1, \dots, J$$

$$\int_\phi W'^s \frac{\partial f^s}{\partial g^s} dF^s(\phi) + \lambda^s \left\{ -c^s + \sum_{i=1}^{J} \bar{t}_i^s \int_\phi \frac{\partial x_i^s}{\partial g^s} dF^s(\phi) \right\} = 0 \tag{21a}$$

$$s = 1, \dots, S$$

$$\sum_s \int_\phi W'^s \frac{\partial f^s}{\partial Z} dF^s(\phi) + \sum_{s=1}^{S} \lambda^s \sum_{i=1}^{J} \bar{t}_i^s \int_\phi \frac{\partial x_i^s}{\partial Z} dF^s(\phi) - \mu \bar{c} = 0 \tag{21b}$$

$$\int_\phi W'^s \frac{\partial f^s}{\partial y^s} dF^s(\phi) - \lambda^s \left\{ 1 - \sum_{i=1}^{J} \bar{t}_i^s \int_\phi \frac{\partial x_i^s}{\partial y^s} dF^s(\phi) \right\} = 0 \tag{22}$$

Note that the 'consolidated tax' $\bar{t}_k^s$ which combines provincial and federal taxes plays a role analogous to that of commodity tax in the traditional unitary State framework [see Atkinson and Stiglitz (1980)]. Let us define

$$b^s(\phi) = \frac{W'^s(\phi)}{\lambda^s} \frac{\partial f^s}{\partial y^s} + \sum_{i=1}^{J} \bar{t}_i^s \frac{\partial x_i^s}{\partial y^s} \tag{23}$$

$b^s(\phi)$ can be interpreted as the net social marginal valuation of income, expressed in terms of the federal budget constraint multiplier λ^s as numeraire, of an individual with attribute ϕ in province S, where 'net' means there is an adjustment to the social marginal utility of income for the marginal propensity to spend taxes out of extra income. This extends the interpretation given in Diamond (1975); Atkinson and Stiglitz (1980, p. 387); Ahmad and Stern (1991, p. 55) to a centralized federal State.

The Slutsky equation for private goods is

$$\frac{\partial x_i^s}{\partial p_j^s} = S_{ij}^s - x_j^s \frac{\partial x_i^s}{\partial y^s} \tag{24}$$

Combining (24) with (20a, b), using equation (14) and the definition of b^s (ϕ) in (23), we obtain after re-arrangement the following equations for optimal provincial and federal commodity taxes.

$$\int_\phi b^s (\phi) \, x_j^s (\phi) \, d F^s (\phi) = \bar{x}_j^s + \sum_i \bar{t}_i^s \int_\phi S_{ji}^s (\phi) \, d F^s (\phi) \tag{25a}$$

$$s = 1, \dots, S$$
$$j = 1, \dots, J$$

$$\sum_s \lambda^s \int_\phi b^s (\phi) \, x_j^s (\phi) \, d F^s (\phi)$$

$$= \mu \sum_s \bar{x}_j^s + \sum_s \lambda^s \sum_i \bar{t}_i^s \int_\phi S_{ji}^s (\phi) \, d F^s (\phi) \tag{25b}$$

$$j = 1, \dots, J$$

Equations (25a, b) together imply the following relationship.

$$\sum_{s=1}^S \left\{ \lambda^s - \mu \right\} \bar{x}_j^s = 0$$

$$\text{i.e. } \sum_{s=1}^S \left\{ 1 - \frac{\lambda^s}{\mu} \right\} \bar{x}_j^s = 0 \tag{26}$$

Since the $\bar{x}_j^s$ are all non negative, (26) implies that μ must lie between λ (min.) and λ (max.). We have, thus, established the following proposition.

Proposition I: In the centralized federal State, if the financing of public goods is optimal, then relationship (26) between the mean quantities demanded in the provinces must be satisfied, and the marginal social benefit of federal revenue must lie between the minimum and maximum values of the marginal social benefit of tax revenue in the provinces. Alternatively, the marginal social benefit of federal revenue is a weighted average of those in the provinces.

The first order conditions for optimal commodity taxes [equations (20a, b)] can be re-arranged, using eqn. (14), to obtain the following expressions for λ^s, μ.

$$\lambda^s = \frac{\int_\phi \beta^s(\phi) x_j^s(\phi) - \mu \sum_{i=1}^{J} \int_\phi \theta_i \frac{\partial x_i^s}{\partial p_j^s} dF^s(\phi)}{\bar{x}_j^s + \sum_i t_i^s \int_\phi \frac{\partial x_i^s}{\partial p_j^s} dF^s(\phi)} \tag{27a}$$

$$s = 1, \ldots, S$$

$$\mu = \frac{\sum_s \int_\phi \beta^s(\phi) x_j^s(\phi) - \sum_s \sum_i \int_\phi \lambda^s t_i^s \frac{\partial x_i^s}{\partial p_j^s} dF^s(\phi)}{\sum_{s=1}^{S} \bar{x}_j^s + \sum_{s=1}^{S} \sum_{i=1}^{J} \theta_i \int_\phi \frac{\partial x_i^s}{\partial p_j^s} dF^s(\phi)} \tag{27b}$$

where $\beta^s = \partial W^s / \partial y^s$ is the social marginal utility of income of individual in province s as evaluated by the federal authority.

(27a, b) provide the link between the unobservable (λ^s, μ) and observable variables. Given tax data (t_j^s, θ_j), the mean consumption levels of the provinces ($\bar{x}_j^s$), the demand derivatives ($\partial x_i^s / \partial p_j^s$) from an estimated demand system on provincial expenditure data, and the welfare weights (β^s) from an a-priori specified social welfare function, (27a, b) allow the marginal social benefit of Federal and provincial revenue (λ^s, μ) to be calculated. (26), then, provides a convenient check for the optimality of a centralized federal tax system.

The following further points should be noted.

(i)   (27a, b), which show the mutual dependence of λ, μ on one another point to the need for iterative solution and, also, provide the basis for the proposed computational algorithm for calculating optimal commodity taxes in a federal country. The illustrative numerical evidence, presented later, demonstrates usefulness of the iterative procedures in federal optimal tax calculations, and confirm the validity of Proposition I.

(ii)   The social marginal utility of income β^s depends not only on the planner's inequality aversion between individuals in province s but, also, on his/her aversion to economic disparities between provinces.

(iii)   Since (27a, b) assume that commodity taxes are optimal, λ^s, μ do *not* have any commodity subscript j. In practice, however, commodity taxes are not optimal — in other words, given *actual* tax data, λ_j^s, μ_j will be commodity specific. (27a, b) can, then, be viewed as the limiting case of optimality i.e. when λ_j^s, μ_j are equalized across commodities j. Section V shows that, in the context of an actual i.e. non optimal tax system, λ_j^s, μ_j can be interpreted as the marginal social cost of revenue arising, respectively, from an adjustment of the jth provincial and federal commodity tax. We exploit this link between marginal tax reforms and optimal taxes, i.e. view the latter as a limiting sequence of the former, in proposing the numerical procedures for calculating optimal taxes in a federal set-up.

Since eqn. (26) holds for all $j = 1, \ldots, J$, it follows that

$$\left(\lambda^1 - \mu, \lambda^2 - \mu, \ldots, \lambda^s - \mu \right)(\bar{x}) = 0 \tag{28}$$

where $\bar{x}$ is the $S \times J$ matrix of mean demands.

$$\bar{x} = \begin{pmatrix} \bar{x}_1^1 & \ldots & \bar{x}_j^1 \\ \bar{x}_1^2 & \ldots & \bar{x}_j^2 \\ & & \\ \bar{x}_1^s & \ldots & \bar{x}_j^s \end{pmatrix}$$

Eqn. (28) implies that either $\lambda^s = \mu$ for all s, or rank $(\bar{x}^s_j) < S$. If J (number of private goods) is larger than S (number of provinces) and if the demand vectors are sufficiently varied among provinces, then one can assume rank $(\bar{x}^s_j) = S$, which implies $\lambda^s = \mu$ for all s. We, thus have the following Proposition.

Proposition II: In a centralized federal State where the number of private goods is larger than the number of provinces, *and* consumer preferences vary widely across provinces, optimal financing of public goods implies that the marginal social benefit of government revenue in the provinces and the Centre are all equal.

To compare the optimality conditions for public goods provision under distortionary taxes in the federal set up [equations (21a, b)] with the Samuelson rule, we substitute the Slutsky equation for public goods [equations (12a, b)] in them and obtain, after some re-arrangement, the following equations.

$$\int_\phi b^s(\phi)\, w^s(\phi)\, dF^s(\phi) = c^s - \sum_i \bar{t}^S_i \int_\phi S^S_{gi}(\phi)\, dF^s(\phi) \qquad (29a)$$

$$s = 1, \ldots, S$$

$$\sum_s \left(\frac{\lambda^s}{\mu}\right)\int_\phi b^s(\phi)\, \tilde{w}^s(\phi)\, dF^s(\phi)$$

$$= \tilde{c} - \sum_s \sum_i \bar{t}^s_i \left(\frac{\lambda^s}{\mu}\right)\int_\phi S^s_{Zi}(\phi)\, dF^s(\phi) \qquad (29b)$$

Let us recall the corresponding Samuelson conditions under lump sum taxes and transfers.

$$\int_\phi w^s(\phi)\, dF^s(\phi) = c^s \qquad (30a)$$

$$\sum_s \int_\phi \tilde{w}^s(\phi)\, dF^s(\phi) = \tilde{c} \qquad (30b)$$

A comparison of (29a, b) with (30a, b) shows that the second best rules modify the Samuelson condition in three respects: (i) the distribution effects given by $b^s(\phi)$, (ii) the so-called 'Pigou term' using King (1986, p. 283)'s terminology, given by the second expression on the r.h.s. of (29a, b), and (iii) the ratio of shadow prices of provincial and federal government revenue (λ^s/μ).

The first order condition for optimal poll tax in each province [equation (22)] implies, using the definition of $b^s(\phi)$ in equation (23), the following

$$\bar{b}^s = \int_\phi b^s(\phi)\, dF^s(\phi) = 1 \tag{31}$$

$$s = 1, \ldots, S$$

To understand the meaning of this condition, let us note that $b^s(\phi)$ measures the aggregate of two effects of transferring a dollar to a household with attribute ϕ: the *direct effect*, measured in federal revenue, and given by the first term on the r.h.s. of (23), and an *indirect effect*, given by the second term, measuring the effect of the transfer on the income of the federal and provincial authorities. The mean $(\bar{b}^s)$ is the net value of giving an equal lump sum payment to everyone in province s. Equation (31) states that if uniform lump-sum payments or taxes were allowed in province s, then the centralized federal State would set them such that $\bar{b}^s = 1$. This is a standard result in the traditional formulation [see, for example, Atkinson and Stiglitz (1980)] — the present discussion extends it to the federal case.

Following the same logic as used in the traditional case of a unitary State, the possibility of individually tailored lump sum transfers in each province causes the $b^s(\phi)$ to be invariant across individuals, i.e. $b^s(\phi) = 1$ which, via (25a, b), imply

$$\bar{t}_i^s = 0 \tag{32a}$$

$$s = 1, \ldots, S$$

$$\mu = \sum_s \left(\frac{\bar{x}_j^s}{\sum_p \bar{x}_j^p} \right) \lambda^s \tag{32b}$$

The use of commodity taxation stems from a pursuit of distributional objectives. Thus, if the utility function is weakly separable
between labour and all commodities, and if individualized lump
sum taxes are available in province s, then, there is no role for
the consolidated commodity tax $\tilde{t}_i^s$ in that province. Recalling that
$\tilde{t}_i^s = t_i^s + (\mu / \lambda^s) \theta_i$, condition (32a) implies that

(a) federal and provincial commodity taxes are proportional across
items, and (b) they differ in sign since $\lambda^s, \mu > 0$. The above result
can be summarized in the following proposition.

Proposition III: In the centralized federal model with leisure/ goods
separability, if a provincial government can freely make individually tailored lump sum transfers, then, at the optimum, (a) provincial
taxes are proportional to federal taxes i.e. $t_i^s = k^s \theta_i$ where k^s is the
constant of proportionality, (b) provincial and federal taxes have
reverse signs i.e. a positive federal tax on an item attracts a subsidy
by the provincial government, and vice versa, and (c) relation (32b)
between the shadow prices of provincial and federal revenue must
be satisfied.

Note that $\tilde{t}_i^s = 0$ does *not* necessarily imply that provincial commodity taxes (t_i^s) equal zero. On the contrary, the above proposition implies that in the presence of individually tailored provincial
lump sum taxes, federal tax ($\theta_i \neq 0$) on an item necessitates a
corresponding provincial tax ($t_i^s \neq 0$) on that item. This distinguishes the centralized federal specification from the traditional
unitary State formulation where, as is well known, the presence
of lump sum taxes renders unnecessary the imposition of *all*
commodity taxes.

Let us extend the analysis to allow the federal government to
impose a lump sum tax, $\bar{l}$, in addition to the provincial lump sum
taxes, l^s. The federal budget constraint becomes

$$S\bar{l} + \sum_{s=1}^{S} \sum_{i=1}^{J} \theta_i \bar{x}_i^s \geq \tilde{c}Z \tag{33}$$

The constrained maximization exercise now implies the following

$$L = \sum_{s=1}^{S} \int_{\phi} W^s \left\{ y_E^s(\phi) \right\} dF^s(\phi) + \sum_{s=1}^{S} \lambda^s \left(l^s + \sum_{i=1}^{J} t_i^s \bar{x}_i^s - c^s g^s \right)$$

$$+ \mu \left(S\bar{l} + \sum_s \sum_i \theta_i \bar{x}_i^s - \bar{c}Z \right) \tag{34}$$

The exercise yields six sets of first order conditions corresponding to the six policy instruments, namely, (i) commodity tax rates (t^s, θ), (ii) quantities of public goods (g^s, Z) and (iii) provincial and national lump sum taxes $(l^s, \bar{l})$. The reader can verify that the first five conditions are the same as before [equations (20a, b), (21a, b), 22]. In other words, the presence of a federal lump sum tax does *not* invalidate any of the Propositions derived earlier. The additional condition, implied by an optimal $\bar{l}$, is as follows.

$$\sum_s \int_{\phi} W'^s \frac{\partial f^s}{\partial y^s} dF^s(\phi) + \sum_s \lambda^s \left\{ \sum_i t_i^s \frac{\partial \bar{x}_i^s}{\partial y^s} \right\} - \mu \left\{ S - \sum_s \sum_i \theta_i \frac{\partial \bar{x}_i^s}{\partial y^s} \right\} = 0 \tag{35}$$

i.e. using the definition of $b^s(\theta)$ given in (23),

$$\sum_s \int_{\phi} \lambda^s b^s(\phi) = \mu S$$

or, in other words,

$$\sum_s \left(\frac{\lambda^s}{\mu} \right) \bar{b}^s = S \tag{36}$$

Using equation (31) i.e. $\bar{b}^s = 1$ implied by optimal l^s in each province, condition (36) becomes

$$\mu = \frac{\sum_s \lambda^s}{S} = \bar{\lambda}$$

We, thus, have the following Proposition.

Proposition IV: In the centralized federal specification, if the provincial and federal authorities can freely impose lump sum taxes and transfers, then the shadow price of federal revenue equals the mean of the shadow prices of revenue of the provinces.

4 OPTIMAL TAXATION IN A DECENTRALIZED FEDERAL MODEL

In a federal country, lower levels of government enjoy fiscal autonomy by deciding independently their taxes and revenue constraints without taking into account the effect of their decisions on each others' resources. The centralized procedure described above does not permit this federal autonomy since the Centre designs federal and provincial taxes taking into account regional as well as intra provincial income redistributional effects, its own revenue constraint and those of the provinces. This contrasts with the decentralized federal model where, while the Centre in designing federal taxes maximizes the nation's *SWF* incorporating inter-province and intra-province welfare weights, the constituent provinces design provincial taxes by maximizing their respective social welfare ignoring the effect of their fiscal decisions on the welfare of individuals in other provinces.

The decentralized federal model, described below, consists of an interactive sequence of fiscal decisions by the Centre and the provinces, based on a roundwise update of notional information on their respective taxes fed by these decision-making units to one another, until convergence.

Step 1: Centre designs optimal federal commodity taxes given the initial (i.e. actual) provincial commodity taxes $t_i^{s\,o}$ i.e. it maximizes the nation's *SWF, SW* [see equation (16)] with respect to θ subject to its own revenue constraint [equation (17)], where the mean demand vector, $\bar{x}_i^s$ is evaluated, conditional on actual provincial taxes $t_i^{s\,o}$. The solution yields first round values of federal taxes $(\theta_i^{(1)})$ which the Centre communicates to the provinces.

Step 2: Using this information, each province s computes optimal provincial commodity taxes by maximizing its own *SWF*, W^s, with respect to t_i^s subject to its own revenue constraint alone, with the provincial commodity demand vector calculated with the federal commodity tax set at $\theta_i^{(1)}$. The solution yields the first round values of the provincial taxes $t_i^{s(1)}$ which the provinces communicate to the Centre.

The Centre re-designs its tax to $\theta_i^{(2)}$ using the updated tax information in computing the new demand vector. The provinces act likewise using the updated federal tax vector $(\theta_i^{(2)})$ to obtain redesigned provincial taxes $t_i^{s(2)}$. The process continues until convergence i.e. changes in θ, ts between successive iterations are less than a pre-specified value. Note that the sequence of tax information used by the Centre and the provinces during the iterations is purely notional and is devoid of actual policy significance.

In Lagrangean terms, therefore, the decentralized procedure involves separate maximization of L_1, L_2^s with respect to $\{\theta_i, \bar{l}\}$ and $\{t_i^s, l^s\}$, respectively, where

$$L_1 = \sum_s \int_\phi W^s \{y_E^s(\phi)\} \, dF^s + \mu\left(S\bar{l} + \sum_s \sum_i \theta_i \bar{x}_i^s - \tilde{c}Z\right) \qquad (37)$$

$$L_2^s = \int_\phi W^s \{y_E^s(\phi)\} \, dF^s + \lambda^s\left(l^s + \sum_i t_i^s \bar{x}_i^s - c^s g^s\right) \qquad (38)$$

$$s = 1, \ldots, S$$

We, thus, have the following sets of first order conditions for optimal federal and provincial commodity taxes.

$$\sum_s \int_\phi W'^s \frac{\partial f^s}{\partial p_j^s} \, dF^s + \mu\left(\sum_s \bar{x}_j^s + \sum_s \sum_i \theta_i \frac{\partial \bar{x}_i^s}{\partial p_j^s}\right) = 0 \qquad (39a)$$

$$\int_\phi W'^s \frac{\partial f^s}{\partial p_j^s} \, dF^s + \lambda^s\left(\sum_i t_i^s \frac{\partial \bar{x}_i^s}{\partial p_j^s} + \bar{x}_j^s\right) = 0 \qquad (39b)$$

The corresponding conditions for optimal lump-sum taxes $(\tilde{l}, l^s)$ are as follows.

$$\sum_s \int_\phi W'^s \frac{\partial f^s}{\partial y^s} - \mu \left(S - \sum_s \sum_i \theta_i \frac{\partial \bar{x}_i^s}{\partial y^s} \right) = 0 \qquad (40a)$$

$$\int_\phi W'^s \frac{\partial f^s}{\partial y^s} - \lambda^s \left(l - \sum_i t_i^s \frac{\partial \bar{x}_i^s}{\partial y^s} \right) = 0 \qquad (40b)$$

Using Roy's identity (eqn. 10) and the Slutsky decomposition (24) in (39a, b), we obtain after some re-arrangement the following equations for optimal commodity taxes in the decentralized federal economy.

$$\sum_s \int_\phi \left\{ \frac{W'^s}{\mu} \frac{\partial f^s}{\partial y^s} + \sum_i \theta_i \frac{\partial x_i^s}{\partial y^s} \right\} x_j^s \, dF^s$$

$$= \sum_s \left\{ \bar{x}_j^s + \sum_i \theta_i \int_\phi S_{ij}^s (\phi) \, dF^s \right\} \qquad (41a)$$

$$\int_\phi \left\{ \frac{W'^s}{\lambda^s} \frac{\partial f^s}{\partial y^s} + \sum_i t_i^s \frac{\partial x_i^s}{\partial y^s} \right\} x_j^s \, dF^s$$

$$= \bar{x}_j^s + \sum_i t_i^s \int_\phi S_{ij}^s (\phi) \, dF^s \qquad (41b)$$

Let us define

$$b_1^s (\phi) = \frac{W'^s}{\mu} \frac{\partial f^s}{\partial y^s} + \sum_i \theta_i \frac{\partial x_i^s}{\partial y^s} \qquad (42)$$

$$b_2^s (\phi) = \frac{W'^s}{\lambda^s} \frac{\partial f^s}{\partial y^s} + \sum_i t_i^s \frac{\partial x_i^s}{\partial y^s} \qquad (43)$$

Note that, following the explanation of the previous section, $b_1^s(\phi)$, $b_2^s(\phi)$, can be interpreted as the social marginal valuation of income, *net* of federal and provincial commodity taxes, respectively, and expressed in terms of the corresponding Lagrangean multipliers (μ, λ^s) as numeraire. $b_1^s(\phi)$, $b_2^s(\phi)$ are the disaggregated counterpart of the comprehensive parameter $b^s(\phi)$, defined in (23), for the centralized federal model.

Equations (41a, b) can, thus, be re-written as

$$\sum_s \int_\phi b_1^s(\phi)\, x_j^s(\phi)\, dF^s = \sum_s \left\{ \bar{x}_j^s + \sum_i \theta_i \int_\phi S_{ij}^s(\phi)\, dF^s \right\} \quad (44a)$$

$$\int_\phi b_2^s(\phi)\, x_j^s(\phi)\, dF^s = \bar{x}_j^s + \sum_i t_i^s \int_\phi S_{ij}^s(\phi)\, dF^s \quad (44b)$$

$$s = 1, \ldots, S$$

Where $\bar{S}_{ij}^s = \int_\phi S_{ij}^s(\phi)\, dF^s$ is the mean Slutsky response in province s.

Using the definition of $b_1^s(\phi)$, $b_2^s(\phi)$, the conditions for optimal lump sum taxes [equations (40a, b)] become

$$\sum_s \int_\phi b_1^s(\phi)\, dF^s = S$$

$$\text{or } \bar{b}_1 = 1 \quad (45)$$

and $$\bar{b}_2^s \equiv \int_\phi b_2^s(\phi)\, dF^s = 1 \text{ for all } s \quad (46)$$

Lump sum taxes in the decentralized federal model, by equating to unity the mean values of b_1 (over all provinces) and b_2^s (in each province s), thus, perform a role similar to that in the unitary State model. Using the same argument as advanced in the traditional case and re-stated in the previous Section, the availability of individualized lump-sum taxes by the federal and provincial authorities, coupled with the assumption of leisure/goods separability, implies that $\theta_i = t_i^s = 0$ i.e. no commodity taxes need to be employed. The traditional unitary State model is, thus, closer to the decentralized federal model, rather than to the centralized model of the previous Section where, as already noted, individually tailored lump sum taxes do *not* necessarily imply the absence of commodity taxes. Unlike in the centralized federal State, the federal resource constraint multiplier, μ, need not lie between the minimum and maximum values of the provincial resource constraint multiplier, λ^s.

5 COMPUTATIONAL PROCEDURES FOR OPTIMAL COMMODITY TAX IN A FEDERAL STATE WITH ILLUSTRATIVE NUMERICAL EVIDENCE

We now show how the theory outlined above can be made operational and the principal analytical result stated in Proposition I checked from actual tax data. This section proposes and applies a computational algorithm to calculate optimal commodity taxes under the alternative models of fiscal federalism considered above. We extend the optimal tax algorithm proposed in Murty and Ray (1989) in the context of a unitary State. The computational procedures are based on a federal extension of the analysis of marginal tax reform provided by Ahmad and Stern (1991).

The central concept behind the proposed procedure is the 'social marginal cost' of public funds generated via increase in the ith tax. If we denote the social marginal cost for federal and provincial government funds by μ_i and λ_i^s, respectively, then in the centralized federal case these are given by

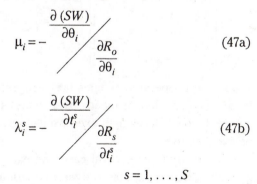

$$\mu_i = - \frac{\partial (SW)}{\partial \theta_i} \bigg/ \frac{\partial R_o}{\partial \theta_i} \qquad (47a)$$

$$\lambda_i^s = - \frac{\partial (SW)}{\partial t_i^s} \bigg/ \frac{\partial R_s}{\partial t_i^s} \qquad (47b)$$

$$s = 1, \ldots, S$$

where SW has been defined in (16). R_s, R_o, which are the net revenue requirements of the provincial, federal authorities, are defined by (17), (18) respectively. We can interpret μ_i as the marginal social cost of raising an extra unit of federal revenue from increasing the federal tax of good i; the numerator in (47a) represents the welfare cost of a unit change, and the inverse of $\partial R_o/\partial \theta_i$ tells us the magnitude of the change in θ_i required to raise one extra unit of federal revenue. If $\mu_i < \mu_j$, then we increase welfare at constant revenue by increasing θ_i and decreasing θ_j, and the reverse if $\mu_i > \mu_j$. A similar interpretation holds for λ_i^s, and we have a corresponding analysis of marginal provincial tax reform based on a comparison of λ_i^s, λ_j^s. Optimality requires that μ_i and λ_j^s are independent of i.

The computational procedure is based on the simple rule that items with an above average marginal social cost of raising revenue have their taxes lowered, and increased otherwise. The principle is adhered to in successive iterations which recalculate the simulated demand levels and elasticities at post iteration prices. Optimal commodity taxes are obtained on convergence i.e. when the marginal social cost of all items are equal. As shown in Murty and Ray (1989, pp. 661–2), the optimal taxes are revenue neutral with respect to the set of initial taxes.

The computational algorithm is given by

$$
\begin{bmatrix} \Delta \theta_j \\ \Delta t_j^l \\ \Delta t_j^s \end{bmatrix} = \begin{bmatrix} k\,0 & \ldots & 0 \\ 0\,k & \ldots & 0 \\ 0 & \ldots\ldots & k \end{bmatrix} \begin{bmatrix} \bar{\mu} - \mu_j \\ \bar{\lambda}^l - \lambda_j^l \\ \bar{\lambda}^s - \lambda_j^s \end{bmatrix} \qquad j = 1, \ldots, J \quad (48)
$$

where the Δ operator denotes tax changes between successive iterations. $\bar{\mu}$, $\bar{\lambda}^s$ denote means over items in each iteration, and $k\ (> 0)$ denotes step length fixed exogenously for a particular set of calculations.

In the centralized federal case, the expressions for λ_j^s, μ_j are given by (27a, b) expressed over a continuum of individuals. In discrete form, and expressed in terms of social welfare weights and price elasticities, these are given by

$$\lambda_j^s = \frac{w^s \sum_h \tilde{\beta}_h^s p_j^s x_{jh}^s - \mu^s \sum_i \theta_i e_{ij}^s X_i^s}{p_j^s X_j^s + \sum_i t_i^s e_{ij}^s X_i^s} \qquad (49a)$$

$$\mu_j = \frac{\sum_s \sum_h w^s \tilde{\beta}_h^s x_{jh}^s - \sum_s \sum_h \sum_i \lambda_i^s t_i^s e_{ij}^s \left(\dfrac{X_i^s}{P_j^s}\right)}{\tilde{X}_j + \sum_s \sum_i \theta_i e_{ij}^s \left(\dfrac{X_i^s}{P_j^s}\right)} \qquad (49b)$$

where h denotes individual, $\tilde{\beta}_h^s$ is 'social marginal utility' of income of h in province s as evaluated by that provincial authority, w^s is province s's welfare weight, and e_{ij}^s is the aggregate price elasticity in province s. X_j^s is aggregate demand for j in province s, and $\tilde{X}_j = \sum_s X_j^s$ is the total demand for item j in the nation as a whole. Note that $\beta_h^s = w^s \tilde{\beta}_h^s$ is the social marginal utility of income of h in province s as evaluated by the federal authority. This welfare weight depends not only on the planner's 'inequality aversion' to income disparities between individuals within the province but, also, on economic disparities between provinces.

The corresponding expressions for the social marginal cost parameters in the decentralized case are given by

$$\lambda_j^s = \frac{\sum_h \tilde{\beta}_h^s p_j^s x_{jh}^s}{p_j^s X_j^s + \sum_i t_i^s e_{ij}^s X_i^s} \qquad s = 1, \dots, S \qquad (50a)$$

$$\mu_j = \frac{\sum_s \sum_h w^s \tilde{\beta}_h^s x_{jh}^s}{\tilde{X}_j + \sum_s \sum_i \theta_i e_{ij}^s \left(\dfrac{X_i^s}{P_j^s}\right)} \qquad (50b)$$

Given initial values of taxes, estimates of demand parameters, data on expenditure distribution, a priori chosen values of the 'inequality aversion' parameter ϵ, equation system (48), used in conjunction with (49a, b) or (50a, b) yields on convergence the full set of optimal federal and provincial taxes that are revenue neutral with respect to the set of initial taxes. We ensured that the illustrative optimal tax estimates for India reported below are truly optimal by checking their invariance to alternative sets of revenue neutral taxes as starting values, and to the step length k.

Estimates of federal and provincial optimal commodity taxes, for a nine commodity disaggregation of consumer expenditure, under both the federal variants have been calculated for all the fifteen major provinces in India and reported in Murty and Ray (1990). The data set is the table of urban consumer expenditure in the 38th round of the National Sample Survey (1983-4) available in Government of India (1986). Table 1 presents the estimates for the provinces of Bihar and Andhra Pradesh. To save space, we report here only the optimal tax estimates corresponding to a particular level of 'inequality aversion' ($\in$ = 2.0). The detailed results, available upon request, show that the taxes vary significantly with $\in$ in a manner consistent with the latter's economic interpretation [see, also, Ray (1986); Murty and Ray (1989)]. The results, presented in Table 1, establish sensitivity of optimal taxes to federal specification. They further confirm that, unlike in the centralized case, under decentralized fiscal federalism, the shadow price of federal revenue need not lie between the minimum and maximum values of the shadow price of revenue of the constituent provinces of the federal Union.

6 SUMMARY AND CONCLUSION

We have attempted an integrated analysis of the optimal provision and financing of public goods in a federal system of government. This chapter extends the traditional framework to meet the peculiar characteristics of a federal nation. These principally include the simultaneous levying of taxes, partly on the same base, by many levels of government, and a distinction drawn between a 'national' and a 'local' public good based on the government organ that supplies it and finances its production. The chapter illustrates the usefulness of duality concepts in consumer theory by extending some of the well-known results in optimal taxation and public goods supply to the case of a federal nation.

An analysis of the consequences of fiscal federalism on optimal taxation under alternative assumptions about decision making in the federal State is offered in this chapter. These include a centralized model involving fully co-ordinated actions between the federal and provincial authorities, and a decentralized federal State where the provinces set their decision variables in the light of their (provincial) objectives, and subject to their own resource constraints. The analysis of Sections III, IV suggests that, in general, the optimal tax estimates are unlikely to be robust between the alternative federal specifications, and that the properties of the centralized model do not hold in the decentralized case. The latter retains a well-known property of the traditional unitary State model in implying that the presence of individually tailored national and provincial lump sum taxes renders unnecessary the imposition of commodity taxes. In contrast, in the centralized federal framework, such individualized lump sum taxes are quite consistent with non-zero commodity taxes though they do require federal and provincial commodity taxes to be proportional across items.

An interesting result, derived in this paper, relates the shadow price of the federal resource constraint to those of the provinces. The relationship is derived in a form that provides a convenient check for the optimality of a given federal fiscal system from available tax and budget data. The paper reports illustrative optimal tax calculations for India which show that the alternative federal models presented above can be made fully operational, and confirm the principal analytical result stated in Proposition I. The preliminary results on Indian budget data also show that both the federal models discussed above yield plausible estimates of federal and provincial taxes. We also present in the centralized federal context analytic expressions to Pigou's argument on the impact of distortionary taxation on the supply of public goods. The sign of the so-called 'Pigou term' is not only ambiguous, contrary to what Pigou had originally suggested, but, crucially in the present context, it is shown to depend on the distribution of the shadow price of provincial revenue to that of the Centre i.e. the federal government.

The recent interest in 'fiscal federalism' stems largely from an appreciation of the limitation of traditional models of public finance in analysis of fiscal issues of many major countries which have federal forms of government. Recent events e.g. the reunification of Germany and the forthcoming economic integration of the member countries of the EEC have stimulated fresh interest in this subject. This paper raises several issues for further research. These include (a) empirical evidence on the federal and provincial tax-rates under alternative federal specifications, and (b) empirical estimation of the demand for public goods in a federal framework. Optimal tax calculations in a unitary State, let alone a federal one, are complex enough to merit a separate chapter. The plausible optimal tax magnitudes in the federal context, reported in this chapter, promise considerable potential for further research.

TABLE 1

OPTIMAL COMMODITY TAXES UNDER ALTERNATIVE FEDERAL MODELS[a]

$(\in = 2.0)$

Commodity	Centralized Federalism			Decentralized Federalism		
	θ_i	t_i^1	t_i^2	θ_i	t_i^1	t_i^2
1. Cereals	−.027	−.003	.050	−.119	−.063	−.012
2. Milk and Milk Products	.110	.133	.217	.137	.135	.237
3. Edible Oils	.073	.087	.171	.047	.070	.155
4. Meat, Fish and Eggs	.094	.100	.192	.088	.101	.193
5. Sugar	.071	.095	.174	.045	.069	.154
6. Other Food	.086	.102	.182	.071	.088	.178

Commodity	Centralized Federalism			Decentralized Federalism		
	θ_i	t_i^1	t_i^2	θ_i	t_i^1	t_i^2
7. Clothing	.133	.142	.246	.179	.163	.272
8. Fuel and Light	.047	.070	.138	-.006	.029	.104
9. Other Non Food	.121	.138	.224	.158	.149	.254
	μ	λ (min.)	λ (max.)	μ	λ (min.)	λ (max.)
	.168	.143	.206	.141	.146	.198

Note: [a] Province 1 is Bihar, Province 2 is Andhra Pradesh

REFERENCES

Ahmad, E. and N.H. Stern (1991), *The Theory and Practice of Tax Reform in Developing Countries*, Cambridge: CUP.

Arnott, R. and R. Grieson (1981), 'Optimal Fiscal Policy for a State or Local Government', *Journal of Urban Economics*, 9, pp. 23–48.

Atkinson, A.B. and N.H. Stern (1974), 'Pigou, Taxation and Public Goods', *Review of Economic Studies*, 41, pp. 119–28.

Atkinson, A.B. and J.E. Stiglitz (1980), *Lectures on Public Economics*, New York: McGraw Hill.

Diamond, P.A. (1975), 'A Many Person Ramsey Tax Rule', *Journal of Public Economics*, 4, pp. 335–42.

Gordon, R.H. (1983), 'An Optimal Taxation Approach to Fiscal Federalism', *Quarterly Journal of Economics*, 97, pp. 567–86.

Government of India (1986), *Tables with Notes on Consumer Expenditure*, 38th NSS round, Dept. of Statistics, New Delhi.

King, M.A. (1986), 'A Pigovian Rule for the Optimum Provision of Public Goods', *Journal of Public Economics*, 30, pp. 273–91.

Mintz, J. and H. Tulkens (1986), 'Commodity Tax Competition between Member States of a Federation: Equilibrium and Efficiency', *Journal of Public Economics*, 29, pp. 133–72.

Murty, M.N. and P.B. Nayak (1989), '*A Normative Approach for Resource Transfers in a Federal State*', Working Paper No. E/137/89, Institute of Economic Growth, Delhi, August.

Murty, M.N. and R. Ray (1989), 'A Computational Procedure for Calculating Optimal Commodity Taxes with Illustrative Evidence from Indian Budget Data', *Scandinavian Journal of Economics*, 91(4), pp. 655–70.

—— (1990), '*Fiscal Federalism and Optimal Commodity Taxes: A Comparison of Centralised and Decentralised Decisions*', Working Paper No. E/147/90 of Institute of Economic Growth, Delhi.

Oates, W.E. (1990), '*Public Finance with Several Levels of Government: Theories and Reflections*', Paper presented at 46th Congress, International Institute of Public Finance, Brussels, 27–30 August.

Pigou, A.C. (1947), *A Study of Public Finance*, 3rd ed., London: Macmillan.

Ray, R. (1986), 'Sensitivity of "Optimal" Commodity Taxes to Alternative Demand Functional Forms: An Econometric Case Study of India', *Journal of Public Economics*, 31, pp. 253–68.

Rosen, H.S. (1988), *Fiscal Federalism: Quantitative Studies*, Chicago: University of Chicago Press.

Samuelson, P.A. (1954), 'The Pure Theory of Public Expenditure', *Review of Economics and Statistics*, 36, pp. 387–9.

—— (1955), 'Diagrammatic Exposition of Theory of Public Expenditure', *Review of Economics and Statistics*, 37, pp. 350–6.

Stiglitz, J.E. and P. Dasgupta (1971), 'Differential Taxation, Public Goods and Economic Efficiency', *Review of Economic Studies*, 38, pp. 151–74.

Varian, H.E. (1978), *Micro Economic Analysis*, New York: W.W. Norton & Co.

Wildasin, D.E. (1984), 'On Public Good Provision with Distortionary Taxation', *Economic Inquiry*, 22, pp. 227–43.

Wilson, J.E. (1991), 'Optimal Public Good Provision with Limited Lump Sum Taxation', *American Economic Review*, 81(1), pp. 153–66.

12

Energy and Development: Some Macroeconomic Constraints for Energy Planning in India

Ramprasad Sengupta

1 INTRODUCTION

The per capita consumption of commercial energy of a country is accepted as one of the indicators of level and quality of living of its people. The commercial energy-intensity of economic activity or gross domestic product is, on the other hand, considered as an indicator of its energy efficiency. After the oil price shocks of 1970s the developed capitalist countries restructured their production economies, particularly their product-mix, technology and trading patterns in order to improve the rate of profit on investment through reduction of the commercial energy intensity and energy cost of output or value added. A major concern of energy policy has been how to raise the intensity of energy consumption per capita along with per capita income while reducing the commercial energy intensity of GDP of an economy at the same time. The advanced capitalist countries have in general been able to ensure the opposite movement of these two indicators of energy intensity. The situation has, however, been different for many of the developing economies like India which experienced simultaneous increase in the per capita commercial energy intensity and the commercial energy intensity of GDP over the last two decades. The state policies of such economies which supported the growth process have been characterized as neglecting the need for energy conservation and encouraging energy inefficiency. It is however the differential nature of energy-economy interaction and the varying political economic considerations in deciding energy supply policy which have made the differences in the energy intensity of GDP across the countries. Any rise in the commercial energy intensity of output in India would involve a rise in the real cost of supply of the social product. For a poor country like India a sudden rise in energy price leads to no less distress than what it would be in the case of a developed country. The political economic process of a country determines the *organic* nature of its economic growth and its fuel policy. These would in turn lead to certain intertemporal pattern of behaviour of commercial energy intensity and fuel composition of the economy.

In any case, as of today most of the commercial energy is derived from exhaustible fossil fuels in the world. There is also an environmental impact of energy intensity of an economy through the various greenhouse gas emissions, solid waste arisings and other types of degradation of natural environment. Environmental concerns of energy production and use have led people to think how soon the GDP growth and the energy consumption can be delinked. In order to be able to appreciate if such slogans for delinking economic growth and energy would be realistic, we analyse in this paper the relation between economic development and commercial energy intensity on the basis of cross-country data of several developing economies including India. We shall further derive the implications in respect of energy intensity and fuel composition from the projections of future energy demand for the Indian economy as worked out by the author for this paper. We also analyse in the following sections the macro-economic implications of the projected fuel intensities and energy demand and challenges of energy planning under realistic Indian conditions. The major issues of energy policy which are crucial for the sustainability of our development process have also been discussed in this paper.

2 Energy and Development

The energy consumption of the developing economies has increased quite rapidly between 1970 and 1991. Their share in global energy consumption has gone up from one fifth at the beginning of the seventies to one third at the end of the eighties in spite of the oil price shocks and instability experienced during this period. Both the per capita consumption of energy and the energy intensity of GDP are in general found to be going up in the early phase of industrialization and urbanization of a developing economy. As the commodity structure of the economy shifts in favour of higher energy intensity with economic development and as the income-effect of development and the process of urbanization raise the per capita energy consumption of the household, such observations are quite expected. The intensity of commercial energy use per unit of GDP, however, attains a peak value at a certain stage of development of such economies followed by a decline. Such a reversal of the trend is explained by the increasing share of the service sector in the GDP of an economy in its mature phase and the reaching of the stage of commercial energy saturation by the household sector. Once all the houses of a country have been electrified, it is not surprising that the elasticity of electricity consumption with respect to personal income will decline as the scope of growth of electricity consumption through fuel substitution will be diminished. Similarly, when the motorization of a society is almost complete, the income-elasticity of oil consumption is likely to decline because of the diminishing scope of further modal shift of transportation in favour of automobiles. An analysis of cross-country data for selected developing economies on the growth of per capita GDP and per capita commercial energy consumption shows that the energy-intensity of GDP consumption has been declining for China, South Korea, Indonesia, Malaysia and Thailand between 1980 and 1991 while it has increased for countries like Brazil, India, Philippines and Pakistan for the same period.

TABLE 1

GROWTH OF COMMERCIAL ENERGY
INTENSITY OF GDP IN SELECTED DEVELOPING COUNTRIES

Countries	GNP Per Capita US $ in '91	Rate of Growth of Energy Intensity (per cent)		
		'70–80	'80–91	'70–91
Bangladesh	220	6.5	3.4	4.78
India	330	3	1.8	2.32
China	370	2.3	–4.1	–0.76
Pakistan	400	0.4	0.4	0.40
Indonesia	610	2.7	–0.8	0.97
Egypt	610	1.4	–0.2	0.61
Philippines	730	–2.0	0.8	–0.65
Thailand	1570	0.8	–0.5	0.17
Algeria	1980	12.3	12.1	11.62
Iran	2170	3	2.3	2.54
Malaysia	2520	–2.5	2.2	–0.27
South Africa	2560	0.7	1.6	1.08
Brazil	2940	0.7	2.2	1.35
Mexico	3030	2.4	0.2	1.28
S. Korea	6330	0.5	–1.7	–0.53
Low Income Countries	350	2.5	–0.4	1.06
Middle Income Countries	2480	NA	1.1	NA
High Income Countries	21050	–1.4	–1.4	–1.4
OECD Countries	21530	–1.4	–1.4	–1.4
World	4010	–0.6	–0.5	–0.53

Source: World Development Report 1993.

It may appear surprising that the energy intensity has declined in the low income countries as a whole while it has increased for middle income countries during the eighties. This may be explained by the low availability of commercial energy, slow pace of industrialization and low level of affordability of energy consumption for this group of countries.

It should however be noted that there is no uniquely defined level of per capita income in US $ at which the energy intensity of GDP of a country would attain its peak. The level of the peak value of energy intensity and the corresponding per capita income differ from country to country depending upon the structure of the economy, geography, climate, size of population, natural resource endowments, level of technological development for both energy use and energy supply and the consequent level of fuel efficiency. These factors also explain the apparent absence of any relation between the level of per capita GDP and the commercial energy intensity of GDP across the countries as observed in Table 2.

We thus find in Table 2 that in spite of having a per capita GDP that is 26 per cent higher, China's commercial energy intensity of GDP was 42 per cent higher than that of India. Similarly, the per capita GDP of South Korea was more than four times that of Thailand in 1991, while the latter had a lower commercial energy intensity of GDP in the same year. Table 2 also shows opposite relationship between per capita GDP and commercial energy intensity in some other cross country comparisons.

What then, do we mean by the relationship between the level of development of an economy and the energy intensity? The major point here is that each country follows a time path of energy intensity showing first a rise followed by a decline as per capita income grows continuously. The timing and the stage of industrialization or urbanization characterizing the attainment of the peak is determined by the specificities of socio-economic environment, resource-technology configuration as well as political values of a country. The organic process of growth specific to each country will characterize the path and the peak. It is well-known that India's commercial energy intensity in steel, textile, sugar, chemicals and other energy intensive industries can be reduced per unit of their products if all the energy inefficient plants with outmoded technologies can be demolished by bulldozers overnight with or

TABLE 2

COMMERCIAL ENERGY INTENSITY OF
GDP AND GDP ELASTICITY OF COMMERCIAL ENERGY
CONSUMPTION IN SELECTED DEVELOPING COUNTRIES

Countries	Population Million	GDP Per Capita US $ 1991	Commercial Energy Intensity of GDP 1991 (Oil eq. kg)	GDP Elasticity of Commercial Energy 1980–91	Commercial Energy Consumption Per Capita 1991 (Oil eq. kg)
Bangladesh	110.6	212	0.27	1.79	57
India	866.5	256	1.32	1.33	337
China	1149.5	322	1.87	0.56	602
Pakistan	115.8	348	0.70	1.07	243
Indonesia	181.3	642	0.43	0.86	279
Egypt	53.6	565	1.05	0.96	594
Philippines	62.9	714	0.31	1.73	218
Thailand	57.2	1631	0.27	0.94	438
Algeria	25.7	1271	1.54	5.03	1956
Iran	57.7	1681	0.64	2.05	1078
Malaysia	18.2	2581	0.41	1.39	1066
South Africa	38.9	2344	0.97	2.23	2262
Brazil	151.4	2735	0.33	1.88	908
Mexico	83.3	3392	0.41	1.17	1383
S. Korea	43.3	6535	0.30	0.83	1936
Low Income Countries	3127.3	294	1.28	0.93	376
Middle Income Countries	1401.0	2616	0.52	–	1351
High Income Countries	822.3	20739	0.25	0.52	5106
OECD Countries	783.1	21231	0.24	0.52	5122
World	5351	4044	0.33	0.83	1343

Source: World Development Report 1993.

without replacement by new capacity. This would contribute to the fall in output, income and employment along with the decline in energy intensity leading to a situation which would be politically unacceptable. India's commercial energy intensity of GDP has been continuously rising over time barring short run fluctuations. India is yet to reach an organic stage of development where the substitution of commercial for noncommercial energy due to industrialization or commercialization has reached its maximum extent warranting the attainment of the peak commercial energy intensity of GDP. It may be noted here that one third of Indian villages have no connectivity by an all-weather road as of today. As large a fraction as 69 per cent of Indian rural households have no electricity connection today. Most of the 42 per cent of entire Indian households which have the load connections receive a very unreliable supply of electricity. Once such connections and reliability of energy supply improve, it would inevitably have an upward effect on the commercial energy intensity of GDP. This effect would, it is very likely, more than offset the effect of conservation of commercial energy due to the technological upgradation of the production activities of our economy for some considerable time in the future.

However our observations on energy intensity and energy conservation have been made with reference to commercial energy only. The changes in commercial energy intensity per unit of GDP in developing countries often tend to overstate the case of their energy inefficiency. The situation would look a bit different if we consider the behaviour of total primary energy resource (i.e., commercial as well as noncommercial energy) use per unit of GDP or national income of an economy over time. It has been often observed that the growth of total primary energy consumption per unit of GDP has been lower than that of commercial energy intensity (See Table 3). This has been particularly true for countries like Bangladesh, India, Brazil, Algiers, Thailand among the selected countries as given in Table 3. The reason for this difference can possibly be explained by the fact that with increasing income and level of development of economic activities there

TABLE 3

COMPARATIVE GROWTH OF TOTAL
PRIMARY ENERGY INTENSITY AND COMMERCIAL ENERGY
INTENSITY OF GDP FOR SELECTED DEVELOPING COUNTRIES

Countries	Primary Energy Intensity of GDP 1989 (kg of oil eq./US $)[*]	Annual Average Growth Rate of Total Primary Energy Intensity of GDP 1973–89 (per cent)	Annual Average Growth Rate of Commercial Energy Intensity of GDP 1970–91 (per cent)	Primary Energy Consumption Per Capita 1989 (kg oil eq./US $)[*]
Bangladesh	0.36	4.4	4.78	0.06
India	0.71	1.3	2.32	0.21
Pakistan	0.64	1.2	0.38	0.21
Indonesia	0.38	2.4	0.97	0.23
Egypt	0.58	1.7	0.61	0.55
Philippines	0.48	0	−0.65	0.29
Thailand	0.47	−0.9	0.17	0.44
Algeria	0.45	6.7	11.62	1.08
Iran	0.40	5.5	2.54	1.15
Malaysia	0.50	2.1	−0.28	1.01
South Africa	1.75	2.4	1.08	2.81
Brazil	0.40	−0.2	1.35	0.66
Mexico	0.67	2.8	1.28	1.36
South Korea	0.65	0	−0.53	1.89
OECD Countries	0.4	−1.7	−1.34	4.79

[*]   GDP or growth rate of GDP estimated on the basis of 1985 US $ and exchange rate.

Source: World Development Report 1993 and 'Global Energy': The Changing Outlook 1992, International Energy Agency/OECD Publication.

is a clear shift in energy consumption away from noncommercial energy to commercial energy forms. To the extent such substitution occurs, commercial energy use as an indicator of the level of energy consumption would be covering a broader base or a higher proportion of total energy consumption in every successive year. Thus an analysis based only on commercial fuels often tends to overstate the rate of growth of energy intensity in developing countries and widen the gap in energy intensity between the developing and the developed (OECD) economies. In terms of total primary energy intensity of GDP the performance of non-OECD countries in the period 1973 to 1989 has not been as bad as an analysis based on commercial energy intensity tends to suggest. One should also notice here that substitution of less efficient noncommercial fuels by more efficient commercial fuels in fact has contributed to the moderation of rise of primary energy consumption per unit of GDP in developing countries.

It remains, however, true that the primary energy intensity of the GDP of our country is quite high. Its estimate has been as high as 0.71 kg oil equivalent per US $ of GDP in 1989 as expressed in 1985 prices and exchange rate while the same has been 0.40 for the OECD countries. One of the major factors behind the high energy intensity of GDP of countries like India is the high pressure of growth of population. The Table 3 shows how per capita energy intensity has been remarkably low for most of the populous Afro-Asian developing countries. The per capita primary energy intensity was as low as 0.21 (oil eq. metric tonne per inhabitant) in India while the same was 4.79 for the OECD countries as a whole in 1989. The rate of growth of per capita primary energy consumption has, however, grown at 3.6 per cent for India while the same increased at a lower rate of only 0.2 per cent for the OECD countries as a whole. In spite of such relative growth of energy intensity per capita, the level of per capita energy intensity of developing countries like India is far below the average level of the developed world. There exists in fact enormous potential of increased energy consumption for the household sector of the developing economies with a rise in income. While energy conservation measures may tend to moderate the growth of primary commercial energy intensity of GDP, it is unlikely to be able to reverse its rising trend in India in the near future in view of the pressure of growing per capita household consumption of commercial energy. Increased rural electrification, greater accessibility to electrical appliances with increased urbanization, higher connectivity of villages by all weather roads leading to greater use of motorized transport, rising level of use of personal transport with increased income, and finally, the growing size of urban population would all contribute to the rise of per capita commercial energy consumption in our country. With the rising share of commercial energy resources in the total use of primary energy, it is thus inevitable that the absolute level of consumption of commercial energy would be growing substantively over time in India for the order of GDP growth as indicated in the perspective plan of the eighth plan document. As we shall find in the following sections, the growth of commercial energy demand for even a lower GDP growth than the plan projection would create pressure on both the energy industry and our macroeconomy.

3 PATTERN OF ENERGY CONSUMPTION IN INDIA

The energy resources which supply the energy requirement of India may be classified into the two categories of traditional (non-commercial) fuels and commercial fuels. Traditional fuels — like fuelwood, agro-waste, dung cakes, etc., — are cheap as their cost of supply includes only the cost of collection. However, the efficiency of these fuels is very low and their end-uses are mainly confined to cooking and water and space heating in the households. As already noted, the use of commercial energy — coal, oil, natural gas and electric power — on the other hand, grows with income, level of industrialization and urbanization of economies. However, the major problem with commercial fuels has been the supply side constraints. First of all, commercial energy is derived mostly from exhaustible fossil fuels in India. Secondly, its supply in various forms, particularly electricity, is highly capital intensive. The gestation lag of investment in this sector is also quite high. Finally, the price of oil — a large part of the use of which is nonsubstitutable — suffers from instability giving rise to serious economic uncertainties from time to time. However, in spite of these problems and a rising cost of supply of commercial energy in India, the share of commercial energy in the total use of primary energy resources has increased from 25.7 per cent in 1953-4 to 62.0 per cent in 1990-1. The changes in fuel composition of primary energy resources in India are given in Table 4.

TABLE 4

SHARE OF ENERGY RESOURCES IN TOTAL
PRIMARY ENERGY RESOURCES CONSUMPTION IN INDIA (PER CENT)

	1953-4	1970-1	1980-1	1990-1
1. Coal and Lignite	20.39	24.47	28.05	33.1
2. Uranium for Power	–	0.50	0.44	0.50
3. Hydel Power	0.29	1.50	1.98	2.10
4. Liquid Hydrocarbons	4.97	13.28	16.59	20.7
5. Natural Gas	–	0.41	0.69	3.6
Total Commercial Energy Resources	25.65	40.16	47.75	62.0
6. Fuelwood	48.21	38.63	33.77	25.8
7. Dung cake	13.10	10.69	9.36	7.2
8. Agro waste	13.04	10.52	9.12	7.0
Total Non-Commercial Energy Resources	74.35	59.84	52.25	40.0
Total Primary Energy Resources	100	100	100	100

Note: The figures of the table are estimated by the author himself from the data complied from the various sources of Planning Commission and other ministries.

For the purpose of an analysis of the pattern of energy consumption and for making future projections it is, however, important to distinguish between primary energy resource use and final energy consumption of an economy. A part of the energy value of energy resources is lost while converting primary energy resources into final energy products like coal into electricity or crude oil into petroleum products, etc. This loss represents conversion loss only and does not account for the difference between the gross calorific value and the useful heat value of a fuel.

TABLE 5

FUEL CONSUMPTION OF FINAL
COMMERCIAL ENERGY CONSUMPTION IN INDIA

	Solid Fuels (Coal & Lignite)	Hydrocarbons	Electricity
1953–4	77	20	3
1970–1	57	34	9
1980–1	47	42	11
1990–1	36	48	16

Source: Author's Own Estimate on the Basis of the Data Obtained from the Planning Commission, Government of India.

The composition of final energy use in the form of commercial fuels in the Indian economy has also undergone a significant change over time. Table 5 shows that the share of coal and lignite has declined from 77 per cent in 1953 to 36 per cent in 1990–1 and that of oil has increased from 20 per cent to 48 per cent during the same period. These estimates are based on the calorific value of electricity as taken on an output basis. Such estimates have thus shown that the share of electricity in the final energy consumption has gone up from 3 per cent to 16 per cent during the same period. Although the share of coal in the aggregate of primary energy resources has been increasing over time and is presently the dominant fuel of the economy, its direct or final use is of declining importance. Coal is now being predominantly used for power generation and the direct use of coal is being replaced by such indirect energy use. The growth of the shares of electricity, oil and gas in the total final energy consumption is understandable in view of the higher efficiency of use of these fuels, industrial and urban growth, and the increasing importance of transportation in the development process. The sectoral composition of final energy use has also undergone significant changes over time in India as shown in Table 6.

TABLE 6

SECTORAL SHARE IN TOTAL FINAL
COMMERCIAL ENERGY CONSUMPTION IN INDIA (PER CENT)

	1953–4	1970–1	1980–1	1990–1*
Household	14.32	14.64	10.44	13.8
Agriculture	1.44	2.37	5.88	9.0
Industry	42.15	45.39	54.74	50.4
Transport	39.98	34.00	24.96	24.5
Other Sectors	2.11	3.58	3.98	2.3
Total	100	100	100	100

*   Estimates quoted from Eighth Plan Document.

Source: Author's Own Estimates on the Basis of the Data Obtained from the Planning Commission, Government of India.

TABLE 7

SECTORAL COMPOSITION OF FINAL
USE OF COMMERCIAL ENERGY IN INDIA IN 1990 (PER CENT)

	Solid Fuels	Petroleum Products	Natural Gas	Electricity
Household	1.1	20.7	0.6	14.9
Agriculture	–	10.7	–	23.5
Industry	89.0	10.9	14.2	50.2
Transport	5.6	40.5	–	2.0
Others Incl. nonenergy	4.3	17.2	85.2	9.4

Source: National Energy Data Profile 1970–2010, Planning Commission, Government of India.

It is also of importance to analyse the pattern of utilization of the different commercial fuels across the sectors as experienced in 1990. This is as given in Table 7.

The industrial sector of India is presently the dominant consumer of commercial energy as per Table 6. Transport comes next in importance. The share of the household sector which follows the transport sector in the ordering has fluctuated around 13 to 14 per cent. The share of agriculture has been on the other hand steadily increasing over time because of the technical changes in Indian agriculture. The share of transport has declined because of the replacement of coal by High Speed diesel in the railway fraction, the latter having a much higher efficiency of use as compared to the former. The scene of sectoral distribution of final energy consumption would however look very different if we consider the noncommercial energy consumption as well in the final use of energy. Assuming that all noncommercial energy is consumed by the household, we find the time trend of the share of household in the total final energy consumption to be as given in Table 8.

TABLE 8

SHARE OF THE HOUSEHOLD SECTOR IN
TOTAL FINAL ENERGY CONSUMPTION IN INDIA (PER CENT)

	1953–4	1970–1	1980–81	1990–1
Total Fuel	83.7	70.8	64.7	55.6
(a) Commercial Fuels	3.3	5.0	4.1	5.9
(b) Noncommercial Fuels	80.4	65.8	60.6	49.7

Source: Author's Own Estimate on the Basis of the Data from the Planning
Commission, Government of India.

The share of commercial energy has thus been around 10.6 per cent only in the total final energy consumption of all kinds by the household sector in 1990–1.

Finally, the fuel wise analysis shows that industry is the major consumer of electricity and accounted for about 50 per cent of total electricity consumption of the Indian economy in 1990, agriculture and residential sectors having shares of 23 per cent and 15 per cent respectively. Transport, on the other hand, was responsble for 41 per cent of the total oil consumption in the economy in 1990 and the residential sector accounted for 21 per cent of the same fuel in that year. From the point of view of oil use as a share of the total fuel use by a sector, the transport sector has the highest oil dependence. Oil constituted 89 per cent of the total fuel used in that sector in 1990. The agriculture and the household and commercial sectors were also dependent on oil for 57 per cent and 70 per cent of their respective requirements of commercial energy in the same year. The Planning Commission's estimates of oil application ratio and oil use ratio as presented in the Eighth Plan document have brought to focus the nonsubstitutability of oil in these two important sectors. The high dependence on oil of transport, agriculture and residential sectors makes the Indian economy dependent on energy import and vulnerable to oil price fluctuations giving rise to the problem of energy security.

TABLE 9

OIL APPLICATION RATIO AND OIL
USE RATIO IN INDIAN ECONOMY IN 1990

	Oil Application Ratio (OAR)	Oil Use Ratio (OUR)
Industry	0.107	0.11
Transport	0.405	0.89
Agriculture	0.107	0.57
Residential, Commercial & Public Services	0.207	0.70

$$OAR = \frac{\text{Oil Consumption in Sector}}{\text{Total Oil Consumption in the Country}}$$

$$OUR = \frac{\text{Oil Consumption in Sector}}{\text{Total Energy Consumption in Sector}}$$

Source: National Energy Data Profile 1970–2010, Planning Commission, Government of India.

What are then the implications of energy — economy interaction in the context of the growth process of the Indian economy? Before working out the energy implications of possible future macro-economic growth rates, we would like to caution the reader about the interpretation of the growth of commercial energy consumption as referred to in section 8.12 of the Eighth Plan document of the Planning Commission. It may be noted here that the Planning Commission estimates in the plan document show the growth of commercial energy consumption to be 4.52 per cent per annum in the eighties while the same is supposed to be 7.2 per cent as per the World Development Report of the World Bank. The difference is explained by the definition of consumption of commercial energy. While the Planning Commission of India implicitly defines such consumption to be the *final* consumption of commercial energy taking electricity on the output basis for calorific value, the World Bank document means by the same terminology all uses of commercial energy resources — final use and use for power generation. Power has thus been implicitly taken on *input* basis for calorific value calculation in the World Development Report. Our presentation of sectoral and fuel wise composition of final energy consumption in Tables 5 to 8 has been given above, taking power on output basis for calorific value along the line of the Planning Commission. However, it is extremely important to keep this distinction in mind while interpreting the GDP elasticity of commercial energy consumption and commenting on the trend of energy conservation in India as these will be sensitive to the definition.

In any case, it is of fundamental importance to analyse the behaviour of the GDP-elasticity of final energy consumption of an economy for future energy planning. The pattern of growth of demand for commercial energy resources can be derived therefrom depending on the choice of fuel for power generation and the conversion efficiency of energy resources. As per the National Energy Data profile compiled by the Planning Commission, we find the GDP elasticities of the different commercial fuels in India to be as given in Table 10.

TABLE 10
GDP-ELASTICITIES OF FINAL CONSUMPTION OF COMMERCIAL ENERGY

	Coal	Oil	Electricity	Total Final Commercial Energy
1970–71 to 80–81	0.99	2.1	2.08	1.34
1980–81 to 90–91	0.32	1.11	1.59	0.94

Source: Author's Estimate on the Basis of the National Energy Data Profile 1970–2010, Planning Commission.

The GDP elasticity values of different commercial fuels as given in Table 10 are however unstable as their measures are based on point to point growth rates of GDP and of the concerned fuel. As the annual GDP growth rate fluctuates due to the influence of monsoon, such point to point estimates of elasticities are affected by the choice of the terminal years and the fluctuations in GDP level. However, it is undeniable that the GDP elasticities of coal, oil and electricity declined over time and reflected the effect of oil price shocks and rising cost of purchase of energy in the country. However, the sharp fall of the elasticity of coal consumption has been due to the substitution of coal in the final uses by oil or electric power like steam traction being replaced by electric traction in the railways; kerosene and LPG replacing soft coke, high quality imported coal replacing larger quantities of inferior domestic coal in steel industry, etc. The decline in the GDP elasticity of coal has been induced more by fuel substitution than by the measures of energy conservation. It should also be noted that once the fuel substitution has reached its maximum extent to replace coal, the elasticity value would mainly reflect the effect of conservation of the final use of coal. It should not in fact be surprising for such GDP elasticity value of coal to rise in future once such a stage has been reached in the process of substitution, although it is very likely that such elasticity value would remain lower than unity. It is only for coal that the GDP elasticity of final consumption (or direct use) of coal has been less than unity while similar elasticities of oil and power consumption have been greater than unity for the eighties. The GDP-elastic demand for oil and electricity has led to the rise in the intensity of these two fuels per unit of GDP in spite of their rising real cost of supply over time.

4 FUTURE ENERGY SCENE OF INDIA

What is the future energy scene of the Indian economy? Will we be able to reduce the commercial energy intensity of GDP, particularly the oil or the power intensity? We present below some updated projection of demand for commercial energy (with fuel wise break up) based on the broad method of (a) assuming some realistic GDP growth rates for the eighth, ninth and tenth five years plans of India, and (b) using normative elasticity values of final consumption of the different fuels with respect to GDP. These elasticity values have built in themselves the effect of policy initiatives for energy conservation and fuel substitution on grounds of efficiency. We present below the aggregate demand projection of the different commercial fuels based on the annual average GDP growth rate of 4.5 per cent during the eighth plan, 5 per cent during the ninth plan and 5.5 per cent during the tenth plan, taking the actual fuel consumption level of 1991–2 as the base for projections. In view of the decelerated growth rate of the GDP of the Indian economy during the period of transition for structural adjustment as experienced in the recent two years, we have considered 4.5 per cent as the most optimistic assumption regarding the growth rate for the eighth plan. We have further assumed moderate acceleration of the GDP growth rate during the ninth and the tenth plan keeping in view the possible constraints on growth of trade, inflow of foreign savings and our ability to service foreign capital on time.

For the calculation of final demand of coal, oil and electricity we have assumed the following GDP elasticities of demand for the respective fuels for the different plan periods. (See Table 11) For the eighth plan the normative GDP-elasticity values for oil and

TABLE 11
NORMATIVE GDP-ELASTICITIES OF
FINAL DEMAND FOR COMMERCIAL ENERGY

	Coal	Oil	Electricity
Eighth Plan	0.8	1.1	1.5
Ninth Plan	0.75	1.0	1.4
Tenth Plan	0.7	0.95	1.3

electricity have been assumed to be approximately the same as those for the eighties while for coal it has been higher. In a period of decelerated growth the decline in the growth rate of fuel consumption is likely to be less than the decline in GDP growth rate because of the insensitivity of a certain part of the growth of fuel consumption with respect to growth in income. The Annexure Table A1 shows the major sectoral demand components of each of these three fuels and their determining causal variables in India. Our impression of the realistic norms of GDP-elasticities has been based on some underlying detailed sectoral demand analysis not presented here which uses the framework of the Annexure Table. We have further assumed a very moderate decline in the GDP-elasticity values of final demand for coal, oil and power over the plan periods in order to build in the effects of some policy initiatives regarding energy-conservation. We have deliberately assumed a very moderate decline in the elasticities in order to balance the concern for conservation with the distributive consideration of meeting the energy needs of a growing population. Finally, in view of the administered character of prices and the controlled nature of energy markets in India, it is quite difficult to trace a reliable relationship between price and fuel consumption. This explains the neglect of the role of price in our estimated demand projections as given in Table 12.

So far as the fuel demand for power is concerned, we have been broadly guided by the mix of generation technologies as indicated by the projections given in the National Energy Data

TABLE 12

FUTURE DEMAND FOR COMMERCIAL ENERGY IN INDIA

Fuels	1991–2	1996–7	2001–2	2006–7
1. Electricity (TWH)				
(a) Consumers' demand	230	319 (312.64)	447	671 (622)
(b) Gross generation (incl. non-utility)	316	422 (448)	580	853 (753)
2. Coal (mill. t.)				
(a) Direct use	80.04	96	115	143
(b) Use for power generation	151.9	177	234	327
(c) Total (a) + (b)	231.94	273 (301)	349	471 (460)
3. (a) Petroleum (mill. t.)				
(i) Final use	54.15	69	90	122
(ii) Total incl. share of power	56.9	73	95	127 (125)
(b) Crude oil equivalent	60.9	78	101	135
4. Natural gas (mill. t. of oil equiv.)				
(a) Final use	7.0	12.3	21.3	37.2
(b) Total incl. share of power	11.3	19.1	32.3	54.6
5. Total commercial energy (mill. t. of oil equiv.)				
(a) Final demand	119.35	155	205	285
(b) Primary commercial energy resources	180.1	221	292	406

Source: The Figures in Bracket Refer to the Perspective Plan Figures Given in the Eighth Plan Document of the Planning Commission.

Profile 1991–2010 of the Planning Commission and the actual mix of generation in 1991–2. We have assumed improvements in T&D loss and auxiliary loss over time while estimating the gross generation requirement.

The projected consumption of gas in the country has been, on the other hand, assumed to be supply determined. We have been guided by the same National Energy Data Profile for India of the Planning Commission in respect of future trend of growth of gas availability in India from domestic or foreign sources, while the absolute level has been adjusted according to the actual level of gas availability and consumption in 1991–2. The data of fuel consumption for 1991–2 have been obtained from the sources of Planning Commission, Indian Petroleum and Natural Gas statistics of the Ministry of Petroleum, and the Economic Survey, 1993–4 of the Ministry of Finance.

For the derivation of the oil equivalent of projected demand we have assumed the calorific values of the fuels to be 860 kcal for 1 kwh of electricity, 10,000 kcal for 1 kg of oil, 4000 kcal for 1 kg of power grade coal, 4800 kcal for 1 kg of other coal, 9237 kcal for 1 m^3 of natural gas. For obtaining the estimate of requirement of primary energy resources, we have assumed the efficiency of hydel resource and nuclear resource to be 100 per cent and 33 per cent respectively in power generation.

The projected levels of future fuel demand as given in Table 12 immediately yields the long term growth rates and GDP elasticity of energy consumption as given in Table 13.

The projected pattern of future consumption of commercial fuels thus shows the implicit GDP elasticity of fuel consumption (final use) to be marginally lower for oil and electricity than what such elasticities values were for the period 1980–1 to 1990–1. However, the projected GDP elasticity of final consumption of coal is shown to be higher than what it was during the eighties. The reaching of maximum extent of substitution of coal may explain such reversal of the trend of elasticity value in future. These GDP elasticity values of fuel consumption thus imply the fuel-intensity of GDP to rise for electricity and oil and for the commercial energy

TABLE 13

PROJECTED GROWTH RATES AND GDP ELASTICITY OF
COMMERCIAL ENERGY CONSUMPTION (1991–2 TO 2006–7)

Items	Annual Average Growth Rates	Long Run GDP-Elasticity	Annual Average Rate of Growth of Fuel Intensity of GDP
(1)	(2)	(3)	(4)
GDP	5.0	–	–
1. Electricity			
(a) Consumers' Demand	7.40	1.48	2.4
(b) Gross Gen.			
Requirement (Utility)	6.85	1.37	1.85
2. Coal			
(a) Direct Use	3.97	0.79	–1.03
(b) Total Use	4.83	0.97	–0.17
3. Petroleum	5.47	1.09	0.47
4. (a) Final Use of			
Commercial Energy	5.98	1.20	0.98
(b) Primary Commercial			
Energy Resources	5.56	1.094	0.56

as a whole. The coal intensity of GDP, on the other hand, is
expected to decline because of replacement of coal in final use
by other fuels and reduction in the share of solid fuel in the total
gross generation of power in future. In view of the oil deficit nature
of our economy, the moderately rising trend of oil intensity of
GDP will have its obvious macroeconomic implications.

The growth rate of future gross generation of power per unit of
GDP is however projected to be lower than that of final use of
power per unit of GDP due to the assumptions of possible improvement in the transmission and distribution of the power system. The GDP-elasticity of gross generation of power has raised

the primary energy resource intensity of GDP, although very moderately at 0.56 per cent rate annually in the next 10 to 15 year horizon. However, the final commercial energy usage per unit of GDP would rise almost at the rate of 1 per cent annually on the average. It is thus unlikely that a power energy starved vast populous country like India will be able to enter the phase of declining commercial energy intensity of GDP soon. For the annual average population growth rate of 1.69 per cent for the period 1991 to 2006 as indicated in the Eighth Plan document, our projection of future energy demand would imply the long run future growth rate of per capita primary energy resource intensity to be 3.87 per cent per annum approximately.

5 MACROECONOMIC IMPLICATIONS OF DEMAND PROJECTION AND ENERGY POLICY ISSUES

Issues on Power

What are the macro-economic implications of the projected future growth rate of commercial energy in India for the fifteen year period from 1991–2 as presented in the preceding section? The estimate of annual average future growth rate has been obtained as 6.85 per cent for gross generation of power, 4.83 per cent for all coal together and 5.47 per cent for petroleum. In view of the high capital-output ratio of the commercial energy sector, the realization of such growth rates of supply of the different fuels would cause serious pressure on the financial resources of the economy, particularly on that of the public sector. For electricity the incremental capital-gross value added ratio (without adjustment for gestation lag) as implicit in the projections of sectoral investment and GVA in the eighth plan document has been as high as 17.0. Assuming that the normative over all PLF for the utility system would be rising from 47.4 per cent in 1991–2 to 55 per cent in 2006–7, we obtain the projected requirement of installed gross generation capacity in the utility system over the time horizon 1991–2 to 2006–7 as given in Table 14. The required addition to capacity in the utility system would thus be about 19280 MW during eighth plan, 28620 MW for ninth plan and 49270 MW during the tenth plan. A cumulative addition of capacity of the order of 97170 MW is thus required to be achieved over the fifteen year horizon from 1991–2 for supporting an annual average GDP growth of 5 per cent.

TABLE 14

PROJECTED REQUIREMENT OF POWER (UTILITY) CAPITAL UNIT MW

	1991–2	1996–7	2001–2	2006–7
Gross generation capacity (MW)	69080	88360	116980	166250
PLF	47.4	50	52.5	55.0

The major problem in the creation of power capacity in India is not the availability of a suitable energy resource. The potential availability of solid fuel and hydel resources of the country poses no serious problem for the sustainability of development of our power sector. Although Indian coal is poor in quality, beneficiation of coal by washing can make the indigenous coal based power near-competitive with the imported coal based power. If the availability of natural gas improves, the cleaner fuel will make the supply situation of power easier in an environment friendly manner. The problem lies with the capital resources. The capital cost of thermal power plants has shot up from Rs 1.1 crores per MW in mid-eighties to a level anywhere within the range Rs 2.5 to 3.5 crores per MW now depending on the loan arrangement for the project made by the State Electricity Board. The component of interest during construction in the project cost would be high or low depending on the extent and the term of loan for the power company or power board. The foreign investment projects in the power sector (e.g. Enron in Maharashtra) also show the capital cost to be as high as more than Rs 4 crores per MW. The Enron project would, in fact, involve a capital investment of Rs 8480 crores for a capacity of 2015 MW based on gas fractions. It should also be noted that the capital cost advantage of gas based technology over solid fuel has disappeared over time for reasons not very clearly understandable from the technological point of view. It is the imperfections of the market which have been mainly responsible for this change in relative capital cost. The hydel projects which are site specific, are generally more capital intensive than the thermal ones and have a lower PLF. The lower average PLF of the hydel plants is partly inevitable for their use for peaking and this makes the incidence of capital servicing cost per unit of electricity for peak hours quite high. The major problem with the growth of the electricity sector is thus the mobilization of adequate financial resources for the creation of capacity. India would need a fund of Rs 291510 crores for the generation capacity of power for the 15 year period from the eighth to the tenth plan. Even if we assume a moderate capital cost of Rs 3 crores per MW, the investment requirement of the supporting T&D facilities for the evacuation and distribution of power would be at least 70 per cent of the generation investment. We thus face the challenge of mobilizing resources of the order of Rs 496000 crore over the three plan periods from the eighth plan if the Indian economy is to move on to a path of 5 per cent GDP growth in the long run.

In order to meet the challenge of resource mobilization of such a high order and reduce the pressure on the fiscal system, the government of India has opened up the power sector to foreign investors and to domestic private entrepreneurs during the eighth plan. For the eighth plan the official plan target of capacity addition has been 30,538 MW. The problem of resource mobilization is likely to constrain the extent of creation of new capacity to not more than 20,000 MW during this plan period. However, as per our own estimate we should not require more than this realizable capacity addition to support an annual average GDP growth rate of 4.5 per cent which is very unlikely to be exceeded during the eighth plan. This however assumes some improvement in generation, transmission, distribution and end-use efficiency of power. In any case, the share of the private sector is now targeted to be around 1500 MW out of the realizable capacity addition of 20,000 MW with no share for the foreign participators during the eighth plan. It is, however, expected that the foreign participation in the power sector will contribute to capacity addition during the ninth and the tenth plan.

Even if we grant that the government of India will be successful in mobilizing foreign savings to finance the growth of the power sector taking advantage of recession in the developed capitalist countries, some problems would remain. The high order of capital cost of the foreign investment projects and the government policy of guaranteeing high return (16 per cent) on foreign investment in dollar terms would cause a significant burden on the State Electricity Board and ultimately to the government's fiscal system. It may be noted that the capital cost of foreign investment projects would be 33 to 60 per cent higher than that of the indigenously built and financed projects. If the political economy of our country cannot sustain a sufficiently high tariff for power which can cover the servicing charge (including guarantees etc.) of such foreign capital investment, there will be a chronic and serious financial problem of a crisis order for the state sector of power. This would inevitably lead to reduction of investment in the state sector of the power industry offsetting at least partly the social gains of foreign investment in terms of capacity creation. The quantitative inadequacy of capacity may be compounded with the qualitative inadequacy of technology because of the shortage of state funds for generation as well as transmission and distribution of power. In order to avoid such a situation the political and economic forces of India will possibly again force a power subsidy onto the system to be financed by the state. This would mean ultimately the shifting of the burden of responsibility of the state to supply power from the capital account to the current account of the government budget.

We do not however mean to suggest here that there is no way out of this impasse. First of all, the capital cost of power can be reduced by the use of indigenous plant and equipment or by an appropriate bargain with the foreign investors in power. The foreign investors will have a vested interest in raising the capital cost in view of the sovereign guarantee of the rate of return on investment. They would also like to build in a premium over the true capital cost so that they may get back a substantive part of their investment through equipment supply by appropriating the premium even before the plant is commissioned.

Secondly, the current power tariff structure of India is highly irrational. It encourages wasteful use of power and sometimes causes unwarranted subsidization. Power is wasted in rural India because it is too cheap. It is not true that our power tariff corresponds to the willingness or the ability to pay the marginal consumer and that the rural and the urban market cannot bear anything above the current rate. The very fact of the fast growth of power generation in non-utilities over the recent years implies that the consumers of such power are willing to bear and are able to pay a higher cost at the margin. It may be noted that the cost of captive generation is substantially higher than the grid power. Apart from industries, a large part of upper middle class and the rich population of the urban metropolis are consumers of such captive power. It is the reliability of power supply for which such consumers are willing to pay more at the margin.

Thirdly, the thrust on technological upgradation of the power sector particularly for the improvement of T&D loss and political will for the elimination of waste and theft of power would also greatly help to improve the financial situation of our power industry.

Even with all these it is quite likely that the participation of foreign and Indian private capital would require some subsidy from the state if there has to be significant reliance on foreign investment for power. The different segments of the power market have different abilities to pay. In view of the consideration of social justice the political economy of this country cannot afford to ease any significant segment of the population out of the market by charging tariff as per the long run marginal cost pricing. Besides this, the problem of high long run marginal cost of supply of power during peak hours would in any case remain. No private or foreign investor would set up a plant with low PLF while there would remain an upper bound on the ratio of peak to average load demand for the utility system. In such a situation it would in fact be much wiser for the state to become the dominant leader in the direct creation of power capacity by providing higher priority to such an infrastructural sector in the public sector plan allocation than depend on high cost foreign investors. Avoidance of the cost of guarantee of return and that of overinvoicing equipment price by the foreign suppliers would enable us to reduce the ultimate dependence on state financed subsidy from the current account government budget. In spite of our efforts for reforms, the technical as well as the political and economic specificities of the problems of this utility sector would not possibly permit withdrawal of the state from this sector in India. The Indian state should withdraw from many of the non-infrastructural sectors and mobilize resources for such infrastructural sectors as power, transport, etc. The problem of the power sector is financial. Its solution has to be sought mainly through appropriate institutional policy initiative.

Issues on Fossil Fuels

As we have observed, the supply of commercial energy in India is primarily based on fossil fuel — coal and hydrocarbons. With coal we do not have any immediate quantitative problem of reserves. We have, however, a serious problem of quality with this fuel resource. In view of the favourable geological configuration like seam depth, thickness, incline, etc., it is possible for our coal industry to supply one of the cheapest fuel resource to the economy closely competing with natural gas. As per the estimate worked out by the present author in 'Energy Modelling for India' published by the Planning Commission, India has mineable coal reserves of about 100 billion tonnes which are not yet projectized as mines and can provide a supply of coal for about 230 years at the current rate of production of 240 million tonne approximately per annum. (We assume here about 56 per cent recoverability from mineable in-place coal reserves.) However, the long run marginal cost of supply of coal would be rising with cumulative depletion of coal as we shall have to exploit deeper reserves. In any case, concern for higher factor productivity, beneficiation and better utilization of coal can ensure competitiveness of Indian coal with imported coal except in the use for metallurgical purposes.

The situation is however quite different for hydrocarbons. Our estimates of balance of recoverable reserves of oil and natural gas stand at 0.8 billion tonnes and 735 billion m^3 respectively. These would supply our requirement of production of oil for 26 years at the low rate of production of 30 million tonnes per annum of 1991–2 and that of natural gas for 40 years at the rate of production of 18.6 billion m^3 per annum of 1991–2. We are all aware that with the low rate of production of 1991–2 the country has had to depend substantively on imports to meet the requirement of oil. It is to be noted with concern that our index of self reliance in oil (i.e., share of import in total POL requirement) has gone down secularly from 70 per cent in 1984–5 to as low as 42 per cent in 1992–3. It is, however, the serious technical problems of Bombay High oil fields which has caused a decline of production in the short run. It is expected that crude oil production will pick up and reach a level of plateau around 45 million tonnes of crude per annum at the turn of the century. This would imply a reserve to production ratio in the range of 17 years for oil even if the balance of re-coverable reserves can be maintained stable at current level of 0.8 billion tonnes. Similarly, our gross production of natural gas can be expected to go up to 31 billion m^3 of rich gas per annum and about 25 billion m^3 of lean gas per annum towards the end of the decade of nineties. These levels of production of rich gas and lean gas are likely to describe the level of plateau with reserve to production ratio of about 24–25 years. Such an assertion also assumes that the balance of recoverable reserves is maintained at the current level.

The major problem with oil or gas is the inadequacy of dis-covery of economically viable fields of reserves. Most of the accretions of reserves in new fields happen to be small and scat-tered ones whose cost of development would be quite high. The geologists and oil industry experts are currently of the opinion that the accretions would be able to just compensate for the depletion for some time at the plateau level of production of oil and gas as described above. It is apprehended that we would possibly have to face a situation of declining oil and gas production as well as hydrocarbon reserves towards the end of the tenth plan period.

Our projection of the future energy scenario has shown the oil demand to grow at 5.47 per cent per annum for a target long run average annual growth rate of 5 per cent, reaching a level of crude oil equivalent of 103 million tonnes in 2001–2 and 138 million tonnes in 2006–7. This would imply the best achievable self-reliance index in oil to be 44 per cent at the end of the ninth plan and 33 per cent at the end of the tenth plan. This presumes that the plateau of production can be stretched till 2006–7. However, the absolute size of import of crude equivalent of oil would then require to grow at more than 6 per cent rate per annum on the average in long horizon upto 2006–7 with the 1992–3 level of oil import as base which is itself very high. Such a long run trend in the projected requirement of oil import raises the problem of both oil security and macroeconomic security of the economy. This is particularly true in view of the current trend and future prospect of oil price rise and the possibility of decline of Indian production from plateau level during the tenth plan period or soon after 2006–7.

It is at present a matter of short run concern that the crude oil price has risen from a level of US $ 14.5 per bbl in 1993–4 to the current US $ 17.5 per bbl. Although this sharp rise might be partly due to the current Nigerian strike and recent rise in American oil demand, there is a noticeable trend of firming up of world oil prices. This is explained by the prospects of long run growth of global demand of oil and the increasing share of OPEC countries in the market due to their controlling share of 77 per cent of the world reserves of oil. There are expectations of oil price rise to a level of US $ 22–3 per bbl as per a Canadian projection or US $ 30–2 per bbl as per the projection by a major multinational oil company. Even with an oil price of US $ 22 per bbl at the end of the ninth plan, there will be rise in the import bill of oil reaching a level of around US $ 9079 million, i.e., Rs 28700 crores in 2001–2 as per our demand projection at US $ 1 = Rs 31 exchange rate. This would imply an annual growth of 7 per cent per annum of oil import bill over the time horizon upto 2001–2 in constant 1992–3 US $ and exchange rate. This will in turn lead to a rise in the share of the oil import bill in the total export earning at 1992–3 US $ over the already high level of 32 per cent of 1992–3. This share of the oil bill in exports would grow at 2 per cent per annum on the average if our exports grow at the same rate of the GDP in the long run.

One may, however, wonder if the conservation of use of oil, or its substitution by other fuels can improve the situation. The problem arises from the fact that the oil use ratios as observed for the transport and the household sector indicate very limited substitutability of oil by any other fuel. It may be noted that most of the nonconventional energy sources like solar power, wind energy, electricity out of biomass, etc., may contribute to the supply of power by replacing coal or nuclear resources but would not come to the rescue of our oil problem. While low grade solar thermal devices or gas out of biomass may provide cooking energy, these are yet to be upgraded and organized for supply at commercial scale. The problem of commercialization arises not always due to our inability to make a technological breakthrough. An institutional problem of organizing the supply of biomass resources arises due to property relations defining the distribution of ownership of the livestock or other biomass resources like agro-waste in the rural economy. It may be noted here that none of the energy supplies through nonconventional routes has as yet been significant enough to figure anywhere in any of the energy balance statements of our country — whether published by public or private sources. Even if these supplies assume any critical proportion of the total energy supply warranting explicit consideration in such balance statements, most of the new technologies would be ones of power supply replacing fossil fuel or uranium. They would contribute little to replace kerosene or LPG and nothing to fuel substitution for transport in foreseeable future. Our overriding consideration of food security would not also permit any diversion of land use for the development of agrobased alchohol industry to supply motor gasolene in India. The only way of ensuring both the energy security and the macroeconomic security of the nation would be to target the following:

(a)   growth of exports in dollar terms in a sustained manner in the long run,

(b)   conservation of oil use by technological upgradation

(c)   acceleration of exploration efforts of oil in new fields and efforts for extended recovery of oil in the existing fields.

So far as natural gas is concerned, the supply will create its own demand. Its demand will grow as it is a clean fuel and has higher marginal value productivity in most of the end uses than the competing fuel or feed stock resources. This is true about the use of gas in power, fertilizer, petrochemicals, etc. The economics of its use and the demand for it would however be dependent on its future price as well. The relative environmental friendliness of gas based technologies and the imperatives of pollution control would also create pressure on its demand and may necessitate the import of LNG. The latter would also add to our problem of financing the energy import bill and balance of payments emphasizing the need for accelerating our exports and efforts for discovery of oil-gas resources.

It is also a fact that the resource constraint of the Government of India has made it apparently necessary for the country to depend today on foreign investors for the exploration and development of new oil/gas fields in our geological basins. It is interesting to note that in spite of efforts of inducing the foreign investors to enter this field of oil/gas industry over the last 7–8 years, not a single exploration well has as yet been drilled by any foreign bidder in Indian land or water. The reason for the resource constraint for the public sector oil industry is not that the domestic petroleum product prices are irrational or subsidized. The price situation is quite different in the case of petroleum from power. Indian final consumers of petroleum products pay approximately the international price. The household consumers of kerosene and LPG are only cross subsidized by the consumers of motor gasolene and other high value products. The real problem of financial resources arises from the fact that what consumers of oil pay does not accrue to the oil-gas industry. A large part of the value paid by the consumer is appropriated by the government as Oil Industries Development Cess apart from as royalty. For crude oil and natural gas supply the Government of India has appropriated Rs 2200 crores in 1992–3 in the form of such cess in addition to royalty to the order of another Rs 2200 crores in the same year. While the royalty is a payment for the ownership right of the state on these exhaustible resources, the OIDC is supposed to be used for the growth of the industry at least in principle. However, most of this cess which has contributed between 2000 crores and 2900 crores per annum since 1988–9 has been used for meeting the current account government expenditure.

The political-economic process of Indian energy market has thus led to a situation where the Indian consumer of energy is subsidized by the state when he is consuming it in the form of electric power, while he subsidizes the Indian state when he consumes in the form of hydrocarbons obtained from indigenous sources. The problem of self-reliance in oil needs some rationalization in the use of OIDC. At least a significant part of this cess may be used for (a) more intensive exploration of hydrocarbons with higher technologies and better rates of success, (b) field development for better recoverability of oil and (c) infrastructural development for the marketing of gas. The use of OIDC for such purpose would enable us to avoid or reduce our dependence on foreign bidders for oil/gas exploration whose terms of contract are often expensive for a nation like India with limited ability to pay. The rationalization of use of such funds of cess needs to be accompanied by the efforts for economization of government revenue expenditure in order to remove the anomalies faced by the planners within the energy industry.

6 CONCLUDING REMARKS

The growth of commercial energy intensity of GDP of India at the best can be moderated but not reversed to indicate a decline at the current stage of development. Any choice of a growth rate of the economy would imply a certain challenge for meeting the requirement of supply of the commercial fuels in different forms. The Indian state has to play the leading role in the energy industry as an explorer of energy resources and as the producer and supplier of commercial energy. There is a necessity on the part of the Indian consumer of energy to politically accept the rationalization of energy prices along economic lines. The Indian state has also to reduce the exploitation of oil consumers for financing its consumption expenditure. The Government of India has therefore to economize its current account expenditure in order to relieve the oil and gas industry. The economy also needs to be reoriented towards the growth of exports for meeting the foreign exchange requirements for the inevitably growing oil deficit of the economy. The concern for energy conservation through continuous technological upgradation is also of importance subject to the constraint of our affordability. It is all these measures together which would enable us to combine energy security with the overall macro-economic security of the nation. This would also help us to target our pace and choose the strategy of development more wisely.

ANNEX TABLE A1

MAJOR DETERMINING VARIABLES (FACTORS) OF SECTORAL DEMAND FOR COMMERCIAL ENERGY IN INDIA

Sectors	Electricity	Coal	Petroleum
1. Agriculture:			
(a) Pumping	Potential availability of ground water and electrification of pumpsets	–	Potential availability of ground water and electrification of pumpsets
(b) Land preparation	–	–	Agricultural output
2. Industry and services (excl. transport and power):	Demand estimated at aggregate level		
(a) Steel and coke ovens	–	Exogenous information based on sectoral perspective plans	Considered along with 2 (c) in the estimation
(b) Fertilizer	–	Exogenous information based on sectoral perspective plans	Exogenous information based on sectoral perspective plan
(c) Other industries and services	–	Value-added in non-agricultural sector	Value added in non-agricultural sector

Annex Table A1 (cont.)

Sectors	Electricity	Coal	Petroleum
Overall 2	Value-added in non-agricultural sector	–	–
3. Transport	Railway freight and passenger traffic	Exogenous information based on the perspective of railways	Freight and passenger traffic of road and railways
4. Household	Private final consumption exp.	Private final consumption exp.	Private final consumption exp.
5. Power:			
(a) Captive	–	Value-added in non-agricultural sector	–
(b) Utility	–	Fuel policy model for power	Fuel policy model for power
6. Other sources of demand	–	Exogenous information	–

REFERENCES

International Energy Agency and OECD (1992), *Global Energy: The Changing Outlook*, Paris.

Government of India, Ministry of Finance, *Economic Survey 1993-94*, New Delhi.

Government of India, Ministry of Petroleum and Natural Gas, *Indian Petroleum and Natural Gas Statistics 1992-93*, New Delhi.

Government of India, Planning Commission, *Eighth Five Year Plan 1992-97*, New Delhi.

Government of India, Planning Commission (1992), 'National Energy Data Profile India 1970-2010', Presented in the 15th W.E.C. Congress, Mimeo.

Government of India, Planning Commission (1993), *Energy Modelling for India: Towards a Policy for Commercial Energy*, Study Carried Out by Ramprasad Sengupta, New Delhi.

Government of India, Planning Commission in Collaboration with ESCAP, UNDP and Government of France (1991), *Sectoral Energy Demand in India*, New Delhi.

Sengupta, Ramprasad (1989), Pace of Economic Development and Long Run Requirement of Commercial Energy in India, *Urja*, New Delhi.

The World Bank, *World Development Report 1993*, New York: Oxford University Press.

Index